The Stormrider Guide

Europe

A Low Pressure Publication

LOW PRESSURE

First published in 1992 by:
Low Pressure Publishing Ltd.
186 Kensington Park Road,
London W11 1EF
Telephone: 071 792 3134

Typeset by:
Jonathan Dear Associates,
366 Kennington Rd.
London SE11.

Colour Separations:
Cover: Power Graphics, London
Insert: C & C Offset Printing, Hong Kong

Printed by:
Butler & Tanner Ltd. Somerset

Printed on:
Sylvan Coat & Corona Offset (100% recycled material)
Supplied by Paperback Ltd. London

Authors: Oliver Fitzjones, Timothy Rainger

The Stormrider Guide: Europe (1992)
ISBN: 0 9519275 07pb

Front Cover: Maurice Cole, Hossegor. *Photo*: Alex Williams
Back Cover: Tom Curren, La Piste. *Photo*: Tim McKeena

Publishing Editors:	Oliver Fitzjones, Timothy Rainger
Assistant Editor:	Andrea Loerzer
Layout & Design:	Matthew Le Maistre Smith, Petra Pryke & Phil Armstrong
Sub Editor:	Stephanie Bretherton
Production:	Sarah Johnson Shiela Fitzjones
Translation:	Andrea Loerzer, Anton Betaudier, Cat Bituad Mihai Badelescu, Cécile Aubague, Marcelo
Editorial Contributors:	Racheal Sutherland, Jamie Blair, Roci Allan, Ian Hill, Thomas Buckley, Jamie Knox, Ms Margaret O'Brian-Moran, Pete Jones, Carwyn Williams, Phil Holden, Wave Graffitti Crew, Peter Cade, Rick Abbott, Jason, Chris Power, Alex Williams, Chris South, Guy Penwarden, Jamie Jamison, James & Grant, Simon Crawford, The Hindley family, Nick Noble, Gary Rogers, Gabriel & Peter Davies, Chris Mason, Steve Wilkinson, Gibus de Soultrait, Belly, Javier Amezaga, Borga Peñeñori, Juan Pedro Sansinenea, Alejandro Nebrada, Gonzalo Campa Villegas, Diego Méndez, Carlos & Lali Bremón, Marco Almaraz, Jordi Fraguas, João Valente, Nick Uricchio, Eduardo & Alvaro Costa, Luca Garibaldi, Carlo Marazzi, Bob Earll, Chris Hines, Partrick Harty, Tom Curren, Antonio Miguel Garcia
Without our friends and family none of this would have been possible. Thanks to:	Sheila & Jake Fitzjones, Sarah Johnson, Camilla Lowther and Charles Aboa, Camilio Gallardo, Matt Nash, Alan Whyte, Leslie & Harrison Whyte, Deborah Whyte, Maureen Grinter, Marguerite MacCurtain, Brie Burkeman, Daniel Allan, Dr. David Wheeler, Dr. Jamie Bartram, Michaela Merrit-Jones, Christine Berry, Mark Hare (Dreadhead), Gary Rowland Associates, Jenny Hildreth, Diana Burtt, Sarah Wyndham-Lewis, Susan Lorentz, Derek Henderson, Regan Cameron, Jon Dear & Susie Williamson, Emily & Polly Fitch, Robert, Tory & Dan Bean, Maurice Cole, Max, LB, Sean, Burn, Dion, Greg, Dieter, Tep, Sharon, Carla & Matthew Loerzer, Julie & Bill Rainger.

Special thanks to:

patagonia

Yvon, Bob, Drew, Nathalie

contents

introduction

Surf sports are exploding across Europe. People are taking to the waves on all manner of surf crafts at a spiralling rate and this book is a response to the wider needs of that expanding community.

We have attempted to compile a body of information which both describes the character of the European coastline and contains the necessary facts which make surf sports accessible. To do this we have been fortunate to have had the enthusiastic assistance of many of Europe's most respected surf personalities. Collectively they have passed on centuries of ocean law that display a remarkable consistency of tone – 100% stoked!

Although we have identified most of the popular and accessible locations, contributors have deleted some locally sensitive material. This is firstly out of respect for local feelings and secondly in the belief that much of the pleasure of adventure sports lies in their discovery. Traditionally surfing has been a male-dominated sport but we hope that this book will prove a source of enjoyment for everyone.

It was always obvious with a project of this nature that problems of marine pollution are a disturbingly pressing concern in what is obviously one of the world's most industrialised (and thus polluted) continents. With the material discussing water quality, we have attempted both to inform and to encourage action. Much serious thought and hard work will be needed in future years if Europe's coasts are to remain beautiful.

The photographic content comes from a cross section of young photographers, the quality of whose work made editing extremely difficult. We have chosen the most informative set of images that we could within the constraints of budget and space presented by a project of this nature.

Finally, we hope that this publication helps to engender a spirit of camaraderie in the oceans which we all communally own. Surfing is a sensation of pure pleasure and in a troubled world, great care should be taken to ensure that the problems of stress induced by modern life do not encroach further into one of mankind's most sacred pursuits.

Tim Rainger

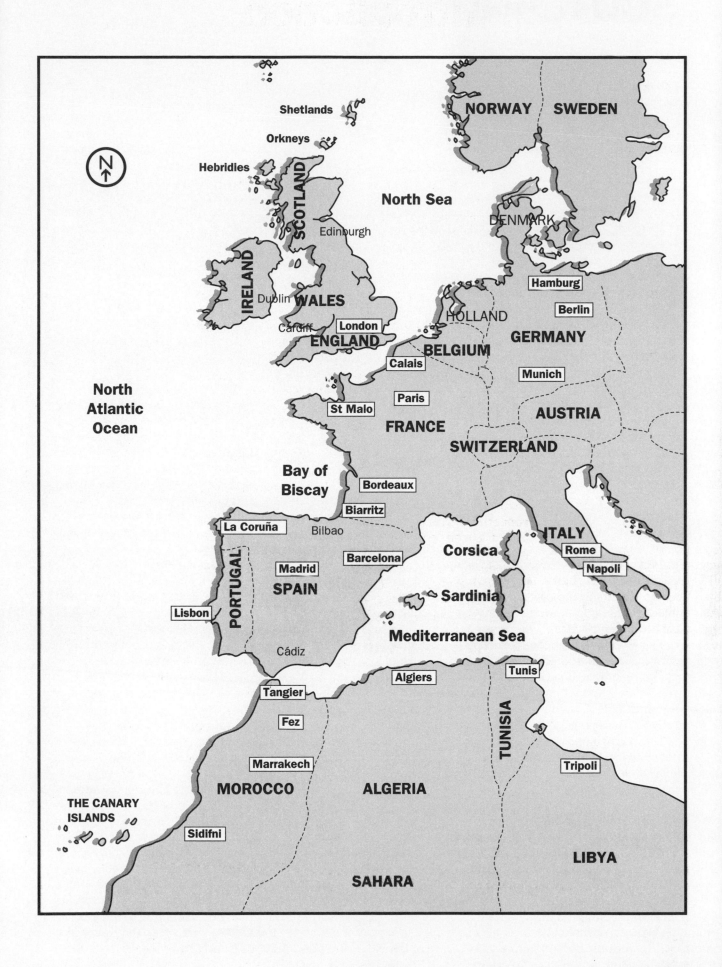

Shetlands

Orkneys

Hebridies

NORWAY   SWEDEN

North Sea

SCOTLAND

DENMARK

Edinburgh

IRELAND

North Atlantic Ocean

Dublin   WALES

Hamburg

Berlin

HOLLAND

Cardiff

London

BELGIUM   GERMANY

ENGLAND

Calais

Munich

Paris

St Malo

FRANCE   AUSTRIA

SWITZERLAND

Bay of Biscay

Bordeaux

Biarritz

La Coruña   Bilbao

ITALY

Barcelona   Corsica   Rome

Madrid   Napoli

PORTUGAL   SPAIN   Sardinia

Lisbon   Mediterranean Sea

Cádiz

Algiers   Tunis

Tangier

Fez   TUNISIA   Tripoli

Marrakech

MOROCCO   ALGERIA

THE CANARY ISLANDS

Sidifni   LIBYA

SAHARA

SCOTLAND

Capital: Edinburgh
Population: 530,000
Area: 30,414 miles²
Time: GMT (summer time GMT+1)
Languages: English and Gaelic
Currency: Scottish Pounds (£)

THE PEOPLE

Scotland is the northernmost constituent nation of the British Isles. Glasgow (897,000) and Edinburgh, the capital (1,453,000) are the two largest cities; the majority of the remaining inhabitants live along the eastern seaboard, with their numbers decreasing the more northern the latitude.

Scottish politics are, at present, an extension of the English system – Scotland has its own Home Secretary but is not autonomous. Traditional industry has centred around the Clyde River/ Glasgow area. Elsewhere farming, fishing and whisky (once Britain's largest export) have been the economy's mainstays. Recently, oil, forestry and nuclear energy have been developed by the government in an attempt to halt depopulation, with some statistical success but questionable long term merit.

Scotland is historically a melting pot of Gaelic tribes from the north, Picts from the east, Norse raiders and Anglo Saxon conquerors from England; there is a strong tradition of animosity and separatist feeling between the Scots and the English, particularly since the Stuart Kings acceded the English throne in 1603. 150 years later, the English had established a firm grip on the monarchy, outlawed clans, declared kilts and bagpipes illegal, and ruthlessly suppressed highland culture.

The Scottish still maintain a certain distance, marked by distinctive accents, schools, judicial system and currency. The predominant language is English (Scottish), though Gaelic is still spoken in the north and west. Accents differ markedly between its various geographically isolated regions. All are a joy to uninitiated ears. Don't be afraid to politely make your non-comprehension clear – they know most people have trouble with the tongue and are far from ashamed of it.

Some Gaelic Words

beach ....traigh
beautiful ....boidheach
big...more
black ....budh
boat ....bata
cold..fuachid
England...Sasainn
God..Dig
good..math
house ....tigh
land ....tir
point...nes
river ....abhainn
small ....beag
swell ....sumainn
town ....baile
water..uisage
wave ....tonn/stuadh
wind ....gaoth
white ....geal
yes ....seadh

THE SURF

The surf breaks in Scotland fall roughly into five area groups. They are:

North Shore
Moray Firth
East Coast
Mull'O'Kintyre
Scottish Islands (Shetlands, Orkneys, Hebrides)

Northerly swells affect Scotland's **North Shore** independently of most other beaches. Between Ackergill and Sandwood Bay, on a stretch of coastline as beautiful as it is varied, break some of Europe's most powerful waves. Whilst the Thurso area is well surfed (by Scottish standards), much of the remaining coastline offers classic solitary surfing conditions. The reefs and beaches hold a variety of world class waves.

The **Moray Firth** coast from Inverness to Aberdeen receives the lion's share of the North Sea swells, occurring most frequently in the deep winter months.

The **Edinburgh/Southeast Coast** is more heavily populated and polluted, and less spectacular, with cooler waters. However, an abundance of reefs and points break swell. Predominant wind direction is offshore, and winter sees quite a lot of strong wave action.

The **Mull'O'Kintyre's** beauty is legendary, and the waves here are well worth surfing and sailing. It picks up W swells from the Atlantic and S swells from the Irish Sea.

The inner islands of **Coll, Tiree** and **Islay** are regularly surfed and windsurfed offering a vast array of wind and swell direction and protection. The Outer Hebrides present the largest unexplored coasts in Europe and their isolation makes them an explorer's dream. They pick up all available swells produced by lows in the North Atlantic and at this time are surfed only by the adventurous. We've heard stories about the locals of **Orkney** being regularly in the water in these extreme northern latitudes, but so far very few visitors have been able to confirm this.

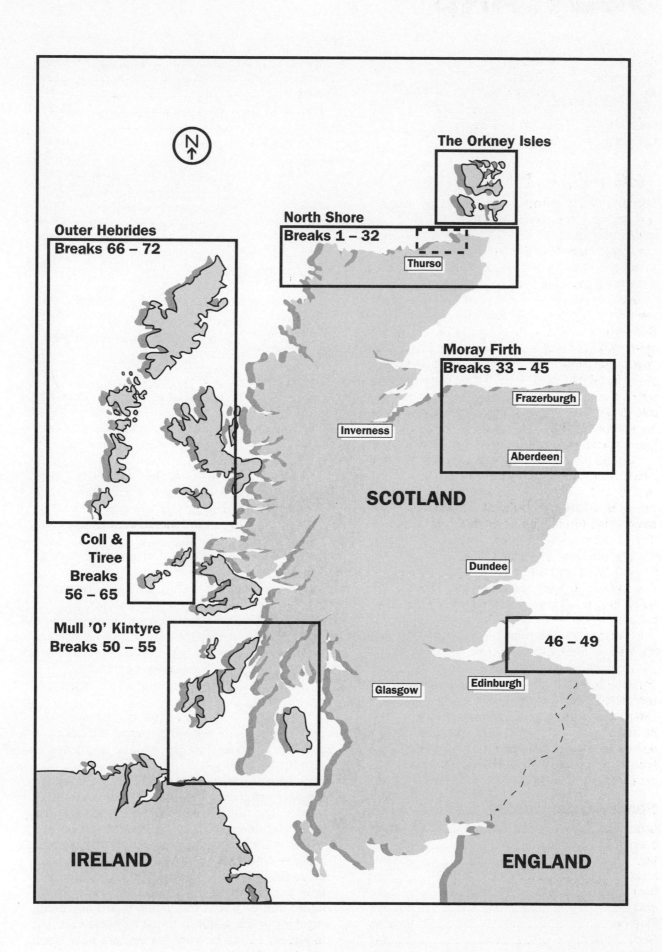

The Orkney Isles

North Shore
Breaks 1 – 32

Thurso

Outer Hebrides
Breaks 66 – 72

Moray Firth
Breaks 33 – 45

Frazerburgh

Inverness

Aberdeen

SCOTLAND

Coll &
Tiree
Breaks
56 – 65

Dundee

Mull 'O' Kintyre
Breaks 50 – 55

46 – 49

Glasgow

Edinburgh

IRELAND

ENGLAND

TRAVELLING AROUND

The best way to enjoy Scotland is in your own vehicle but if you're relying on public transport, the two main options are the bus or train, the latter being more comfortable but also more expensive.

Scottish Tourist Boards
Scottish Tourist Board
19 Cockspur Street
Trafalgar Square
London
Tel: 071 930 8661
Mon-Fri 9.00-6.00
Main Office
23 Raveston Terrace
Edinburgh EH4 3EV
Tel: 031 22433
Publishers of *Scotland: Where to Go and What to See*, available in 8 languages.
Greater Glasgow Tourist Board
35-39 St. Vincent Place
Glasgow G1
Tel: 041 2274880

EMBASSIES AND CONSULATES
All Embassies are in London.
Foreign Consulates in Edinburgh
Australia: Hobart House
Hanover St
Tel: 031 226 6271
France: 7 Wemyss Place
Tel: 031 225 7954
Germany: 16 Eglington Crescent
Tel: 031 337 2323
Italy: 6 Melville Crescent
Tel: 031 226 3631
Norway: 50 East Fettes Ave
Tel: 031 552 7101
Portugal: Gogar Park House
Tel: 031 339 5345
Spain: 51 Larderdale St
Tel: 031 447 1113
U.S.A: 3 Regents Tce
Tel: 031 556 8315
EMERGENCY MEDICAL TREATMENT
As for Britain, the NHS covers emergency medical treatment, for E.E.C. members and other countries with a reciprocal agreement (eg. Commonwealth countries). For immediate emergency treatment anyone can go to the casualty department of the local hospital where you'll be stitched up for nothing. However, if you're not covered by the NHS and you have to stay in hospital, it'll cost minimum £120 per day and that's just bed and meals.

EDINBURGH FESTIVAL
Major cultural festival in Europe occurs during the last 2 weeks of August.
Festival Box Office
21 Market St
Edinburgh EH1 18W
Tel: 226 4001
YOUTH HOSTEL ASSOCIATION:
7 Glebe Crescent
Stirling Central FR8 2JA
London: Y.H.A. Services
14 Southampton St
London

Scotland is a funboarder's dreamland. North Atlantic low pressure systems often extend over the islands, providing frequent strong SW and W winds which are cross-shore on many west coast breaks.

The surfing population numbers a few hundred. They are concentrated mainly in Thurso, Fraserburgh, Edinburgh and Aberdeen, though Glasgow has about half a dozen and there are various folk scattered the breadth of Scotland with a surfboard under the house for the occasional classic paddle.

Surfing here is still at a formative stage. For many, the idea is still inconceivable, but humans being what they are, cold climates can be adapted to. For the young folk of Scotland presently taking up surfing, (as for the Irish) there has been little or no precedent for their new sport. The communities' attitudes towards surfers are also still largely unformed. In all areas we urge respect and encouragement, both in and out of the water. With a good wetsuit and a brave heart you'll find Scotland an excellent destination.

The North Shore

Scotland's North Shore is divided between two counties and two broad geographical areas. **Caithness** is flat. Not dead flat with sharp horizons, but like a gently shaking quilt with subtle, organic suggestions of movement. Lying on this plain are a domestic splatter of croft houses, villages and straight, well built roads. The patchwork of fields is broken by a huge variety of fencing. The pinks, burgundies and browns of heather and scrub, and the greens and blacks of the peat bogs add local colour.

The county lies on a bed of hard grey stone which is flat, regular, and splits easily. In the early nineteenth century, its potential in the paving and construction industry was grasped and, until the Second World War, was a major economic resource. These same stones, jutting into the Atlantic in huge slabs, are the breaking surface for some of Europe's hairiest waves. There are some beautiful beaches in Caithness, however it is the reefs which make this a world class surfing area.

Travelling west from Melvich one enters the district of **Sutherland** and the flagstones disappear. Great glacial river valleys rake down into the ocean and their moranic remains form boulder reefs and sandy beaches. North Sutherland is both less populated and more mountainous – a vast prehistoric landscape of peat bogs and highland tussock leading onto glorious sandy beaches. One look at an ordinance survey map will reveal a good deal of virgin wave potential.

North Shore swells are generated by intense low pressure systems forming high in the North Atlantic, most often in autumn, winter and spring. In summer, you can surf all day and most of the night if there's swell – it's only briefly dark around 3am!

Several of the breaks, **Brims Ness** especially, experience strong current and tidal water movements as the Atlantic flows along the coast to meet the North Sea. The tidal reach is vast on full moons and spring tides. Often it is the tide pushing

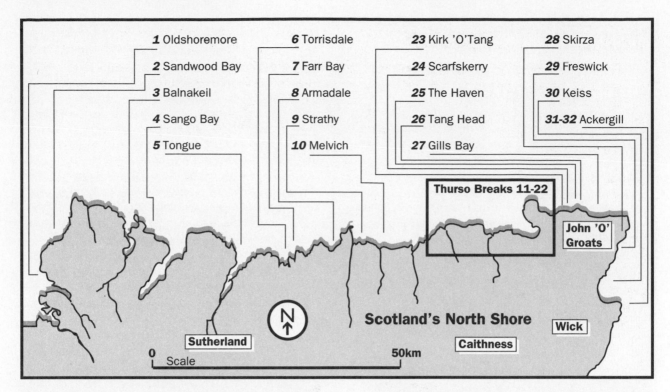

1 Oldshoremore	*6* Torrisdale	*23* Kirk 'O'Tang	*28* Skirza
2 Sandwood Bay	*7* Farr Bay	*24* Scarfskerry	*29* Freswick
3 Balnakeil	*8* Armadale	*25* The Haven	*30* Keiss
4 Sango Bay	*9* Strathy	*26* Tang Head	*31-32* Ackergill
5 Tongue	*10* Melvich	*27* Gills Bay	

Thurso Breaks 11-22

John 'O' Groats

Scotland's North Shore

Wick

Sutherland

Caithness

N

0 Scale   50km

into a swell which gives the waves their extra power and it pays to exercise extreme awareness, especially on big days. There are few people around able to help should you encounter difficulties, which can be easily compounded by cold water conditions.

Thurso is obviously the centre of surf activity on the North Shore...and there are some good locals, who you're bound to run into if there is good surf, people like Neil & Nicola Harris, Billy, Pat Kieran, Jamie Blair from Glasgow, Andy Bennets and others. Should you stray north during the winter months, you'll probably be a welcome sight; they get lonely surfing by themselves.

It's a spooky experience – the green black water, the general desolation of the country side, the knowledge that you're on a latitude comparable to Alaska, the big seals in the line up, the lack of surfers, the absence of people in general, the reefs...the North Shore has a presence all of its own which demands respect.

Surf Breaks 1 – 32

1. Oldshoremore

A sheltered bay facing southwest, receives waves on a strong W or even N swell, better at higher tides. It's a useful indicator for Sandwood – if Oldshoremore is even one or two feet, Sandwood is on. Offshores are NE. Just north of Kinlochbervie.
Water Quality: Excellent.

2. Sandwood Bay

The mile long beach at Sandwood is one of Britain's finest, and save for the birds and an occasional walker, it'is a deserted wave factory. No fewer than nine different bars/reefs work on all stages of the tide. The bay faces northwest, with reefs at both ends, two separate rock clusters marking its length and high cliffs offering protection from N and S winds. It receives as much swell as any other Scottish beach. The only access is a 4 mile track located just north of Blairmore. The first two miles or so are navigable in summer by car – otherwise its strictly a walk through the peat bog. The walk is as stunning as the beach and its wave quota.
Water Quality: Excellent.

3. Balnakiel Bay

A sweeping sandy beach facing west into the Kyle of Durness, picks up W and N-W swells that may miss other breaks further east. Protected from N winds and swells. Offshore breezes are E.

Water Quality: Excellent.

4. Durness (Sango Bay)

Below the town of Durness, sheltered by the limestone bluffs and rich sheep farming pastures, lies Sango Bay, a small sandy beach facing northeast. It picks up N swell with offshores from the S and is protected from a W. Located near the spectacular 'Smooo Caves,' a world renowned pot-holing site. Other breaks in the vicinity of Durness include the beach at **Ceannabeine (Rispond Bay)** and **Rabbit Islands**. There's parking above the bay.

Water Quality: Excellent. ·

5. Kyle of Tongue

A sheltered glacial bay, works in huge swells, offering protection from most other than N winds. An area surfed very rarely, waves are rideable for hundreds of metres up both sides in the right conditions.

Water Quality: Excellent.

6. Torrisdale

Beach break with a good righthand rivermouth. The best bars are near the river...check for sinking sands along the riverbanks. Offshore is in the south, with low to mid tide generally the best for surfing.

Water Quality: Excellent.

7. Farr Bay

Due to its northeasterly aspect Farr Bay also picks up swell that may miss Thurso with lefts better at mid to high, and rights that can work at low. Walk through the dunes after taking a turn off at the Farr Bay Inn. Don't forget to close the gate as it's farmed land.

Water Quality: Excellent.

8. Armadale Bay

Faces due north and is visible from the main road. Another good beach break with lefts and rights better at high tide. Either follow the rivermouth or walk from the town.

Water Quality: Excellent.

9. Strathy Bay

Another rivermouth with a good high tide righthander off the rocks at the eastern end of the bay. Well protected from westerly winds but also from westerly swell. Take the road to the graveyard, then walk over the dunes to the beach. Paddle out in the river or off the beach.

Water Quality: Excellent.

10. Melvich

Melvich is another deserted bay with a river dominating the sandbar formations. Good left bars break best from mid to high tide. Park with

consideration at the end of the access road to the big house. The definition between private and public land appears uncertain here. Sunbathing seals are a common sight.

Water Quality: Excellent.

11. Sandside Bay

Another classic beach/reef set up. Sandside faces north. Lefthanders break into the bay from the harbour with occasional left and right bars on the beach. It works on an average north or big west swell, best at mid to high tide (the left gets rocky at low). Sandside Bay lies twelve miles west of Thurso, just after the village of Reay. It's within a stones throw of the reactor at Dounreay.

Water Quality: Sandside's lefts are surfed regularly despite the ominous presence of the nuclear power plant... Dounreay is the UK's oldest experimental reactor. Paradoxically, the town needs the employment it has provided, yet it's well known there is a leukaemia 'cluster' around Thurso and the Orkneys. Draw your own conclusions. The UK Atomic Energy Commission is considering contracting commercial dry storage for imported spent nuclear waste up here... When will the madness end?

12. 13. 14. Brims Ness 'Graveyards'

Brims Ness is Nordic for 'Surf Point' and that's what it is. Three distinct breaks:

THE BOWL, as the name suggests, is a bowly righthander breaking in shallow water. The swell comes out of deep water fast, best on mid to high tide on the in, up to 8ft. Offshore SE.

THE COVE has a similar set-up to the Bowl. Not as rapid fire, 100mtrs away and works on similar tide and wind.

THE LEFT has a classic lefthand point break, rideable for 100mtrs or more on a reasonable swell, best at low to mid tide in clean conditions. (It's easily blown-out.)

Whilst the walk over the paddock makes this a bit of effort, especially in the cold, these three breaks on the same point catch most of the swell in the area, and Brims can be overhead when Thurso's flat. When seen from the road, size can be misleading. Look for the silos and the waves on the point (visible from the main road 3 miles west of Thurso). Right turn just after the point is visible, down to the farm buildings – parking is amongst the sheds and machinery. It's private property, enough respect!

Water Quality: Assuming no nuclear nasties float around from Sandside, the water quality is good. Can we safely assume this?

15. Thurso Reef, The Shit Pipe, The Sewer Pipe

Just off the breakwater on the west side of the Thurso River. A north-facing reef which breaks left

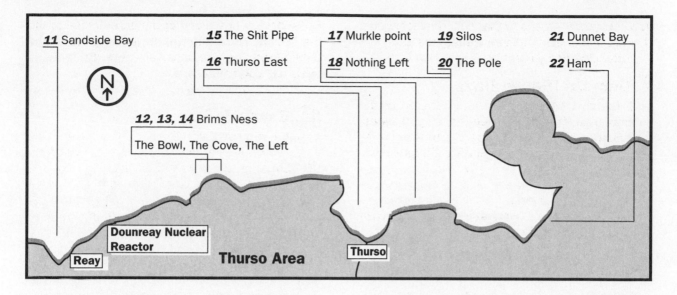

Thurso Area

11 Sandside Bay
15 The Shit Pipe
17 Murkle point
19 Silos
21 Dunnet Bay

16 Thurso East
18 Nothing Left
20 The Pole
22 Ham

12, 13, 14 Brims Ness
The Bowl, The Cove, The Left

Dounreay Nuclear Reactor

Reay

Thurso

and right in a small to medium sized swell. Becomes a righthander in big swells. It's called the Sewer Pipe for obvious reasons – you'll see the congregations of seabirds in the same spot on a still day. The wave breaks on a small swell near where the pipe comes out. Access is off the beach at lower tide, or off the harbour wall at high.

Water Quality: Town sewage from 9,000 people receives maceration and is discharged approximately 400mtrs from the low water mark. Unfortunately the water quality has not yet been publicly monitored.

16. Thurso East, Castle Reef, The Mecca

A classic righthander. Long tubes break on a flat, kelp covered northwest facing reef. A slowish take off and a long tube section subside into a fast, smaller inside section. Works at all stages of the tide (swell depending), but regarded as best on an incoming from mid, wind direction SE. Paddle out either off the point or in the bay on bigger days. Has been surfed at 12ft+. A large bombora breaks in the middle of the bay when the swell is max N – it hasn't been surfed yet. When the bay gets big enough for The Bombora to break, outside sets can close out from the Shit Pipe across to Thurso East, so even a brave paddle out in the river could be a terminally bad move. One day maybe. Access is by public road down to the most northern part of the Estate of Lord Thurso. Parking is generally fine adjacent to the break.

Water Quality: The water always looks brown/black but it's not shit – peat flows down the Thurso River which gives it the colour.

17. Murkle Point

Lying between Thurso and Dunnett Bay are various rock outcrops and formations. A beautiful left breaks off 'the Spur' into the bay on a large W or N swell. Offshores are in the S. Turn north off the A836 in the village of Murkle. A short one-way road leads to the harbour.

Water Quality: One outlet pipe discharges sewage from 1,000 people below the low water mark. Water quality depends on wind and swell direction.

18. 19. 20. Nothing Left, Silos, The Pole

Facing northeast three reef formations between Murkle and Dunnet provide thick lefthand peaks in W or N swells. Rarely surfed as access is tricky. Find them and surf them if you can.

Water Quality: Good.

21. Dunnet Bay

Six miles east of Thurso, a three mile long beach break facing west to northwest. Lefthand waves break at the southern end of the beach by the old flagstone quarry, average sandbars along its length and excellent rights at the northern end. W swell gets in as does a large N. Two righthand reef/points further out at Dunnet Head also need checking out. The A836 runs along its length, with parking and foot access over the dunes at various points.

Water Quality: Two pipes service a population of 200 people. Macerated sewage is discharged below the low water mark.

22. Ham

A lefthand reef breaking into deeper water around the harbour. Offshores are from the S with some protection from a W wind. From Ham you can see down the coast to other reefs in the area.

23. 24. 25. Kirk'O'Tang/ Scarfskerry/ The Haven

A series of reefs visible at various points from the main road, facing north. Wave quality depends on the swell direction.

Water Quality: Good.

26. Tang Head

A mid to high tide, northwest facing reef at the

rivermouth. Depending on where it's breaking, paddle off the rocks or in the river. Offshores are from the south. Turn left off the A836 from Thurso at the village of Mey.

27. Gills Bay

The furthest east of all the breaks on the north coast, partially protected from the north by the Island of Stroma. Gills offers lefts at the western end of the bay and rights at Ness of Quoys. To get out there, park near the graveyard and walk over the fields. The road to the pier is signposted off the A836.

Water Quality: Good.

28. Skirza Harbour

The most northerly mainland break facing the North Sea. Three or four miles southeast of John'O'Groats is a man-made harbour inside a lefthand breaking reef. Faces southeast and offers superb lefts, very long and very heavy. The water temperature here is noticeably colder than at Gills Bay. It's sign-posted 'Skirza' off the main road and 'pier' to get you to the harbour – either jump off the harbour wall or rocks.

Water Quality: Excellent.

29. Freswick Bay

A beautiful rivermouth with waves breaking on a sand and boulder reef in the same bay southwest of Skirza harbour, usually bigger. Access is off the road to Skirza. The first road right leads to the beach. The access down to the big house in the middle of the bay is private property.

Water Quality: Good.

30. Keiss (North Beach)

Keiss is the name given to the northern end of Sinclairs Bay. Lefts form off a sand rock reef to the north and sand bars create peaks down the bay, best near the river mouth in the middle. The south end of Sinclairs Bay is named Reiss, which works in similar conditions to Keiss. The beach is visible from the A9 along its entire length.

Water Quality: Good.

TRAVELLING AROUND

Tourist Information
Fraserburgh (Summer)
Tel: 28315

Weather
Aberdeen
Tel: 8091
Radio – BBC Radio Aberdeen 93.1 MHZ

H.M. Coastguard
Peterhead
Tel: 4278 (Information) 999 (Emergency)

---

31. & 32. Ackergill

Between Reiss and Noss Head near the castle at Ackergill are two righthand reefs with thick breaking waves that work best at low to mid tide, when a SE swell wraps around the point. Offshores are in the SW quarter. Both reefs want to show through the wave – an ominous portent.

Water Quality: O.K.

Moray Firth

Steep cliffs and sandy beaches line an area known as 'The Granary of the North,' a countryside of small fishing villages and quiet inland farms.

The swell patterns here are different to those experienced west of the Orkney's. North swells generate in an area west of the Shetlands to Norway and north, most frequently in late autumn and winter months. It is the North Sea, and whilst further south than the North Shore, is always 1 - 2°C cooler without the warming presence of the Atlantic Drift. Due to the predominant SW airflow, offshores are consistent.

The further east you travel, the bigger the waves get. On any given day, Banff Reef, Fraserburgh and Inveralocchy would be a metre bigger than conditions at Lossiemouth and Cullen. This is due to the shape of the sea bed and the sheltering effect of Duncansby Head on swell patterns. For further information on predicting swells in the North Sea, see *England: East Coast.*

Rattray Head to Lunan

South of Rattray Head, the coast receives similar swells but many locations orientate southeast and shelve steeply into the North Sea. Strong N or S swells produce good conditions on many unidentified reefs as well as the main locations listed below. The monolithic castle of Dunnotar was where Bram Stoker dreamt up Dracula and where Samuel Johnson and James Boswell couldn't sleep "for the stench of the pillows stuffed with seagull feathers and the relentless roar of the waves..." (Road to the Isles, 1766). This stretch of coastline was also once the centre of a thriving smuggling trade in illegal spirits.

Unfortunately the North Sea's polluted state should come as no surprise and this stretch of coastline is definitely not the cleanest, with Lossiemouth East, Banff and Fraserburgh beaches all failing to meet the EC guidelines for safe bathing water. Some of the smaller coves and bays are beautiful but concentrations of pollutants near populated areas are high.

No guide to Europe would be complete without noting the lashing given this coast and its inhabitants by deep swells in the winter months, and the dedication and hardiness of the locals here who surf and sail in water as cold as anywhere in

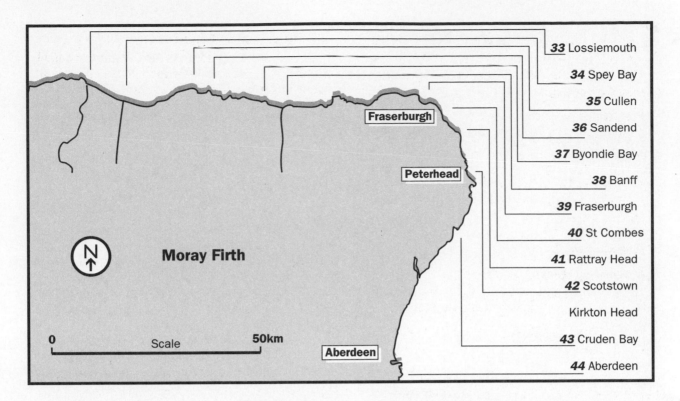

Map showing surf breaks along the Moray Firth coastline:

33 Lossiemouth
34 Spey Bay
35 Cullen
36 Sandend
37 Byondie Bay
38 Banff
39 Fraserburgh
40 St Combes
41 Rattray Head
42 Scotstown
Kirkton Head
43 Cruden Bay
44 Aberdeen

Europe. Fraserburgh and Aberdeen are the places to find other surfers and facilities, and the folk here come from a long sea faring tradition and, whilst not numerous, we once again urge respect.

Surf Breaks 33 – 45

33. Lossiemouth

Lossiemouth is the first real surf spot east of Inverness. The town is situated at the western ond of several miles of average beach break that work generally better at high tide in big swell. Offshore winds are SW to S.

Water Quality: Lossiemouth East has failed EC guidelines for safe bathing water several times. The western beach is cleaner.

34. Spey Bay

Once an important centre of the salmon fishing industry. Conditions required are similar to Lossiemouth. Various peaks.

Water Quality: Variable.

35. Cullen

Fast breaking rights and lefts are very visible from the main road (A90). The bay faces north to northeast. Facilities by the Golf Club, on the foreshore overlooking the bay. Paddle out off the beach or in the rivermouth.

Water Quality: Town sewage Is a problcm.

36. Sandend

East of Cullen and more exposed to varying winds from the south, Sandend Bay is dominated by the rivermouth. Offshores are SW, best from low to mid tide.

37. Byondie Bay

The coast road from White Sands leads around to and down Byondie Bay. A long righthand reef in front of the Pavilion at the eastern end of the bay. Works best at mid tides in small to medium surf but breaks through to high when the swell gets bigger. Reefs at the western edge of the bay break in deeper water on bigger swells. Offshores are from the south. It's visible from the look out. Ample parking in front of Banff Sands Hotel.

Water Quality: Dubious.

38. Banff

The River Deveran still dominates the sand bar formations on the small beach east of the town. Best waves are the lefts breaking into the river over a sandy rock reef which can work on all tides. Offshore is prevailing S – SW. Ample access and parking available on the sea shore on the eastern fringe of the town.

Water Quality: Variable.

39. Fraserburgh

One of the busiest and most impressive ports in the NE, Fraserburgh faces the North Sea and Moray Firth at the end of Kinnards Head. Various spots including a left at the harbour wall and two miles of good beach break.

Water Quality: Variable, has failed EC guidelines.

40. Inveralocchy/Charleston/ St Combs

Between Cairnbulg Point and Inzie Head the coastline is littered with reefs which break at various stages of the tide, usually bigger than Fraserburgh. The area is largely unsurfed and definitely worth exploring. The road to follow skirts the golf course or via the walking track which connects Inveralochy and St Combe.

Water Quality: Good

41. St Combes/Rattray Head

Five miles of beach break pick up all available swell, unfortunately the only access is along the beach. The road joins the beach on the foreshore below the 'Tufted Duck.' Alternatively several roads and tracks leave the A592 to Rattray head, but all involve some walking. Get a map! Secret spots abound.

Water Quality: Good.

42. Scotstown & Kirkton Head

At Kirktown village, a single track road to the cemetery takes you to the coast. Two classic curved bays present golden sands and two good points to the North Sea.

Prevailing winds are offshore. Access is off the A952 between Fraserburgh and Peterhead. From the track you can drive over two closed fields to the beach.

43. Cruden Bay

Recently voted one of Britain's finest 100 beaches. Two miles of crescent shaped sands are accessible over the Ladies' Bridge at a small rivermouth to the north end. It's a powerful beach which works mostly in winter.

44. Aberdeen

The Don Ythan Coast stretches north of Aberdeen for 15kms. It's largely uninspiring, though small groyne constructions can create good sand bars for Aberdeen's students who practice at the southern end in front of chocolate fudge cake cafes.

45. Lunan

A grand symmetrical arc-shaped bay where fishing nets hang elegantly out to dry, backed by high dunes and drawn in by rocky points. Sandbars form at both ends and usually work better at high tides.

EDINBURGH AREA
Surf Breaks 46 – 49

This stretch faces north-northeast and prevailing winds are offshore SW, which can make for some good surf days (not weeks). Any bay can be easily reached within a day from Edinburgh, a beautiful city built on a series of ancient volcanoes.

It's a dramatic backdrop for good night-life and a fantastic festival of music, plays, street theatre and films happens in August, when the city really comes alive.

46. The Gegan (Tantallon)

A small and beautiful sandy bay facing due north, the waves are not at their biggest here, but the setting is worth it in itself. Here you can bob up and down below the ruins of Tantallon Castle and gaze out to islands in the Firth. Access is through a small farmed estate off the A198 from North Berrick.

47. John Muir County Park

The following breaks all face northeast away from the prevailing winds. John Muir was a 19th century pioneer of ecology who emigrated to the United States in his passion for all things wild.

RAVENSHEUGH SANDS definitely has some good waves, best at low to mid tide but beware of partially submerged rocks. Access is between Whitekirk and Tyninghame where there's a long straight single track road called Limetree Walk running east of the A198. You have to walk about – a mile to the beach through woodland, heading northwards to Ravensheugh and straight ahead to Tyne Sands.

TYNE SANDS is an estuary and not a lot works there but a paddle out on the rip towards a possible lefthander off a point named St Baldred's Cradle could be a good call.

BELHAVEN BAY is one worth getting up for! The beach is long, the bars form well sufficiently far out and waves roll in in great long lines. Good at mid to high but again currents are strong. Access is from the car park at Belhaven (home of Edinburgh's finest real ale) next to the town of Dunbar.

48. Pease Bay

Faces due north and nestles at the foot of high cliffs, the road winds down to holiday caravans, parking is free and there are loos and a shop.

Off season when the waves are big, the whole place is quiet, bar 5 - 10 surfers from Edinburgh, Glasgow and Newcastle. It's the most popular and reliable bay for miles, it is also the most accessible. If there's a wave to be had, you'll find it at Pease Bay although some days are easier than others and it can get blown out completely. Under these conditions the southern end cleans up faster and is generally held to be better. Access is off the A1 to Newcastle-upon-Tyne.

For the determined there are a number of rocky points around Pease; they are **Barns Ness, Reed Point, Siccar Point, The Wheatstack , St Abb's Head and The Cove.**

49. Coldingham Bay

Faces due east, nice place where the waves are squeezed in and rise to quite a size. A pumpy alternative to Pease and it has the advantage of two small hotel-cum-pubs but no campsite. Access is through Coldingham village towards St Abb's Head, and take a right hand track to the beach.

Rachel Sutherland

Mull'O'Kintyre

Due to the sheltering presence of Scotland's Western Islands, the western mainland of Scotland has very few surf breaks. These can be found only at the extreme north of the country or on the Mull'O'Kintyre, in a small swell window south of the Islands of Islay and Jura. North swells are sheltered by the islands and South Atlantic swells (other than those generated in the Irish Sea) are blocked by Ireland. But when depressions move north offshore Ireland, a fair amount of swell gets in here.

Were it not for a tiny isthmus, Kintyre would be the innermost of the Hebrides and it possesses much of the feeling and individuality of an island. Campbeltown may have been the capital of the ancient Celtic kingdom of Dalriada, but the present town and its name belong to the early 17th century.

As the crow flies, Campbeltown is 65 miles from Glasgow but by road it is 135. The drive is spectacular all the way. Due to short daylight hours in autumn and winter, the best bet would be to plan a stay minimum of three or four days.

Surf Breaks 50 – 55

50. Bellochantuy (The Graveyard)

A 2 mile strip of beach north of the graveyard at Bellochantry. Faces west and works best on a rising tide. The break is over the sand bars which shift continually. Offshores are E.

Water Quality: Excellent.

51. Westport/Port a'Bhorrain /Caravan Parks

Westport offers jacky righthand bars especially

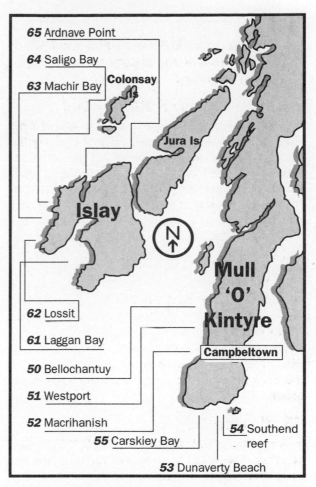

65 Ardnave Point
64 Saligo Bay
63 Machir Bay
Colonsay Is
Jura Is
Islay
Mull 'O' Kintyre
Campbeltown
62 Lossit
61 Laggan Bay
50 Bellochantuy
51 Westport
52 Macrihanish
55 Carskiey Bay
54 Southend reef
53 Dunaverty Beach

at mid to high tide. The beach picks up all available swell to 6ft or so when reefs further out begin to break. South of Bellochantuy, parking is at the end of the road leading to the beach.

Water Quality: Excellent.

52. Macrihanish

When the swell is bigger and the wind too far south for Westport, Macrihanish can be a more manageable break. Three and a half miles of sand run north to Westport giving rights and lefts best at mid water rising.

A store doubles as a beach cafe in summer and perhaps in winter if you can press your case. Access is from the foreshore by the village. Otherwise beach access is on foot.

TRAVELLING AROUND

Macrihanish Airport:
Cambletown
Tel: 0586 52571

Loganair Ltd:
Glasgow Airport, Abbotsinch, Paisley PA3 2TG
Tel: 041 889 3181

Mechanics:
West Coast Motors Ltd, Bennhor Garage, Campbeltown , Tel: 0586 52319

Accommodation:
Caravan Park at Westport

Tourist Information:
Area Tourist Office
MacKinnon House, The Pier, Campbeltown
Tel: 0586 52056

53. Dunaverty Bay

Mid to high tide rights break off the rocks at the western end of the bay. Lefts on the beach break at various stages of the tide depending on the swell. Ten miles south of Campbeltown, through Conie Glen to South End, Dunaverty Bay is west of the golf course.

54. Southend Reef

A road leads through the golf course to the old launching ramp at the eastern end of Dunaverty Bay. Off the headland is a submerged kelp-covered reef which gives classic waves around low tide. A bowly right with serious tube potential, the left has a longer wall. N offshores.

55. Carskiey Bay

Tradition has it that Saint Columba first set foot here in 560AD and a ruined chapel is dedicated to him. Behind the chapel is Saint Columba's well where the water is considered holy. The waves at Carskiey Bay are normally lefts and rights on a sharply shelving beach and righthanders off the rocks to the western end.

Normally best at low tide. Offshores are northerlies. Continue west from Dunaverty one mile. Keil Point lies between Dunaverty and Carskiey.

The Inner Hebridies

TIREE

Tiree is the most popular destination of all the Hebrides for surfriders, and to date the most visited by wave sailors and a regular competition venue.

The shape and small size of the island combined with a great selection of beaches and reefs, make Tiree an ideal place to surf and sail. Tiree receives so much swell! But it's a flat exposed island (very few trees survive here as a result) and winds pass over the island with no breaks. This is a bonus if wind is your prime energy source, but can be a disadvantage for surfers. Whilst winter can be a tough time to visit, empty waves and some of the highest recorded levels of early summer sunshine make this a spring gem.

COLL

Tiree's strange and barren neighbour is another flat, swell-drenched, Hebridian island and has 3 or 4 bays along its northwest facing coast. Definitely worth a trip for the 'remotest of all' experiences. There are hostels to stay in (Ballyhough 08793 44)

TRAVELLING AROUND

FERRIES
Caledonian MacBrayne has a subsidised monopoly on all island crossings, sailing on Monday, Wednesday and Friday from Oban.
GETTING THERE
By Ferry – Caledonian Mac Brayne car ferry from Oban to Coll and Tiree. Mon, Wed, Fri and Sat in summer; Tues, Thurs and Sat in winter. Tel: Gourock 33755
By Plane – Loganair Ltd run a weekday service from Glasgow to Tiree. Currently no facility for taking sailboards by air but surfboards possibly O.K.
Tel: 041 889 3181
GETTING ABOUT
Car Hire – Tel: 08792 469/644/555/9??
Bike Hire – Tel: 08792 428
The roads are single track with "pockets" (passing places) and there are two petrol pumps, one at the ferry pier and one at Brown's store in Balemartine. The garage is at Crossapol, "The Old Forge" also does repairs
Tel: 08792 644 (day) 548 (night)

TOURIST INFORMATION
Oban – Tel: 63122/63551
COASTGUARD
Oban – Tel: 63720 – 999 (Emergency)
MAIN TOWN
The main town is Scaranish (from the Norse: Scara – Gull, Nes – point) consisting of no more than 20 houses around an old harbour built in 1771 and little used now, but once a prosperous port bringing in fuel and sending out sheep and cattle.
ACCOMMODATION
There is rental accommodation at the Coll Hotel and in a number of self catering cottages and caravans.
On Tiree the Tiree Lodge Hotel, 7 days B&B £104 – £155; 3 days B&B £50 (prices seasonal) Tel: 08792 368. Self catering from £70 a week. Special prices for R.Y.A. courses and associate members.
Pre-booking rooms and cottages is advisable and rates vary from season to season.

Contact the Tourist Board.
Camping
Open, or "free" as they say, yet permission to pitch should be sought out of common courtesy from the nearest house around...if there is one. The dunes around the Maze and Hough provide excellent camping grounds. Tiree is a clean, fresh and tidy island, with a quiet and friendly host population...so keep it so!
WEATHER
Glasgow Weather Centre –
Tel: 041 284 3451
Television BBC Weather at 6.20 & 9.30
Oban Windsurfing – Tel: 0631 64380
Tiree Windsurfing Club – Tel: 08792 559
Scottish Windsurfing Association – Tel: 0224 315218
LANGUAGE Gaelic is spoken by 70% of the people. Most place names are Gaelic, although a significant number are of Norse derivation from the 300 years of Norse occupation of the Isles.

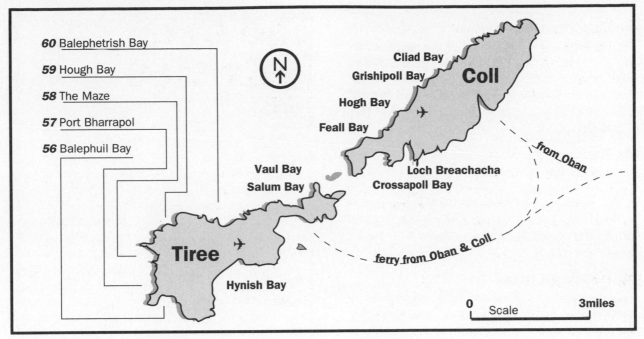

Map labels:
60 Balephetrish Bay
59 Hough Bay
58 The Maze
57 Port Bharrapol
56 Balephuil Bay

N

Cliad Bay
Grishipoll Bay
Coll
Hogh Bay
Feall Bay

Vaul Bay
Salum Bay

Loch Breachacha
Crossapoll Bay

from Oban

ferry from Oban & Coll

Tiree

Hynish Bay

0   Scale   3miles

and the usual open camping.

Much of the western seaboard is bright shell sand heaped into huge dunes (some up to 100ft high) knitted by 'machair' grass. A few prosperous farms raise sheep and cattle and there is one small town, Aringgour. Coll is slightly less exposed than Tiree but remains a great island to surf on.

Surf Breaks 56 – 60

56. Balephuil/Travee

A mile and a half of white shell sand beach faces S/SW but surprisingly picks up good amounts of swell. Rights and lefts break on the beach and Kenavara Point could also hold secrets.

57. Port Bharrapol

A magnificent rock and sand bay at the bottom of high cliffs. Faces west and catches heaps of swell. From 'The Glassery,' (a restaurant and vantage point between Bharrapol and Middleton) you can see up and down the coast.

58. The Maze

The most popular spot on the island for windsurfing and scene of The British Wavesailing Nationals. The Maze is a long sandy beach wide open to all W swell. Long and fast peaks break on the beach and off the point. If you climb the remnants of a World War II radar station at Ben Hough, all will be revealed.

59. The Hough

Faces W-NW. More beach waves receive some protection from 'The Hough Skerries' but a left hand reef break merits further investigation.

60. Balephetrish

A large pebble and sand beach with interesting bars at its mouth.

ISLAY

The closest and most varied of the surfable Inner Hebrides, lies 16 miles west of Kintyre. It is relatively lush and hilly, and the bays work under different conditions.

Given its accessibility and fertility, Islay is, by island standards, 'wealthier,' with thriving, pretty villages. Tourism plays a significant part in the island economy as do sheep and cattle, (large numbers are all are free to roam around at random.) It's a nice island with enough folk around to push my van off the beach... Thank God.

Surf Breaks 61 – 65

61. Laggan Bay

The largest bay on the island, and it's humungous. It stretches for miles but faces SW, into the prevailing wind, and requires a good swell when clean regular bars form 3 miles out at the mouth of the bay. It works well on all tides. Access is to the south of the golf course. Park outside the Machrie Hotel and follow the stream to the beach. Or, to the north, take a turn off to Island House and follow the track running SW of the house, through two or three gates (saying "No Camping"), through open grazing and small forestry plantations to the dunes.

62. Lossit Bay

Lies at the bottom of high cliffs and you'll get some good waves if you can get down. NW facing. Access is tricky. Take the track to Lossit Farm. You end up in someone's front yard and there it is likely you'll have to park, so be courteous. From the farm it's a 3km walk around and down the cliffs.

63. Machir Bay

Four kms of sand face west divided from

north/south by a river. The north end works well with righthanders coming off an inside point. To the south the beach shelves more deeply and strong breaks form over sand bars. Works on all tides. Access: It's obvious. Machir Bay is one of the best places to camp.

64. Saligo Bay

A heavy west facing bay, with warning signs of strong currents. Take a long look before paddling out.

The waves here are thick and sucky, lefthanders to the south and righthanders to the north, which is steeper. Inexperienced surfers should 'wave-watch' instead.

65. Ardnave Point and Bay

North facing it requires a good swell but offshores are prevailing. It's more sheltered than other breaks on the island. Access is from Ardnave House and Loch.

The Outer Hebrides

The main islands in the Outer Hebrides are **Lewis-Harris** (one island) **North Uist, Benbecula, South Uist and Barra.** They are separated from the north west coast of the Scottish mainland by 'The Minch' and from the northern islands of the Inner Hebrides by the 'Little Minch'. Together they form a 150 mile stormbreak for the Western Highlands and the northern isles of the Inner Hebrides.

Lewis and Harris form a single island hosting the main town of Stornway, a port and airport, with a population of approximately 25,000 people.

North Uist, Benbecula and South Uist have been joined by causeways to form another single long island and whilst they sport many local differences, they share a particularly beautiful western facing coast of sparkling shell sands, backed by grasslands bright with flowers. Two main ports/ towns are Lochboisdale in the south and Loch-maddy in the north.

Barra is the other serviced island of the group. Castlebay is the main town and harbour whilst an

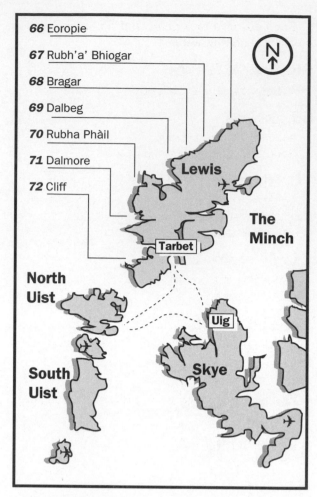

airport which is water covered at high tides, exists in the north of the island.

THE SURF

Without any doubt, the Outer Hebrides receive some of the biggest swells in Europe. 150 miles of exposed coast angles north west into the Atlantic presenting an almost limitless variety of wave breaking surfaces. They, with the other Scottish islands, present fantastic virgin surf opportunities.

Surf Breaks 66 – 72

66. Eoropie

Steep tubey shorebreak. Heavy rips.

67. Rubh 'a' Bhiogar (Lewis)

TRAVELLING AROUND

FERRIES
Caledonian Mac Brayne Ltd.
Car Ferry
Ullapool – Stornway, Mon-Sat
Uig (Skye) – Tarbert, Mon-Sat
Head Office
The Ferry Terminal
Gourock PA19 1QP
Tel: 0475 34531 (Res)
  0475 33755

Mon-Sat 8.30 am – 5.00 pm

BY AIR
British Airways
Glasgow – Stornway, Mon-Sat
Inverness – Stornway, Mon-Sat
Glasgow – Tel: 041 887 1111

TOURIST INFORMATION
Outer Hebrides Tourist Board

4 Sth Beach
St. Stomoway
Isle of Lewis PA87 2XY
Tel: 0851 3088
Coastguard Information
H.M.C.G. Stornway
Tel: 70213/4
  999 (Emergency)
Weather
Stornway – Tel: 702282

Sand covered rock point that holds big swell, breaking in shallow water.

68. Bragar (Lewis)

A long slow right and left peak.

69. Dalbeg

Another protected cove.
Good place to camp on the cliff.

70. Ruhba Phàil (Lewis)

South of Yig Sands, a narrow bay that can also hold some of the island's biggest surf. Sandy beach – best at high tide.

71. Dalmore (Lewis)

Lefthander in a protected cove.
(Not as good as Cliff).

72. Cliff (Harris)

White sand beach break picks up all available swell.

Orkney Islands

Population: 17,077.
Principal Town: Kirkwall.

GEOGRAPHY, HISTORY

The archipelago of the Orkney's is made up of 67 islands and extends for 50km, 5kms north of Duncansby Head, separated from the mainland by the Pentland Firth. Hoy, South Ronaldsay and Mainland islands encircle the Scapa Flow, with Stronsay, Eday, Rousay, Shapinsay, Westray and others to the north. The Atlantic ocean forms the western, and the North Sea the eastern, seaboards.

The first people were living here by 4000BC and the islands have a great wealth of impressive, prehistoric remains. As late as the 19th century Norn, a form of Norse, was the language spoken and it is this Norse heritage which differentiates the Orkneys and Shetlands from the mainland Scotland.

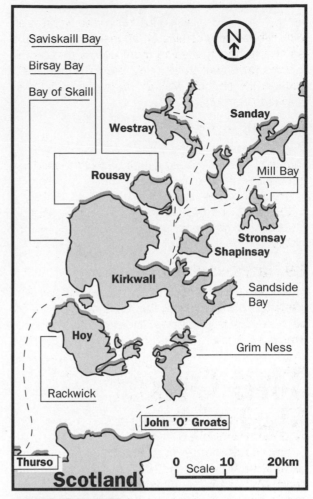

THE SURF

Whilst lying even further north than Thurso, the Orkneys have several strong points of interest for surfers and sailors. Their geography resembles Caithness. There are several reefs, and beach breaks on the mainland alone. Swell comes from both the Atlantic and the North Sea (unlike Thurso and other North Shore breaks) and as swell and wind directions change, one can cross the islands to find cleaner waves or different swell.

Access problems presented by such a large number of small Islands are pertly solved by causeways and an enjoyable ferry service. It has to be said that very little of the island's potential has been realised and like many other regions of Scotland one look at an Ordinance Survey map would present a host of possibilities. We have talked to three locals who confirmed that the sport was alive and kicking on this northern latitude

TRAVELLING AROUND

AIRPORTS
BA daily services to Kirkwall from Glasgow, Inverness and Aberdeen - Tel: 0856 3359
Loganair daily services from Edinburgh,Inverness and Wick
Tel: 0856 3457

FERRIES
"P&O" car ferry from Scrabster to Stromness daily in summer.
"Thomas & Bews" passenger ferry John'O'Groats to South Ronaldsay daily in summer. Tel: 9353
Barrock in winter - Tel: 619
TOURIST BOARDS

Orkney Tourist Board
Freepost
Kirkwall
Orkney KW15 1BR
Tel: 0856 2856
Phones
Dialling the Orkneys – Tel: 0856 then a 4 figure number.

IRELAND

Capital:	Dublin (Republic)
	Belfast (Northern Ireland)
Population:	4,943,405
Area:	70,283 km²
Time:	GMT (summer time GMT+1)
Religion:	Roman Catholic,
	Protestant minority
Languages:	English, Irish
Currency:	Punt (IR£)

THE PEOPLE

Ireland is the whole island west of Britain. Northern Ireland comprises the six counties that have remained part of the UK since the Anglo-Irish treaty in 1921, and the Republic of Ireland (Eire) comprises the 26 counties governed from Dublin. For the purpose of this guide, Ireland is being treated as one country.

It is believed that the first Irish settlers were Mesolithic hunter/fishers who arrived around 6000 BC from Northeast Scotland. These were the people responsible for the vast assortment of Megalithic remains still to be seen throughout Ireland and along the Atlantic seaboard of Europe, from Galicia in Northern Spain to Scandinavia.

The next visitors were the Celtic tribesmen who came up through Europe around 700BC. Theirs was an oral culture in which immortality was to be gained by starring in epic tales. The tribes were left to war amongst themselves as the Romans considered Ireland to be not worth invading.

Centuries later Christianity arrived in a big way. Monasteries were built, Latin was introduced and Ireland slowly gained a reputation for its saints and scholars. Still, as with all of Europe, wars continued and Vikings were followed by Norman and British invaders, who continued to fight for control.

Time passed by and Oliver Cromwell marched through Ireland with a bloodied sword and strengthened the English hold over the land. Laws were enforced forbidding Catholics to hold Mass, or to buy or inherit land. The failure of the Irish potato crop in 1845, 1846 and 1848 threw the island into appalling famine. Irish farmers were utterly dependent on their potatoes, as other foodstuffs were sold to pay extortionate rents to English landowners. In less than ten years the population was reduced by two million. Many left Ireland forever, many were too weak to survive the voyage on what became known as the 'coffin ships.' Long-standing resentment, inflamed by the English connection, deepened to new levels.

On Easter Monday in 1916 a group of Fenians led an unexpected uprising in Dublin and took control of a number of public buildings. After five days they were overrun and systematically executed. This again only strengthened the people's sympathy for the Republicans and their cause. On December 6, 1921 the Anglo-Irish treaty was signed but this did little for the nation except plunge it deeper into civil war.

In 1938 a new constitution came into effect which finally declared Ireland's complete independence by renouncing British sovereignty and this free state became known as Eire. World War II was followed by twenty years of economic stagnation with vast numbers of the young and talented emigrating. In 1959 things had improved and in 1972 the country joined the European Economic Community. However, this has done little to bring the N and S of the country together and to this day the troubles in Northern Ireland unfortunately remain its most reported on topic.

THE LAND

The topography of Ireland is fairly subtle, there are few high mountain ranges and most of the centre is covered by a flat boggy plain. The country used to be covered in great forests but intensive pressure on the land leading up to the great famine of 1845 left the country bare.

Forests have been replaced largely by a patchwork of small grass fields divided by wild untidy hedgerows. The low population in Ireland today means that, over much of the country, there is less intensive land use than in many other European nations. Natural ecosystems such as peat bogs, dunes and wetlands still survive here, having all but disappeared elsewhere under the relentless pace of modern development.

Ireland escapes extremes of weather with the enveloping Atlantic Ocean producing a mild, damp climate. Summers are rarely hot, winters rarely cold and in parts of the West it rains on two days out of three. Such a climate is particularly favourable to the growth of grass and moss, inspiring Dubliner, William Drennan in the 18th century to name it 'the Emerald Isle.'

LANGUAGE

Irish is perhaps the most widely spoken of the Celtic tongues with an estimated 30% of the population competent in its use. It has been compulsory in schools since independence and can be found in newspapers, books, magazines, public notices and signs, and it's commonly spoken on television and radio. English, however, is the main language spoken although the untrained ear may need acclimatisation to some Irish accents.

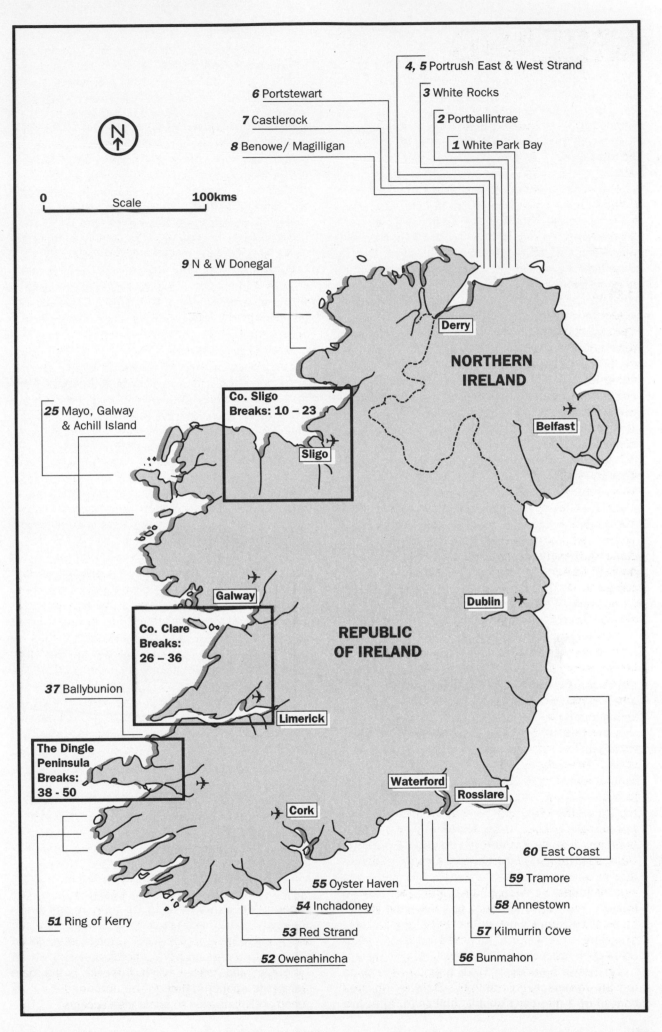

4, 5 Portrush East & West Strand

6 Portstewart

3 White Rocks

7 Castlerock

2 Portballintrae

8 Benowe/ Magilligan

1 White Park Bay

N

0   Scale   100kms

9 N & W Donegal

Derry

NORTHERN IRELAND

25 Mayo, Galway & Achill Island

Co. Sligo Breaks: 10 – 23

Sligo

Belfast

Galway

Dublin

Co. Clare Breaks: 26 – 36

REPUBLIC OF IRELAND

37 Ballybunion

Limerick

The Dingle Peninsula Breaks: 38 - 50

Waterford

Rosslare

Cork

60 East Coast

55 Oyster Haven

59 Tramore

54 Inchadoney

58 Annestown

51 Ring of Kerry

53 Red Strand

57 Kilmurrin Cove

52 Owenahincha

56 Bunmahon

THE SURF

"The best outside Hawaii," said Paul Russell, when describing the surf in Ireland, during a TV interview, and yet Ireland is the country in Europe where surfing has developed the least.

Two thirds of Ireland's population live along the East Coast. There are no towns on the West Coast so with with a population of more than 3,000 within walking distance of a surf spot this is the reason why Ireland has not developed as a surfing nation. The Irish have not been prominent as a seafaring nation either and, due to the country's wet climate, nor have they flocked traditionally to the coasts for their recreation. In amateur surfing Irish organisers and judges have held a number of high level posts at World and European level, but the surfers, with a few notable exceptions, have never quite made the grade. The Irish Surfing Association's decision to concentrate totally on the Under 16 Development Programme may well change that for the better in the future.

The majority of surf in Ireland comes from lows which track across from the United States to Northern Scandinavia, deepening as they go. The surf generally comes from a northwesterly direction as the lows approach Iceland with the winds from the lows blowing from the SW. This means that the north and northwest facing breaks, angled to catch the swell, also have got predominantly offshore winds.

A glance at the map of Ireland will show you the irregular nature of the coastline which provides a very useful variation in the direction of breaks within a short distance. There are countless surf possibilities, but we have identified three main surfing areas.

1. County Sligo
2. County Clare
3. Dingle

These are by no means the only places to surf but for various reasons, are the most popular.

The North Coast receives classic waves, but like County Donegal, Mayo and Galway, access problems present themselves. A more thorough navigation would reveal countless surf discoveries, but for now, they remain unsurfed.

The **South Coast** receives a lot of swell as well as onshore winds.

Most of the surfers in Ireland tend to use the better known breaks. There are no professional or even 'full time' surfers and as there is no real problem with crowds, little time is given to searching for new breaks.

Every surfer in the country will give you a list of places he plans to check out sometime soon. So, if you feel like an exploratory trip, there is plenty of scope.

The best times to visit are spring and autumn. During summer, the swells are a bit sporadic and it has been known for flat periods to last as long as two weeks. During the winter, the surf is almost continuous but the water is cold (3°- 4°C) and the winds can be very strong. April and May are often blessed with the best weather, the water is still quite cool but the winter swells have started to settle and the surf is fairly consistent. September to November is prime time. The winter swells have started to roll in and the water is still fairly warm. If you are used to wearing a wetsuit, you will find the temperature acceptable up until late November.

One basic necessity will be reliable transport. The wind and swell directions can change rapidly and while Ireland does have a lot of surf it's very often accompanied by onshore wind conditions so you do need to travel to find those sheltered spots.

As with Scotland, the sport is at a crucial nursery stage in Ireland. Most people haven't had contact with the sport so it's safe to say that we are all important ambassadors for the sport here. Why should Irish surfers inherit the 'ratbag' image not even entirely deserved in the more chaotic surf communities of the world. Show respect to the locals, drive with consideration and if people want to talk, be friendly. Things go slowly here so be patient – slip into the Irish mode of doing things and you will really enjoy yourself here, and you'll also be a constructive part of an exciting future. "Cead mile failte" or, "a hundred thousand welcomes."

Roci Allan/Irish Surfing Association

WINDSURFING

Windsurfing in Ireland has a large recreational following and also an intensely competitive fleet numbering approximately 200 sailors. The Irish Board Sailing Association is the body fostering the sport in Ireland. The highlight of the year is the I.B.S.A. Irish Championships and the Association is always very willing to provide information on any aspects of sailing in Ireland.

For the experienced windsurfer interested in wave jumping, the West and South West coasts offer a huge variety of beaches where Atlantic swells invite them to take on some of the most challenging conditions they are likely to meet anywhere. To quote top British Windsurfer, Duncan Coombs:

"Ireland's really got it! With thousands of miles of unexplored coastline and reefs everywhere... who needs Hawaii?

"At some points along the coast such as Achill Island, Co Mayo and Brandon Bay, Co Kerry, windsurfing compared to the best of the sport found in Hawaii and the Canary Islands. I now train in Brandon Bay which lies under a 3,000ft range of mountains, these funnel the wind accross the bay which picks up the powerfull swells. The clean waters and uncrowded beaches mixed with the timeless pace of life, and friendly people gives Ireland it's magical beauty."

Irish Tourist Board

TRAVELLING AROUND

Living

Ireland is not an especially cheap place to travel. If anything, basics work out more expensive than in Britain. It's hard to live cheaply but it can be done by renting a cottage between a few friends and cooking your own food. Camping is easy and obviously the cheapest way to live although, considering Ireland's wet climate it's not for everyone. Farm cottages and B&B's are numerous and often very comfortable.

No trip to Ireland is complete without a visit to a pub! Especially in rural areas, the pub is far more than just a place to drink. It's the heart of the Irish village, and often the political centre too. For food, advice and conversation, the pub is usually the place to head for and very often they are venues for local entertainment especially live music.

Money

In Ireland, you spend Irish pounds, also known as the punt, which is divided into 100 pence as in Britain. There is a myth that there's no need to change your cash if you are coming from Britain since the Irish will helpfully accept pounds sterling, which is not at all surprising when £1 sterling is equivalent to about IR£1.15. Change your money in the banks.

Ferry Services

Ireland is serviced by a number of different ferry companies which sail from both Britain and France. Prices vary considerably depending on which season you travel, and outside of the summer period they can be extremely good value. The main advantage of travelling by ferry is that you can bring your car – vital if one is going to get the best out of Ireland's swell pounded coasts. Ferry companies operating to Ireland include: B+I, P+O, Sealink, Belfast Car Ferries,etc.

Flying

International carriers fly to Dublin, Belfast, Cork and Shannon and from these airports it's easy to catch a connecting flight to Ireland's many regional airports. Competition between airlines and ferry companies keep prices cheap and it's advisable to shop around if you want to get the best deal available.

Airlines flying to Ireland include: Air Lingus, Air UK, Britannia Airways, Ryanair, Dan Air, British Airways, British Midlands and Capital Airlines.

Driving

It's well worth remembering that Ireland's roads cater for drivers who are prepared to take their time. You can't get anywhere very fast, so it's best not to try. Savour the slower pace of life and don't try to cover too large an area in too short a time.

Another thing worth remembering is that petrol is expensive (IR£2.80 per gallon) and petrol stations in some of the more remote areas are few and far between.

Still, driving around Ireland from one great reef break to the next is hugely enjoyable and is one of Ireland's greatest delights. As in Britain you drive on the left and most other road signs and markings are similar.

Embassies and Consulates

British nationals do not need a passport to enter the Republic or the North, but it's useful to carry one in case you use the medical services, and for cashing travellers' cheques.

If you don't take a passport, be sure to have some other form of convincing ID. Other EC nationals, travellers from the USA, Canada, Australia, New Zealand and Commonwealth countries simply need a passport and can stay for up to three months.

EMBASSIES (ALL IN DUBLIN):
UK:
31/33 Merrion Rd, Dublin 4
Tel: 695211
US:
42 Elgin Rd, Ballsbridge, Dublin 4
Tel: 688777
AUS:
Fitzwilton House, Wilton Terrace
Dublin 2
Tel: 761517
AIRPORT INFORMATION:
Dublin: 01 370191
TOURIST OFFICES:
Dublin, 14 Upper O'Connell St,
Dublin, 1
Tel: 01 747733
IRISH TOURIST BOARDS:
Irish Tourist Board:
Baggot St Bridge
Dublin 2
Tel: 01 765871
GB:
150 New Bond St,
London W1Y 0AQ
Tel: 071 4933201
France:
33 Rue de Miromesnil,
75008 Paris
Tel: 1 47420336
Northern Ireland
53 Castle St
Belfast BT1 1GH
Tel: 0232 327888
TELEPHONING:
Northern Ireland: As for England
Republic of Ireland
Dialling in code......................353
Dialling out code.......................6
Operator.................................10
Directory enquiries................190
Long Distance Calls 10
International Calls.................114
Telegrams 115
Emergency 999
PUBLIC HOLIDAYS:
Northern Ireland:
As for England,
Republic of Ireland:
1, January
17, March (St. Patrick's day)
Good Friday
Easter Monday
First Monday in June
First Monday in August
Last Monday in October
25, December
26, December

NORTHERN IRELAND – THE CAUSEWAY COAST

'The Causeway Coast' stretches from Ballycastle to Magilligan Point. Surfing first started here in the Easter holidays of 1963 when local customs officer Ian Hill entered the water at Castlerock with a 'Bob Head' board made at Mawgan Porth in Cornwall. Three years later a group of youngsters led by Alan Duke (to be many times Irish champion) started surfing in the Portrush/Portstewart area and began travelling to the West Coast where they met up with other surfers who had just started in the Rossnowlagh, Sligo, Waterford and Tramore areas.

For 20 years the number of Northern Irish surfers stuck at around 20. The advent of body boarding opened up the sport to a younger age group and a proportion of these youngsters progressed to stand-up surfing. Today surfers number about 120 'locals,' mainly from Portrush/Portstewart, and there are quite a few travellers who come up from Belfast on the weekends attracted by both the surf and the night time entertainment on offer. 'Kellys' in Portrush is the biggest disco in Ireland.

The expansion of the sport has also had led to the opening of a surf shop, 'Troggs (The Underground) Surf Shop' which stocks all the well known brands of 'hardware' and 'software' and offers a full hire and instruction service and wave report.

The main surfing season on the north coast is from mid August to mid May when the lows in the northern hemisphere track across from Iceland to Norway. In the summer months the lows tend to be a lot further south in the Atlantic, sending good swells into the West Coast, but Malin Head tends to stop them getting round to the Causeway Coast.

Ian Hill/Troggs Surf Shop

TRAVELLING AROUND

Tourist Offices:
Portrush; Located in the Town Hall
Tel: 0265 823333
Portstewart; Located in the Town Hall
Tel: 0265 832286

Surf Breaks 1 – 9

1. White Park Bay

White Park Bay faces north-northwest offering 2kms of beach break rights and lefts. It's an attractive spot which can make surfing here that much more worthwhile if the waves are good. Surfable on any tide up to 6ft. The car park above the beach is five minutes walk from the sands.

2. Portballintrae

Just to the East of Portballintrae lies a consistent northwest facing bay. The waves here will often be a foot or two bigger, and more powerful than at other nearby beaches. Quality will depend on the state of the sandbanks and wind direction. Any wind with too much west in it will mess up the swell. Good to 8ft. There is a car park in Portballintrae which lies next to the Southwest corner of the beach. From here it's a short walk.

3. White Rocks

White Rocks needs a N swell with a S wind to produce decent rideable waves. With these conditions good rights and lefts can be surfed on any tide up to 6ft. The beach gets crowded in summer but with tourists not surfers. Located on the road from Portrush to Portballintrae (it's signposted) with easy parking next to the sands.

4. Portrush – East Strand

Portrush, like Portstewart is a popular holiday resort for people living in Northern Ireland. On the eastern side of the peninsula, there is a good beach which works best with SW to SE winds. It is also a good spot to check out on a big swell, when the other nearby beaches are closing out. This is due to the protection it receives from the peninsula on which Portrush is built. There's a big car park next to the beach, which tends to get full in summertime.

5. Portrush – West Strand

Northwest facing beach that catches swell when the East Strand is too small. Waves increase in size from east to west. At the western end is **Black Rocks** (Dhu Varren), a leftand reef break which holds surf to 8ft. Drive under the railway bridge to the car park.

6. Portstewart Strand

Just west of Portstewart, is Portstewart Strand. The beach here can provide some of Northern Ireland's gentler waves. Optimum conditions, like most of Northern Ireland's beaches are a N or NW swell, accompanied by a S or SE wind. This will provide some good peaky rights and lefts. The waves are surfable up to 6 – 8ft. Portstewart itself, is a busy seaside resort which gets crowded during summer months. Either park above the beach, or do as the locals do and park on the sands.

7. Castlerock

A little way east of Castlerock is a long stone jetty. The presence of this jetty has helped to create a consistent sandbank. This bank is best surfed around mid tide when it can produce an excellent, long righthander. The wave is best from 3 - 6ft, any bigger and then it will close-out. From low to mid tide the sands are wide and firm and are safe for most vehicles to drive on. You can either drive from Castlerock or, alternatively, it's possible to drive along the beach from Portstewart and paddle out through the river, around the jetty, to the wave.

8. Benowe/Magilligan

The longest beach in Ireland – ten miles of beach break peaks. You can get there via Downhills and Benowe. A superb view from Bishops Road above the beach to Donegal and Londonderry.

9. North and West Donegal

There are only a few coastal areas left in Europe where the possibility of finding perfect undiscovered waves still exists. North and West Donegal is one of these places! It receives so much swell that more often than not one's only real concern will be the wind conditions. These winds can often be very strong and they will generally blow from the N and W. The relentless forces of nature have slowly carved up the desolate coastline around Donegal, consequently little protected little bays and islands have become abundant. Such places offer unlimited potential, all they need is time and energy to explore!

Donegal is sparsely populated due its harsh climate and inhospitable landscape, accessability is therefore limited. **Bloody Foreland, Magheroaty, Dunfanaghy, Gweebarra and Loughros Beg** have been surfed in the past, beyond these breaks you will very possibly be surfing virgin waves.

County Sligo

County Sligo might seem an unusual choice of location, but in Europe it's one of the few places to warrant the title 'a surfers' paradise.' A large portion of its coast is north facing, so it works in the prevailing SW airstream. It presents numerous reefs, points and beaches to the wrath of the North Atlantic and picks up swell from the West, North West and North.

County Sligo still remains an uncrowded place to surf and the reasons it has retained its purity might become obvious when looking at climatic tables. Sligo is wet and windy. Combine that with the cost comparisons between an Irish and a French surf holiday and you'll get an idea of why people have left the Sligo coast to a select handful of surfers.

But when you get there, you'll see waves which make all the cost comparisons not worth the paper they're written on. Two main focal points have emerged in County Sligo – the towns of Bundoran and Easky. Bundoran is the home of some semblance of surf culture. The waves at Bundoran and Tullan are excellent and surrounding areas are beautiful. Competitions have been known on this stretch of coast. But it's the two breaks at Easky which have so far become the best known in Ireland and it's not uncommon to find people of several different nationalities sitting on the point. The town is small and friendly and accommodation is not difficult to find, the shopkeepers know everyone in town and were friendly to us. There are perhaps only one or two resident surfers here and they're quite young, it should be interesting to watch their progress. Needless to say, help them all you can.

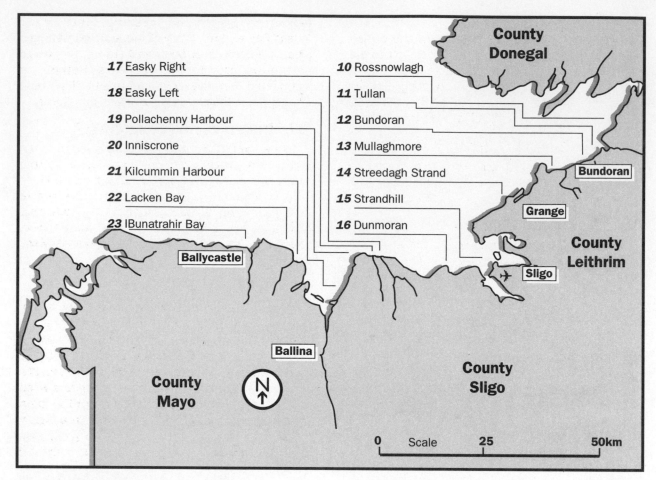

17 Easky Right
18 Easky Left
19 Pollachenny Harbour
20 Inniscrone
21 Kilcummin Harbour
22 Lacken Bay
23 IBunatrahir Bay

10 Rossnowlagh
11 Tullan
12 Bundoran
13 Mullaghmore
14 Streedagh Strand
15 Strandhill
16 Dunmoran

County Donegal

Bundoran

Grange

County Leithrim

Sligo

Ballycastle

Ballina

County Mayo

N

County Sligo

0   Scale   25   50km

Surf Breaks 10 – 23

10. Rossnowlagh

Rossnowlagh is home to one of Ireland's biggest surf clubs and it's here that one may meet some of the rare Irish surfers who can often be found sipping a Guiness in 'the surfers' bar' of the hotel. The waves here can be good but they will tend to be a bit weaker and smaller than those at Tullan. Still, when Tullan is closing out, Rossnowlagh can be a good alternative. The beach faces west and the waves are surfable on any tide, depending on the swell size. There's easy parking by the beach.

11. Tullan Strand

The waves breaking onto Tullan Strand are considered to be some of the best and most consistent beach break waves in Ireland. It's a nice spot, with dunes backing on to a wide expanse of golden sands. The southern end, below the parking area, has the nicest peaks which generally work best around low tide. If it's flat along the rest of the coast, then there can still be a wave here. Good to 6ft. To get there take the first left north of Bundoran, (it is not signposted), and after about half a mile you will come to an area for parking above the beach.

12. Bundoran

Bundoran is home to one of Ireland's best and most surfed waves. With a fair sized W or a bigger NW swell, a peak breaking mainly left will peel and tube its way across the northern side of the bay. It's a low tide break that is at its best in the 4 - 6ft range, with a S or SE wind. When this wave starts getting big, another more sheltered lefthander starts to work. This wave can also be very good. Both break over a rock bottom and both can occasionally get crowded. There's easy parking in front of the waves.

13. Mullaghmore

This sheltered NE facing beach is a good spot to check out when there's a SW wind accompanying a big NW swell. With such conditions one will find nice clean lines pushing into the bay, providing fast rights and lefts. Also, at such times, it can be worth a drive around Mullaghmore Head. There is reputedly a lefthander breaking over some shallow rocks that can hold a 20ft swell! There's easy parking above the southwest corner of the beach.

14. Streedagh Strand (and beyond)

Streedagh Strand faces northwest and needs a fair sized swell to produce worthwhile waves. However, if the sandbanks here are not producing the goods, then your time spent getting here might not necessarily be wasted. Beyond Streedagh, all the way down to Ballyconnell, are numerous unmarked roads leading to numerous virgin little coves and inlets. The possibility of finding an unmarked reef or point break here is high. Streedagh Strand is signposted from Grange and there's parking by the beach.

15. Strandhill

At Strandhill, you can either surf the beach break, or, if you have the energy, paddle out to the sandbars breaking offshore at the southern end of the beach. Both spots often produce high quality rights and lefts that are best surfed with a S or SE wind. The beach here is popular with tourists and locals alike and there is even a place where one can rent a surfboard, worthwhile remembering if your board has been chewed up by some of Ireland's unforgiving reefs! There's easy parking at the centre of the beach.

16. Dunmoran Strand

Dunmoran Strand is a nice out of the way place which can have good beach break waves. It faces north and can hold surf up to 6ft. A good beginners' beach. Park by the beach.

17. Easky Right

Easky Right is without doubt a world class righthander! It's the kind of wave that keeps you rooted to the spot, leaving you with little desire to explore the rest of this wave-rich island. Low tide is best with the wave being rideable from 2-10ft. One of the major pluses for this break is its consistency and the abundant offshore winds you get here. These conditions provide perfect tubes and long fast walls. This wave is located to the right of the old ruin, if it's working you'll definitely see it. There's easy parking in front of the peak.

18. Easky Left

The lefthander breaking on the western side of the harbour wall is another very good reason for spending time in Easky. This wave works under the same conditions as the right but it will break on a smaller swell and it can be surfed whatever the tidal state. The waves break over a rock bottom and can hold up to a 12ft swell. At the end of the harbour wall are steps leading into the sea. The water is usually calm here making the paddle out to the waves easy. Watch out for strong rips, outside sets and shifting peaks. Like the right, this wave can have crowds in summer and autumn.

19. Pollacheeny Harbour

At the mouth of Pollacheeny harbour you will find another excellent reef break. From low to mid tide, there's a righthander that tubes its way over the rocky point giving fast rides of up to 150mtrs in length.

This break, like nearly all of Ireland's breaks is rarely surfed. This, however, is purely due to the lack of surfers and the number of great breaks Ireland has to offer. If any of these waves were in a place like Cornwall or Southwest France, they would always be crowded! Pollacheeny Harbour is signposted from the main road (about 5kms west of Easky) and there's easy parking by the slipway.

20. Innishcrone (Enniscrone)

Innishcrone has a nice, long, north facing beach which can provide fun and easy sand bottom waves. It's a sheltered spot which will only work on a big N swell. At the eastern end, near the harbour an excellent righthander will start to break over a sand and rock bottom when the swell is big enough and it can provide some great long waves. Easy parking.

21. Kilcummin Harbour

When there's a big swell from the N and a S or SE wind, an excellent, long lefthander will break in front of the harbour wall at Kilcummin. Although a S or SE wind is best, the shelter this break receives means that a W wind will not totally ruin it. It breaks over a rock bottom and can have strong rips when it's big. Kilcummin is signposted from the main road. After a few kms you will come to a cross-roads, take the right hand turn following the sign saying 'Humbert's Landing.' The harbour is about 2 kms from there.

22. Lacken Bay

There can be some good beach break waves along this attractive and secluded bay. It works under the same conditions as the left at Kilcummin but it needs less swell to produce rideable waves. Follow the road around from Kilcummin and the beach will come into view. Park where possible.

23. Bunatrahir Bay

Breaking over a rock bottom, at the western side of Bunatrahir Bay is a very nice lefthander. It needs a fair-sized N swell to get it going and a South wind to clean it up. With these conditions, you'll get some great rides. A little way outside of Ballycastle is a road leading to a small unmarked harbour. If the wave is working, you'll see it.

24 & 25 Mayo, Galway
Achill Island

Ireland is a slow-paced, quiet and thinly populated country. Western Ireland is even slower, quieter and more thinly populated. Counties Mayo and Galway virtually stand still. Like Donegal, it's not everybody's ideal surf location, but for those of you who like the excitement of surfing unexplored waters in a wild place, then look no further.

ACHILL ISLAND is Ireland's largest offshore island (connected by a bridge). It's a remote place but there are a few places to stay, making it a good place to spend a few days. There are breaks at **Keel, Dooega, Dooagh and Doogort.**

TRAVEL INFORMATION

Tourist Office:
Galway, Aras Failte, Eyre Sq
Tel: 091 63081

Galway Airport Information:
Tel: 091 52874

County Clare

County Clare, like Sligo, would be one of Europe's most popular surfing destinations, if the weather here was a little more hospitable, as it offers a huge selection of surf spots. These breaks range from mellow reefs and beaches (Lahinch Left and Lahinch Beach) to the biggest, gnarliest tubes you could ever want to ride! (Crab Island and the outside reef at Spanish Point.)

County Clare is exposed to the full influence of the Atlantic ocean, with low pressure systems from the SW, W and NW all sending in swell. Offshores, being predominantly SE, aren't as common as SW winds and consequently this area may be less consistent than many north facing parts of County Sligo, but when it's on, it's right on. To stand above Lahinch Points and see the points break, is a magnificent sight, and it's one of a complement of wicked waves.

Clare also has a very rich culture in traditional music and highly entertaining pubs. Clare is bounded to the west and north by the Atlantic, to the south by the Shannon Estuary and to the west by the River Shannon. It is this geographical isolation that has helped to maintain the county's proud attachment to Irish music.

The town of Lahinch is the centre for surfing in this part of Ireland and for good reason (especially if you're a goofyfooter). It's situated next to a long, white, sandy beach and at its northern end lie three excellent lefthand reef breaks. These waves and the presence of a small surf shop (just off the promenade) have prompted many surfers, wave-ski riders and boogie boarders to take to the water. These surfers are as refreshingly friendly as you'll find anywhere in Europe and they welcome the chance to surf with travelling surfers.

There is a large variety of accommodation available in Lahinch from camp sites, hostels, self-catering flats, and guest houses through to top class hotels. Many of these are open all year round. There is also a hostel in Spanish Point and many hostels in Doolin, also two between Lahinch and the Cliffs of Moher. On rare flat days, visit the Cliffs of Moher and take a little time to tour the Burren in North Clare. This is a unique limestone area resembling nothing else in Europe. If you're interests extend to rock climbing or caving, this area could keep you exploring for a year or so.

There are a few more surf breaks along the coast but access is a major problem and if you insist on trying to find them you could risk antagonising the local farmers, and this would not endear you to the small-but-dedicated local surf community.

The local club is The West Coast Surf Club and may be contacted through the Lahinch Surf Shop Tel: 065 81543 or the Brewsters Pub Tel: 065 81414.

Thomas Buckley/Lahinch Surf Shop

Surf Breaks 26 – 36

26. Crab Island

Not to be taken lightly, firstly because of its distance from Doolin pier (a long paddle), but mostly because of the size of the wave. A big righthander jacks-up suddenly from deep water and can form very frightening tubes if the wind is from the east. Check your leash carefully!

27. Doolin Point

At the point, beyond the car park, there is a fast righthand reef break. Often, various sections will break unevenly, ruining the wave. But, when the swell is clean enough, long walling rides are possible. If this wave isn't working and Crab Island doesn't suit your tastes, then there can be other peaks with decent rides available. Neither Doolin Point nor Crab Island are beginners' waves. Doolin's well signposted and there is a car park in front of the wave.

28. Lahinch Beach

Lahinch is about the closest thing to a surfing town you will come across in Ireland. There's a surf shop, quite a few surfers and plenty of great waves. The more experienced surfers generally ride the reef break leaving the many beginners to practice on the excellent, slow beach break waves. These waves are best from mid to high tide and are rideable up to about 8ft. Easy parking by the beach. There's a rip on the left side of the beach which will help you get out the back.

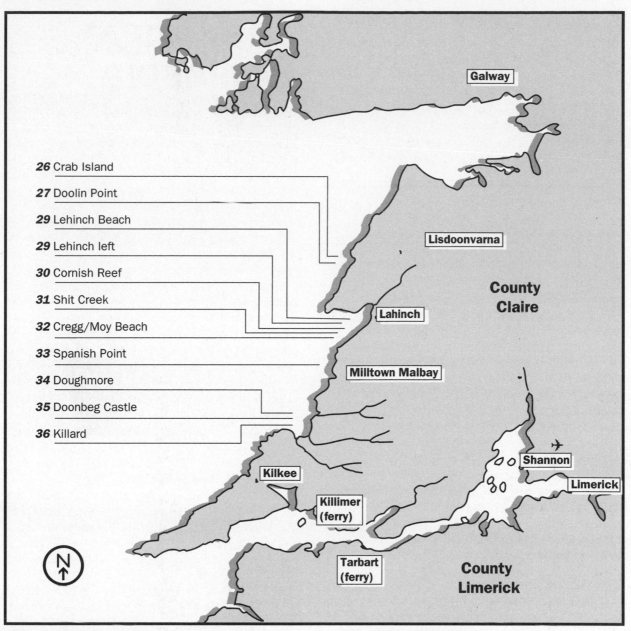

26 Crab Island
27 Doolin Point
29 Lehinch Beach
29 Lehinch left
30 Cornish Reef
31 Shit Creek
32 Cregg/Moy Beach
33 Spanish Point
34 Doughmore
35 Doonbeg Castle
36 Killard

Galway

Lisdoonvarna

County Claire

Lahinch

Milltown Malbay

Shannon

Limerick

Kilkee

Killimer (ferry)

Tarbart (ferry)

County Limerick

29. Lahinch Left

This is by far the most popular wave amongst Lahinch locals. It's a very easy wave to ride, with a simple take-off and long walls with rides of up to 400mtrs.

This spot is Ireland's favourite break with crowds present if there's a decent swell. Still, the locals here are very friendly and hassles in the water are virtually nonexistent.

On a big swell high tide is surfable, otherwise low to mid tide is best. A SE wind is offshore and the wave is surfable up to 10ft. Park in Lahinch and you'll see waves breaking over rocks at the left hand side of the beach.

30. Cornish Reef

Cornish Reef can provide good, sometimes excellent, lefthanders. It works under the same conditions as Lahinch Left but it's a faster, more tubey wave. It also doesn't get as crowded. Mid tide is best and it's surfable up to 10ft. Fairly easy paddle out off the rocks between Cornish and Lahinch Left.

31. Shit Creek

It's the least surfed and the most demanding of Lahinch's reefs. Low tide is shallow, fast and hollow, leaving little room for error. Mid tide is still fast and hollow but safer. High tide is more mellow but with a big swell it can have the best wave of the lot. The main ride is a lefthander but there is also a good right. Lastly, don't be put off by the name, Shit Creek is so called because of murky river water discolouring the sea and not pollution! You'll find it a bit beyond Cornish Reef.

32. Cregg Beach/Moy Beach

This little stony beach can be a good spot to check when there's a big swell accompanied by a SE wind. At such times you will find some fun rights and lefts, with the best size being from 2 - 4ft. Moy Beach is located south of Lahinch. You'll see it from the road. Parking is possible for a few cars. Southwest of Cregg beach is an excellent, if a little rare, reef break called **Aussie Left** – one of the longest waves in Clare. To get there turn off at the sign for Barr Tra Seafood Restaurant.

33. Spanish Point

Spanish Point was so named because it was here that survivors from wrecked Armada ships swam ashore. Unfortunately for them, the High Sheriff of Clare had them all executed. Now, these hazardous rocky reefs can provide some excellent righthanders.

INSIDE POINT needs a big swell with a SE, E or NE wind to produce good waves. It's a short ride that is best at mid tide.

MIDDLE POINT is usually the best of the three reefs, giving fast walls and makeable tubes. Mid tide is best.

OUTSIDE POINT takes the brunt of most swells and is rarely surfed due to the ferocity of the break. Can hold a 15 – 20ft swell! For the Inside Point, park at the car park above the northern end of the beach. For Middle and Outside Point, take a small un-marked road about ½ km north of the car park. There are also good beach break waves.

34. Doughmore

Beach break with outside reef. When every other break is too small this works. When swell is big it dumps right across beach even in offshore winds. However, access is at present a major problem. Check with local surf club if there has been a resolution to this before crossing anybody's land or you could find yourself in serious trouble.

35. Doonbeg Castle

When there's a huge swell with a SW wind a very nice lefthand wave can be found breaking near the old ruined castle by the jetty in Doonbeg. It breaks over a rock bottom and is best from mid to high tide. Head here when all other breaks in Clare are closing out. Turn off the main coast road by the church.

36. Killard

This sandy little bay works under the same conditions as Doonbeg. The waves here are best from low to mid tide and they are surfable to 4ft. There's easy parking by the beach.

37. Ballybunion

Ballybunion has an impressive beach with a couple of good waves. At the northern end, breaking along (and smashing into) the cliffs you will find a sand bottom righthander.

Locals who know this break will sit and wait for the waves just inches away from the cliffs. The take-off is fast and wedgy but otherwise it's an easy wave to ride. High tide is best.

The other is a lefthander that breaks over the rocks further down the beach. This is a low tide break providing some fast hollow waves more suitable for experienced surfers. The beach break can also give good waves. There's easy parking (except summer) at the north end and also by the ruin in the middle of the beach.

The Dingle Peninsula

The Dingle Peninsula is one of the most naturally beautiful areas of Ireland. Even if there's no surf, this area is worth a visit. Fortunately, the breaks are also great.

The Peninsula is mostly mountainous with dramatic sweeps down to the sea. There are climbs which vary from gentle walks to serious mountain challenges with superb views all the way, as well as archaeological sites which you will stumble across. A great place for mountain biking including the highest mountain pass in Ireland.

There is fishing for most tastes from deep sea angling to surf casting for Atlantic bass, from spinning for sea trout to trying to catch their wild mountain lake cousins. The wildlife is generally abundant and the naturalist or ornithologist will find plenty to absorb them.

Everywhere you look there are pubs where "the crack will be mighty." Often there is traditional music played for pleasure and some excellent musicians to be heard. A few pubs specialise in sea food (Spillane's Bar, Fahamore, and Castle-gregory for example) and particularly in Dingle there are excellent, if expensive, restaurants.

Accommodation is no problem. There are camping and caravan parks of varying standards and many bed and breakfast establishments at reasonable rates. It's possible to rent holiday cottages by the week but you would be well advised to book in advance.

A great place for families, there is little chance for getting bored and whatever you choose to do on the Dingle Peninsula, you will not be bothered by crowds. And you are never far from the sea with long golden beaches, surf, wind and waves.

Jamie Knox/Focus Windsurfing School

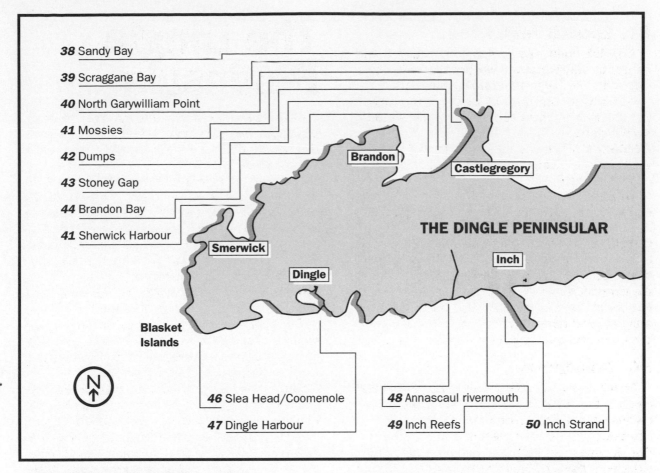

38 Sandy Bay
39 Scraggane Bay
40 North Garywilliam Point
41 Mossies
42 Dumps
43 Stoney Gap
44 Brandon Bay
41 Sherwick Harbour

Brandon
Castlegregory
THE DINGLE PENINSULAR
Smerwick
Dingle
Inch
Blasket Islands

N

46 Slea Head/Coomenole
47 Dingle Harbour
48 Annascaul rivermouth
49 Inch Reefs
50 Inch Strand

Surf Breaks 38 – 51

38. Sandy Bay

Sandy Bay is ideal for beginners and families on holiday. There's plenty of accommodation in the area and safe sheltered beaches with (from June to August) a resident lifeguard. A great place to learn the basics with more challenging waves close by.

It's the site of the Focus Windsurfing School run by Jamie Knox.

39. Scraggane Bay

Take the right fork at the grotto marked 'Green Room Bar' and follow down to the sea. Good place for windsurfing slalom, best on SW, W or NW. Safe intermediate spot.

40. North Garywilliam Point

Warning, this wave is only for the best and most experienced surfers! The take-off jacks up as steeply as any Hawaiin wave with house sized righthand tubes on its best days (NW swell, light E winds). The most exciting surfing sensation you are ever likely to get – wear a brown wetsuit!

NOT TO BE RIDDEN ON LOW TIDE – ROCKY REEF. If you still want to go there after reading this, access is by walking north from Mossies. Go to the end of the point and paddle round to the break.

41. Mossie's

Probably one of the best surfing waves in Europe. Nicknamed after the farmer who first saw surfers at this spot. It's situated opposite Spillane's Bar in Fahamore. Unless you like a long paddle out, access is easiest from Garywilliam Point by driving to the end of the road, walking between the houses and down the cliff to see a peak which breaks left and right. Offshore wind is E and it picks up any direction of swell, good on NW at all tides but best on the incoming. It's a rocky reef so beware at low tide.

42. Dumps

Half way between Sandy Bay and Fahamore close to the road on the Brandon Bay side is a gap in the sandhills. West facing, so crosshore winds from N or S at low to mid tide give you the best waves. At high tide the name Dumps reveals it's origins – you will be dumped onto the stones, so beware!

43. Stoney Gap

Situated between the two Sandy Bay caravan parks on the Brandon Bay side. This can be accessed by driving through the sandhills. For windsurfers the crosshore winds are S to SW, best at mid tide. Good in NW with small swell but **dangerous** in a big swell! Surfing can be good at low tide.

44. Brandon Bay

From the top of Conner Pass (the highest mountain pass in Ireland) you can see the whole horseshoe sweep of Brandon Bay facing NW. For a combination of surfing and windsurfing this is one of the best places in Europe. Within the area from Fermoyle to Scraggane Bay in the Maharees, you can experience all types of conditions suitable for everyone from beginners to pro's. Why spend all your holiday driving?

The winds funnel down between the mountains and the surf is formed by the shelf at the edge of the Brandon Bay Deep. It picks up most directions of swell and works in most winds. East of Fermoyle is Stradbally, a well known windsurf spot. In a sideshore wind (SW), it really picks up the swell with well spaced waves. Some of the best wave riding, jumping and out and out windsurfing in Ireland. West again is one of the best places for surfing and windsurfing for safe fun. Nicknamed 'Three Peaks,' in S to SW crosshore winds it breaks from left to right on a shallow sand bank, best at rising mid tide. When surfing, line up with three white poles on Stradbally golf course for the peak.

45. Sherwick Harbour

Surfing only. Two relatively unknown breaks; a left in the centre of the harbour, and a righthander at Ballydavid are both good in N to NW swells and S to SE offshore winds. The left is not for the fainthearted! The take-off is heavy. Ballydavid has an easy take-off with a long wall and fast finish. Best at mid tide. Access from Ballydavid and the other side of the harbour.

46. Slea Head (Coomenole)

Surfing only. On the end of the Dingle Peninsula lies the southwest facing bay called Coomenole. It picks up all S and W swells and the beach drops sharply into the ocean. Ledgey righthanders break in front of the shipwreck (note well!) and rocky reef. Exercise caution, water movement in the area can be extreme. Fools rush in where angels fear to tread. Low to mid tide is best on the push. Slea Head is signposted and there is easy parking above the waves.

47. Dingle Harbour

On the days when there's no wind take your board and paddle out in the mouth of the Harbour

TRAVEL INFORMATION
Tourist office:
Main Street (June – Sept)
Tel: 066 51188
The Natural Living & Healthy Centre
Tel: 066 58189
Accomodation overlooking Inch Strand. Classes in relaxation, yoga and Shiatsu.
Macrobiotic, vegan and vegetarian food also available.
Ferry to Blacket Islands:
Tel: 066 56146 – 56280
Between 11am and 5pm May to September subject to weather.

to meet and play with Fungi, the famous Dingle dolphin and afterwards try a few pints in the local pier-side pubs!

48. Annascaul Rivermouth

Again for surfing only. Best in SW swell with offshore N to E winds. It's a faster take-off than Inch Reefs with the peak moving around a bit. As it wraps in you get a nice tube and a faster wave.

The paddle out is often quite difficult because of the rivermouth. Good duckdiving needed. Best at incoming mid tide. From Inch Reef make a sharp left to park. The break will be obvious.

49. Inch Reefs

Under inaccessible cliffs west of Inch Strand is Inch Reef. For surfing only. You want a S to W swell and offshore winds from N to E to create righthand waves with easy take-offs and long walls. Good place to watch your mates do their stuff while you make the effortless paddle out around the break.

The best break is at high tide which makes for problems leaving the water. Take care and make sure you have a suitable exit point figured out before catching a wave in. Surfable waves up to 10ft. Access is up to you. Park on the side of the road and find a way down.

50. Inch Strand

Inch Strand juts out to sea for 4 miles. It's a beautiful place which can also provide some good quality beach break waves. It's more of a longboard or beginner's wave, best at mid tide. The northern end is usually the best part of the beach – it receives fairly good protection from NW winds and is the easiest place to paddle out when the waves are big. For windsurfing the prevailing wind is W to SW onshore and therefore it's practically impossible to launch. There's easy parking at the top of the beach.

51. The Ring of Kerry

The 110 mile Ring of Kerry which encircles the Iveragh Peninsula has some great surf amongst some of Ireland's most impressive scenery.

At the northern end lies **ROSSBEIGH STRAND** giving 4 miles of beach break waves similar to those breaking along Inch Strand across Dingle Bay.

Your next port of call should definitely be **BALLINSKELLIGS BAY**. This sheltered bay contains a number of breaks ranging from gentle beaches to excellent reefs and points. With a SW swell, or a big W swell waves will show themselves.

Different breaks work on different tides with different winds so something will nearly always be working here.

Past Waterville is **DERRNANE**, here there is a lovely beach with crystal clear waters which can, when the swell is big enough, provide some pristine little waves.

Surf Breaks 52 – 60

52. Ownahincha

There are a couple of exposed beaches here that will pick up more swell than just about anywhere on Ireland's South Coast. They face SW and consequently need a N, NE or E wind to make the swells clean. Rights and lefts will break from sandbar peaks with mid to high tide being best. Easy parking by the beaches.

53. Red Strand (Dirk Bay)

Red Strand is a small beach with rights and lefts that are more protected against strong winds than other nearby beaches. At the eastern end, lefthanders can be good if the sand bottom is well formed. These waves will break on any tide depending on the swell size and can be surfed up to 4 – 5ft. Red Strand is signposted and there is easy parking.

54. Inchadoney

Inchadoney has an attractive beach with a headland in the middle and a river at each end. The waves here can be good if there's a S or SW swell with a NW to NE wind. When provided with such conditions, it can be a good idea to stop above the beach (where there's an excellent view of the waves) and check to see which sandbanks are working. There's easy parking by the beach.

55. Oysterhaven

Oysterhaven is a beautiful, sheltered bay, ideal for beginners, just ten minutes drive from Kinsale, and 25 minutes from Cork City. The harbour faces out to the southwest, attracting fresh sea breezes ideal for funboarders.

TRAVELLING AROUND

CORK TOURIST OFFICE:
Tourist House
Grand Parade
Tel: 021 273251

AIRPORT INFORMATION:
Tel: 021 313131

WATERFORD TOURIST OFFICE:
41 the Quay
Tel: 051 75788

AIRPORT INFORMATION:
Tel: 051 75589

IRISH BOARD SAILING ASSOCIATION:
Viaduct House,
Castlewhite,
Waterfall,
Nr Cork
Tel: (021) 543268

---

56. Bunmahon

There are countless beaches along Ireland's south coast that require the same conditions as Bunmahon. A S or SW swell with a wind from somewhere up north. When these conditions are present, then Bunmahon can be as good as anywhere but not necessarily better than anywhere. If you find a beach with a well-formed sand bottom, stick around and make the most of it. Swells on the South Coast don't last long. Easy parking by the beach.

57. Kilmurrin Cove

When the swell is closing out other nearby beaches and winds are too strong, there can still be good waves breaking in this sheltered little horseshoe bay. The ride involves a big drop at the mouth with a long gentle shoulder on the inside. Don't go outside the mouth, where there can be strong currents, and large waves break against the cliffs. Works best around mid tide. Easy access from car park.

58. The Perfect Wave (Annestown)

This is a very popular reef break east of Annestown beach reached by walking around the rocks 100mtrs from the beach. The waves here are often bigger and it works at low tide. The rocks are a little too close for comfort unless the surf is over 4ft. Not for beginners.

59. Tranmore Area

Anyone landing in Rosslare at the start of a surf holiday would do well to check out the Tranmore area. Though surf here is often accompanied by onshore winds, it does have moments of perfection. The Tranmore Surf Club has been going strong since the mid 60's, and the current National Junior Champion David Blount comes from Tranmore. Surfboards can be hired at Tranmore beach and lessons are given to beginners. Surfboard manufacturer Henry Moore stocks all surf supplies and also repairs damaged boards.

The South Coast S. C.

(est 1968)
Ms Margaret O'Brien-Morgan
7 Marine Terrace, Tramore,
Co Waterford Tel: 051 865882

---

60. East Coast

The East Coast of Ireland can occasionally have rideable waves. During winter strong S winds will generate some swell. These winds then need to swing round to a more westerly direction to make the swell clean. If you are in the area and these conditions are present, then **Jack's Hole** is worth a look. The Irish Sea is reputedly the most radioactive sea in the world, so even if it looks clean…?

WALES

Capital:	Cardiff
Population:	2,728,000
Area:	20,240km² (7800mls²)
Time:	GMT (summer time GMT+1)
Languages:	English, Welsh
Currency:	Pound Sterling (£)

BACKGROUND

Of the three countries of Great Britain, Wales is the smallest. It is surrounded on three sides by oceans, the Irish Sea, St George's Channel and the Bristol Channel. It is a predominantly mountainous country, although two-thirds of the rural area is farmland and one-third moorland. Coastal areas, especially around Dyfed and the Gower are noted for their scenic beauty and it's this beauty that makes surfing in Wales such a delight.

England and Wales have never had an entirely easy relationship. The country constantly fought off the Romans and then the English until 1282 when Edward I defeated the last native Welsh prince, Llewelyn ap Gruffyd, at which point Wales passed into English rule.

Trouble flared up again with the uprising of Owain Glyndwr in the 15th century, but finally, when the Welsh prince Henry Tudor defeated Richard III at the battle of Bosworth to become King of England, he paved the way for the 1536 Act of Union which tied the English and Welsh in an uneasy but lasting alliance.

The passing centuries have watered down Welsh culture but the Welsh language is still widely used. It can be seen on bilingual road signs all over the country and mostly heard in North and Central Wales. Arguments for self rule are not as strong as in Scotland and nothing like in Northern Ireland but still, many Welsh people have some desire for independence.

Wales was once one of the great mining areas of the world. Coal, slate, steel and tinplate provided work for a large proportion of the population and were exported around the world. Today, mining has greatly diminished and has been replaced by farming, tourism and light industry.

Like the rest of Britain, Wales has a mild, damp climate. The high regions are slightly cooler than the lowlands and have a heavy rainfall (over 200 days a year). This rainfall is very important, not only for Wales but also for England, supplying major cities such as Liverpool and Birmingham with their heavy demand for water.

Atlantic seals breed on Ramsey Island off Dyfed and on small islands off the coast of Anglesey. Many rare birds nest in Wales which is the home of the last few Kites left in the British Isles. Let's hope that in the next century this will still be the case.

THE SURF

Surfing in Wales has a great heritage. I grew up in a spot called Langland Bay where I had to learn some respect for the locals who were, by rights, the best bunch of surfers in the country.

You would never paddle out onto the best breaks in the bay unless you did it early in the morning, or you were encouraged by the crew. Growing up at Langland definitely helped me realise my dream of becoming one of the best surfers in the world. The surf can sometimes be brilliant, but we must be one of the few bunches of surfers who get excited when the forecast is for gale force winds and rain, as Langland never seems to max out no matter what the conditions. I think this in itself breeds the hardcore element into Welsh surfing.

You hear people say it always rains when they visit Wales, but we don't mind that at all as long as there's surf, and when the swell is up, Langland produces a huge variety of waves. The high tide shorebreak close-outs are perfect for trying big manoeuvres in front of the boyz and girlz on the promenade. As the tide drops back, the lefts on the reef start to work – they're slow but pretty perfect. This often turns into what is known as the reef, a right and left normally crowded and pretty slow. As the tide goes out, the middle of the bay might start to work along with the lefts and the shit pipe. At low tide Crab Island starts to become visible and a nice righthander peels off the back of it. This is a great wave but has a heavy crew of older surfers on big boards, along with some of the younger whipper snappers. This wave should stay out of bounds unless you are lucky enough to catch it with no one out (you may live in hope). The other option is the point. This is a really nice right with not too many people surfing it.

When the surf is flat at Langland we normally go to Llangennith at the far end of the Gower. This is the most consistent of all the breaks on the Gower. If there's no wind and you know the tides, there's some nice reef breaks to be found.

It's touch and go whether you'll get perfect waves if you come to Wales but there are a few characters to meet. The nightlife in Mumbles is classic and the sheep are friendly!

Carwyn Williams

WATER QUALITY

This is the biggest problem facing Welsh surfing to date. Take Swansea Bay for example, there's no surf in most of this bay. The amount of sewage milling around is alarming. The government have just this summer (92) awarded Swansea Bay a 3 Star rating yet in the same paragraph they say that swimming here could make you sick!

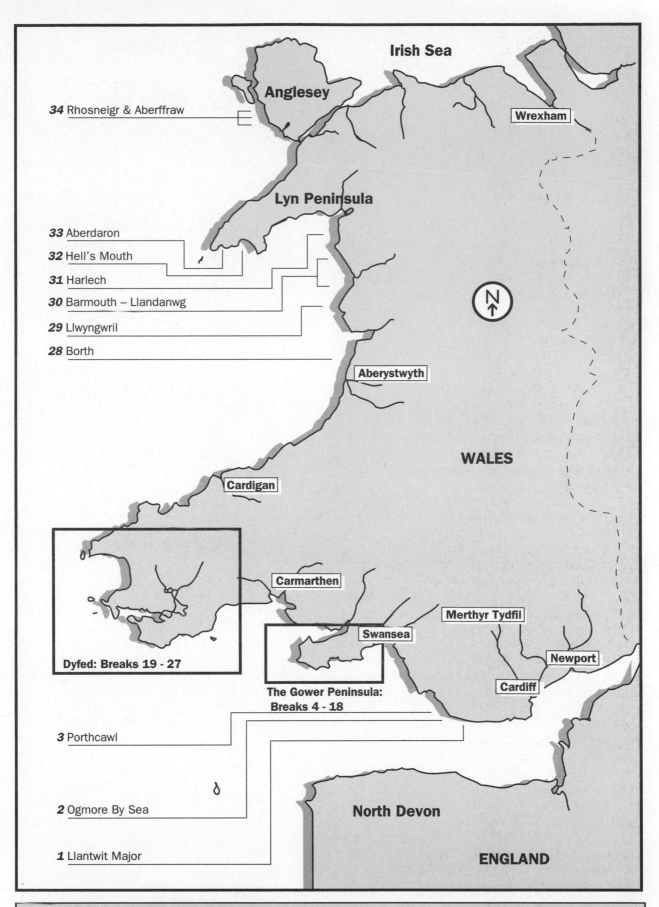

Irish Sea

Anglesey

34 Rhosneigr & Aberffraw

Wrexham

Lyn Peninsula

33 Aberdaron

32 Hell's Mouth

31 Harlech

30 Barmouth – Llandanwg

29 Llwyngwril

28 Borth

Aberystwyth

WALES

Cardigan

Dyfed: Breaks 19 - 27

Carmarthen

Merthyr Tydfil

Swansea

Newport

Cardiff

The Gower Peninsula:
Breaks 4 - 18

3 Porthcawl

2 Ogmore By Sea

North Devon

1 Llantwit Major

ENGLAND

TRAVELLING AROUND

For information on money, public holidays, opening times, visa requirements and driving see England.

Airports: Cardiff, Swansea
Train Stations:
Cardiff: Central Station
Wood Street
Tel: 0222 28000

Swansea: High Street
Tel: 0792 46777
Tourist Offices:
Cardiff: 8 - 14 Bridge street
Tel: 0222 27281

The levels of chemicals in the water are also very alarming and we (SAS) are doing tests on both the water and the surfers to see if any long term illnesses occur that are related to some of the carcinogenic chemicals pumped into Swansea Bay every day (from the likes of BP and British Steel). Unfortunately, we won't know the results for many years so let's hope we are all still fit, healthy and ripping it up. Join SAS! (Break by break information on water quality for the Gower peninsula has also be supplied by Carwyn Williams who's been European champ 5 times, now returning to comps.)

Surf Breaks 1 – 3

1. Llantwit Major (Col-huw point)

Llantwit Major needs a fair-sized swell to work, but can be well worth a visit. Its best wave is a righthander at low tide to the left of the beach, which can be long and fast. As the tide comes in, lefts and rights can be found along the beach. Beginners should take care of rocks and rips caused by the rockpools and try not to swallow too much of the water which can be polluted.

Water Quality: Failed beach!

2. Ogmore by Sea

Where the river meets the sea, on the southern side there is a good lefthander with rides of up to 100mtrs. The wave needs a clean swell, a NE wind and works best from mid up to high tide. It does get very polluted due to the river, which also causes strong rips. The rest of the beach can have some good lefts and rights, depending on the state of the sandbanks. Beginners should definitely avoid the left at the rivermouth!

Water Quality: Failed beach! 140,000, receives secondary other, into river approx 1.6kms from sea.

3. Porthcawl

The west facing beaches of Porthcawl can have good rights and lefts all the way along to Margam sands, but the whole stretch is often badly affected by very common SW, W, and NW winds. It's a popular spot that works best from mid to high tide. Pollution can be bad due to the heavy industrial site of Port Talbot to the north.

Water Quality: Average.

The Gower Peninsula

The Gower Peninsula, Wales' premier surfing area is ideally located to receive swells generated by mid and south Atlantic low pressure systems. The rugged, scenic coastline offers a wide variety of breaks – all within sheltered bays providing waves which smugglers rode in on 150 years ago. These bays now offer untold secrets for the dedicated surfer to find.

Surfing on the Gower started in the early 60s, but many of the early pioneers are now expatriates living and surfing in warmer climes. It wasn't until 1967 when travelling Australian surfing champion, Keith Paull, got into it that the local kids really started. During a classic late summer swell at Langland Bay, he ripped up the shorebreak in his 'silver baggies' and local hotties gawked in amazement – surfing had arrived. Keith Paull, Howard Davies and John Goss were the first to surf Crab Island.

From the mid to late 60s surfing on the Gower was mainly confined to the beach breaks at Langland Bay, Caswell and Llangennith. Heavy boards and the risk of damage to board and body, (leashes only came into use in late 1972) meant the more inaccessible reef and point breaks were only surfed by a handful of very hard-core locals. Pioneers in these early days include Viv Ganz, John Goss, Dave Friar, Robin Hansen, Howard Davies, Paul Connibear and myself.

By the mid 70s most of the reef breaks along the six mile stretch from Port Eynon to Fall Bay had been surfed. During the early 80s, a few extra 'secret' spots were added to the surfing map and first surfed by Carwyn Williams and Rob and Phil Poutney.

From the early 60s to 1974 most of the boards being ridden were imported from Newquay, with Bilbo being the most popular label, closely followed by Tiki boards, then made in Abergavenny! The longest surviving board manufacturer on the Gower is Crab Island Surfboards, still spearheaded by technical 'guru' Pete Phillips. By the late seventies Crab Island boards were used by most of the Gower's top surfers. During this time, travelling airbrusher and surfboard shaper Craig Hughes, (now based in Ulladulla, Australia) started working for Crab Island. Craig provided the catalyst needed to enhance the talents of a very young Langland surfer, Carwyn Williams, who went on to become Britain's most successful professional surfer of the 80s.

The '79 to '82 period was the most influential for the Gower surfers in terms of equipment. Locally made boards were now able to match the imports from Newquay and abroad. Surfing on the Gower had come of age.

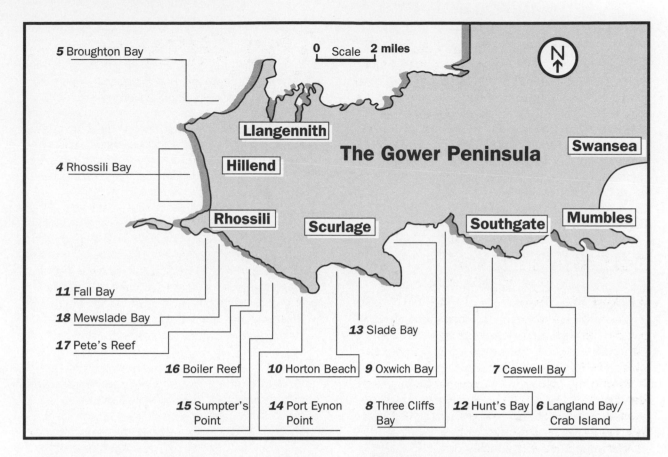

The Gower Peninsula map showing: 5 Broughton Bay, Llangennith, Hillend, 4 Rhossili Bay, Rhossili, Scurlage, Southgate, Mumbles, Swansea, 11 Fall Bay, 18 Mewslade Bay, 17 Pete's Reef, 16 Boiler Reef, 15 Sumpter's Point, 10 Horton Beach, 14 Port Eynon Point, 13 Slade Bay, 9 Oxwich Bay, 8 Three Cliffs Bay, 7 Caswell Bay, 12 Hunt's Bay, 6 Langland Bay/Crab Island. Scale 0 to 2 miles.

Windsurfing on the Gower has only been introduced relatively recently. Early pioneers in 1981 - 82 were Laurie Grove and Keith Sulsh who introduced 'real' windsurfing, i.e. wave riding and wave jumping.

Every Easter Bank Holiday, Port Eynon plays host to the B.F.A. (British Funboard Association) windsurfing championships. Mainly a racing event for longer boards, this event has attracted many 'hot' sailors to the area in recent years. Most notable have been top wave rider Duncan Coombes, who was one of the first to sail Port Eynon Point on a huge swell. Dave Perks (former world champion) and Nick Baker (Britain's hottest wave sailor today) have all sailed the Gower.

After 10 years, there are still only a few local hard-core windsurfers who sail the Gower all year round which is amazing when you compare it with the South Coast of England, where the water can be crammed with hundreds of sails out – sailing on flat water!

The Gower is unique in that within a five mile radius, you can blast along on perfect flat water conditions at Oxwich Bay, test your skills in mast high waves at Llangennith, or have the best of both with flat water and waves at Horton and Port Eynon (and all on the same day!)

With the prevailing SW, always cross-shore somewhere, and with consistent breezes all year round, the Gower really is a sailboarder's paradise. Consistently the most windy time is winter – but with regular gale force winds and water temperatures down to 7°C in January, only the hardiest survive!

Pete Jones/PJ's Surf Shop

Surf Breaks 4 – 18

Pete Jones/PJ's Surf Shop

4. Llangennith Beach (Rhossili Bay)

The indicator beach for the Gower area, Llangennith picks up just about any swell hitting the South Wales coast. With three miles of beach, Llangennith remains relatively uncrowded and surfable at any stage of the tide. When the swell is big, it's one of the hardest places in Britain to paddle out, with few rips to help.

The ideal wind direction for clean waves is E/SE/NE. When the swell is 4ft or less, **Three Peaks** at the north end of the beach has excellent waves and it's a mid to high tide break.

When the swell is huge and wind direction is S/SW/SE the south end of the beach has sheltered waves at Rhossili. You can either walk along the beach from Llangennith or take a 10 minute detour drive to Rhossili village. Access to the beach is through the village. Turn left past PJ's Surf Shop (the biggest for its size in the world) and continue down to Hillend. The local pub, The King's Head, is renowned for its summer raves!

Windsurfing is excellent with N/NW the best wind direction for wave jumping, and SE for wave riding. Always better at low water.

Water Quality: The water here takes on a very murky appearance due to the Lougher Estuary. There's some visible pollution here coming down from Llanelli but you'll get used to that.

5. Broughton Bay

In heavy SW storms, Broughton Bay has some excellent waves best on a S, SW or W wind. It's a high tide break only and one of the longest lefts in South Wales, especially suitable for longboard surfing. Watch out for strong rips, which drag you away from the break – not really suitable for beginners. Windsurfing can also be really good. Best wind directions are NE, N, NW, with mainly flat water sailing. Access is from the village of Llangennith, straight on past PJ's and remember to park outside the caravan park as the local site owner does not take kindly to surfers! Access for windsurfers is best through the village of Llanmadoc. Car park on beach.

Water Quality: Same as Llangennith.

6. Langland Bay

Just over the hill from Mumbles, Langland is one of the most popular breaks for local surfers. Rotherslade lefts, the middle reef and the outside point are good at low to mid tide. On big swells, the shorebreak at high tide has some fast, sucky waves – very heavy.

The most famous wave at Langland is **Crab Island** (located at the SE of the bay – exposed only at mid to low tide). One of the best rights in Wales and is always crowded when it's over 5ft. Watch out for the 'old' local crew here. Langland is the 'Malibu' of South Wales and is always crowded.

Windsurfing can be excellent but only at low water only. The big waves and rocky outcrops make this a spot for experts only. Best wind for sailing is anything from a S to W, once the wind swings to the north it becomes very gusty.

Water Quality: Langland is just 1 mile from where up to 800 million litres of sewage is pumped every day. However, when the wind is offshore for a week or so, it's as clear as a bell.

7. Caswell Bay

Just a stone's throw away from Langland. Best here at high tide and particularly good for beginners. The best wave is the lefthander breaking at the westerly end of the beach. Usually breaks 1ft smaller than Langland and needs a strong SW swell to work properly. Too sheltered for windsurfing here.

Water Quality: Not as polluted as Langland.

8. Three Cliffs Bay

Gower's picture postcard bay rarely works and needs a big swell with offshore winds to work properly. A rivermouth beach break, the waves tend to be very shifty with lots of peaks. Can be good at mid to high tide. Strong undercurrents close to the cliffs are very dangerous for beginners. Access is through Penman – very limited parking.

Water Quality: One of the cleanest beaches on the Gower.

9. Oxwich Bay

A beautiful, crescent shaped bay stretching for miles across to Three Cliffs. The home of Gower's only windsurfing school (open only during summer months). Becalmed for most of the year, Oxwich comes alive during big winter storms and when the wind is howling southwesterly can produce excellent 'hot dog' waves. The beach break only works at high tide and due to the beach currents, is always bigger as the tide turns to drop back. When Oxwich is working, word gets around fast and hence it is usually crowded. Excellent small left and right barrels.

Windsurfing here is excellent for beginners with flat water blasting. Sailable on most wind directions. Can be excellent for experts when the wind is howling E or SE. Access is via a (very expensive!) privately owned beach car park.

Water Quality: Good.

10. Horton

This beach bordering one of Gower's most picturesque villages, faces south. The swell has to be fairly big to work properly (usually when Llangennith is over 6ft). A heavy beach break can produce shorebreak barrels at most stages of tide. Excellent for beginners here as it's usually uncrowded.

Horton and the north end of the beach at Port Eynon are two of the best locations for all round sailing. From longboard sailing to wave riding, this beach can offer all kinds of conditions. Port Eynon Point can offer some really challenging wave sailing during big swells – experts only here. Best wind directions S, SW, W, and NW. There are car parks at both ends of the beach.

Water Quality: Good.

11. Fall Bay

Facing south and right out on the west of Gower, Fall Bay only works when the swell is big, breaking at low to mid tide only. Access is a very long walk through fields from Rhossili.

Water Quality: Good, though most of the seaweed has died here over the last 10 years.

All the point and reef breaks on the Gower have a southerly aspect. Surrounded by some breathtaking scenery, when the wind is N/NE or NW, they produce some of the hollowest waves on the Gower. Moving west from Caswell:

12. Hunts Bay

Best at low to mid tide and needs a solid 5 - 6ft swell to work properly. Very rocky rights and lefts and usually uncrowded. Access is through Southgate village.

Water Quality: Good.

13. Slade Bay

Another 'sometimes' break. Needs a N wind and a solid 5 - 6ft swell, very rocky with good rights and lefts. Access is via Horton car park followed by a very pleasant walk around the footpath at the bottom of the cliffs to the break.

Water Quality: Only really affected by run-offs from a farm.

14. Port Eynon Point

Moving west, this is the first of the more famous Gower reefs, picking up more swell than the breaks to the east. Facing south west, a very sucky righthander breaks in very shallow water over a rock ledge. The take-off and first section are best as the wave peels into deeper water and the face flattens off. A low to mid tide break only. Access is via Port Eynon car park.

Water Quality: Very close to a sewer pipe although it's not big, and as you only surf here at low tide when they don't discharge it's okay.

15. Sumpter's/Overton Point

The easiest of the Gower reefs to surf. Entry into the water is through a deep water gulley, making the paddle out fairly easy, even when the swell is huge. A good, long righthander, but not as hollow as the other reefs. Very heavy first section when it's big, a low to mid tide break only. Access is through the village of Overton with very limited parking.

Water Quality: This is where the sewer pipe is. You walk down it to get to the water!

16. Boiler Reef

The best lefthand reef break on the Gower, with an excellent tubing first section. The wave peels into a deep water gulley, but watch out for the take-off – any hesitation and you'll be picking barnacles out of your back! The strong rip current is constantly taking you away from the take-off zone. A low to mid tide break only. Don't be too late leaving the water, as the bay fills in with the waves slamming against the rocks. Access is via Overton village again.

Water Quality: Mostly affected by run-offs from farms and algae which turns to horrible brown froth in summer months.

17. Pete's Reef

Due to a deep water trench funnelling into this reef, the waves can 'jack-up' here to 2 - 3ft when all the other surf spots are flat. A very shallow wave breaking over uninviting jagged rocks. The righthander is best and barrels on take-off. The lefts can be good as well, but this wave peels into ankle depth water. Exit and entry into the water is difficult, particularly when the swell is 4 - 6ft. Works well during smaller summer swells. A low to mid tide break, with a strong rip on an incoming tide. Access through Overton.

Water Quality: Same as Boiler.

18. Mewslade Bay

More sheltered when the wind is strong NW. This low to mid tide lefthander needs a solid swell to work properly. It's a long walk over fields via Rhossili car park – this tends to keep out the crowds.

Water Quality: Good

Dyfed

Little or no development has taken place to spoil the sand dunes and red sandstone cliffs that shelter the beaches and the surrounding National Park. The occasional ice cream van is often the only source of sustenance here and local surfers are both keen and friendly. The South Pembrokeshire Surf Club has been running for 20 years or more, and information on the area and club is available from the Westcoast Surf Shop near the Castle Wall in Pembroke.

The wild wide openness of Freshwater West extends in both directions. North of Milford Haven from West Dale, the top end of Newgale and beyond to Whitesands and Abereiddy, there are numerous beaches and coves that require only a moderate swell to provide excellent surfing conditions. Many have remained unchanged and some even undiscovered for centuries. Whitesands is the focus for most surfing in north Dyfed. South of Freshwater West, the coastline is indented with a small cove called Broadhaven, a beach break which if the sandbars are right, can have tube take-offs

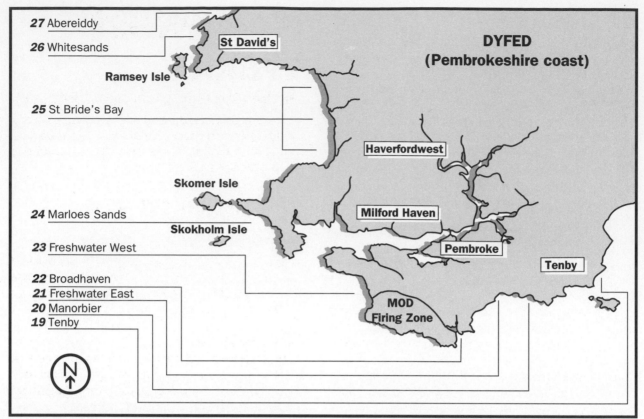

27 Abereiddy
26 Whitesands
St David's
Ramsey Isle
25 St Bride's Bay

DYFED
(Pembrokeshire coast)

Haverfordwest

Skomer Isle
24 Marloes Sands
Skokholm Isle
23 Freshwater West

Milford Haven

Pembroke

Tenby

22 Broadhaven
21 Freshwater East
20 Manorbier
19 Tenby

MOD
Firing Zone

and shifting peaks of world class quality. Manorbier faces into the prevailing winds more than Broad Haven. Its characteristic right has provided endless hours of sheer enjoyment, even in onshore conditions. The appeal of Tenby with its walled town and harbour, draws the tourists in their hoards. Waves are fairly infrequent but in storm conditions, the rides at South Beach can be both fast and numerous.

Phil Holden

Surf Breaks 19 – 27

19. Tenby (South Beach)

When there's a big storm swell with winds from the north and all the other surf spots are blown out, then Tenby South Beach is a worthwhile place to visit. It works on all tides and can have good, fast 2 - 4ft waves with good small barrels to tuck into. The beach does get very crowded with tourists in summer, but for the rest of the year it's fine. A good spot for beginners and also very popular with windsurfers.

Water Quality: Screened/macerated sewage from 25,000 people (dirty but not failed).

20. Manorbier

This is a lovely south west facing sand and rocky beach with an impressive l2th Century Norman castle standing guard over the excellent righthanders. The wave breaks over the rocks and is at its best around high tide, with little or no wind. Gets very crowded but can work well even in onshores. Car park by beach.

Water Quality: Sewage from 520 gets secondary treatment and is discharged at the low water mark.

21. Freshwater East

Faces east and can have good waves when there's a big swell with a SW to NW wind. The north end of the beach picks up the most swell and is best on the incoming tide. Car park by beach.

Water Quality: Raw sewage from 600 people is discharged at the low water mark.

22. Broadhaven (Bosherton)

Good wedgy lefthanders are Broadhaven's speciality. However, facing Southeast, it only picks up the biggest swells and does start closing out at the 6ft mark. The bay works best from mid to high tide with a NW wind but is still able to handle quite a strong W or SW wind. Car park by the beach.

Water Quality: Good.

23. Freshwater West

The heart of Dyfed's surfing is to be found at Freshwater West. As its name implies, the long, sandy beach is both unpolluted and westerly facing. Exposed to the depths of the Atlantic, this corner of Wales will catch any SW swell running.

A series of reefs link two bays with particularly good sand bars in summer months at the extremes of the tides. The southernmost beach is M.O.D. and firing times are indicated by red flags.

The best waves tend to break on the jagged rocks to the south of the beach, giving good hollow rides of up to 100mtrs in length.

Many of Wales' surf contests have been held here since Freshwater West is Dyfed's most consistent beach. Rips can be very strong here, so beware. Easy parking along the beach.

Water Quality: Good.

24. Marloes Sands

Rarely ridden but consistent, with some good peaky waves, Marloes is a great place to escape civilization.

The beach works on all tides but there are some dangerous rocks scattered along the beach. One should also watch out for the incoming tide, which can cover the whole beach. There's a car park from where it's a 10 minute walk down a sign-posted cliff path to the ocean.

Water Quality: Good.

25. St. Bride's Bay (Newgale, Druidston Haven, Broadhaven)

The west facing beaches of Newgale, Druidston Haven and Broadhaven offer 5 miles of consistent beach break waves.

Newgale gets the most swell and is the most surfed of the beaches, being rideable up to 6ft before it starts to close-out. At the very northern end of the beach good waves can be found at low tide when there's a N wind. When Newgale is closing out or blown out, you should head south to either Broadhaven or Druidston Haven.

Broadhaven gets good protection from SW winds and is usually about half the size of Newgale and is also one of Dyfed's most popular windsurfing beaches.

Druidston Haven is not so accessible. It is rarely surfed, but it still gets some good waves and is worth a visit if you want some solitude. The beaches are all safe and are suitable for beginners. There's easy parking for Broadhaven and Newgale.

Water Quality: Good.

26. Whitesands Bay

Sand bottom waves work best from low to mid tide up to 8ft. The water is clean, the locals are friendly and the setting for a surf is impressive. Not surprisingly, it does get crowded (even seals are sometimes seen in the line-up), but when it's working, there are usually enough waves to go round.

When it's big, there's a useful rip at the northern end of the beach which can save you a lot of hard paddling. A good beginner's beach with easy parking.

Water Quality: Good.

27. Abereiddy

A small black sand and rock beach facing west. Like Whitesands it has great scenery all around but with none of the crowds. A bed of rocks at the southern end of the beach can produce a hollow lefthander at mid tide.

The rest of the beach has good rights and lefts and gets good protection from all winds apart from a straight westerly. A good spot to check on a SW to SE wind. Car park by beach.

Water Quality: Good.

Northwest Wales

(& the Llyn Peninsula and Anglesey)

The coastline of Mid and North Wales, including the Llyn Peninsular and Angelesy, is not renowned throughout the world for its surf. But, with patience some decent waves can be found.

Surf Breaks 28 – 34

28. Borth

This is a popular seaside resort with two miles of west facing beach. Works best from low to mid tide and is suitable for beginners.

Water Quality: Good.

29. Llwyngwril

On big swells there's a good lefthander here. It breaks over rocks. Only works at high tide and as it faces north, it's quite often offshore. Beginners should take care as it can be dangerous.

Water Quality: Failed beach! Raw sewage from 370 people is discharged at the low water mark.

30. Barmouth to Llandanwg

With 15 miles of uninterrupted beach breaks, it faces SW and so picks up some swell. Occasionally produces some good waves. Good for beginners.

Water Quality: Good.

31. Harlech

Has 4 more miles of beach break, again facing SW. Gets a bit of protection from SW winds being best from mid to high tide. We mention nearby Harlech Castle as an one of Wales' most awesome.

Water Quality: Average.

32 & 33. Porth Neigwl (Hell's Mouth) and Aberdaron

Facing south west, these two bays are usually the best and most consistent beaches in the whole of North Wales. They both pick up a good amount of swell and both benefit from protection from all but SW winds. Hell's Mouth (so named because of the danger it's caused ships over the years) works on all tides, but rips are strong here so beginners should take care. Aberdaron works best at mid tide and is often the better of the two beaches.

Water Quality: Good.

34. Rhosneigr and Aberffraw

There are a number of nice, quiet beaches on the southwest side of Anglesey that get some rideable surf on big swells. They tend to work best on the incoming tide which brings in a little swell with it. Popular windsurfing venue.

Water Quality: Good.

ENGLAND

Capital:	London
Population:	48,000,000
Area:	130,362km^2 (50,333 miles^2)
Time:	GMT (summer time GMT+1)
Religion:	Church of England
Language:	English
Currency:	Pound Sterling (£)

THE PEOPLE

Despite its island status, English people are of mixed stock. The earliest immigrants were often refugees from tribal warfare and unrest. The Belgic tribesman escaping from Imperial Rome, the Romans themselves, the Angles, Saxons, Jutes, Danes and Normans, all in turn brought genetic variety. Under Roman rule the population of the British Isles numbered about half a million. By the time of the Doomsday Census (1086) it had doubled and over the next 900 years it has become one of the most densely populated countries of the world.

Despite physical proximity to the rest of Europe, England's people have maintained a strong sense of cultural separation. In the past, the surrounding seas have served the English well, protecting them from casual invasion, providing them with food and trade, and being the starting point for their exploration and exploitation of far-flung lands. The British Empire was, for over 200 years, the most powerful in the world and it wasn't until the end of the Second World War that the empire began to disintergrate. In 1947 India and Pakistan became independent and by 1970 nearly every other commonwealth country had done the same.

Today, although not the great power it once was, England retains its place amongst the world's leading nations. English literature, music, fashion and general cultural influences continue to permeate world affairs, and her colonial legacy has produced one of the world's most multi-cultural societies. Deeper integration with Europe should increase its cosmopolitan nature.

THE LAND

England has a gentle landscape. There are no great mountain ranges, deserts or vast prairies and a large proportion of the land has been intensively cultivated. The coastline however is dramatic, especially in the southwest where pounding seas crash onto a variety of landscapes. No part of England is more than 80 miles from England's 7,000 miles of coastline and consequently the English are an instinctively seafaring nation.

Despite its relative position near the Artic, England is favoured climatically. Other countries lying at similar latitudes such as Eastern Siberia and Southern Alaska are much cooler with longer winters and ice-bound coasts. The Gulf Stream is the main reason for England's temperate climate. Most of the UK receives damp, maritime air from the Atlantic Ocean for much of the year, providing a background of mild summers and moderate winters. Other influential climatic changes are brought about by rapidly shifting air masses coming from the continent and the Arctic. Continental air can bring hot weather in summer and bitterly cold weather in winter. Pressure systems pass over England almost daily, bringing the familiar variations of cloud, rain and sunshine that give rise to England's fame for changeability.

The Southwest is England's warmest climatic zone in winter but its weather remains predictable only by its unpredictability. Surfing conditions naturally share this changeability, making knowledge of weather forecasting that much more necessary. The English public is well supplied with easily accessible weather information. BBC Television has excellent forecasts throughout the day (after news broadcasts) and BBC radio is serviced by 'The Shipping Forecast' with detailed information covering all of England. The English have a well-deserved reputation for being pre-occupied with the weather.

There are various surf report numbers run by surf and windsurf shops across the country which are updated daily. These will tell you about the waves on the day of your call but will not help if you are trying to predict a few days in advance. For that, personal knowledge of weather maps is your best bet. Surf report numbers are listed regionally throughout the text.

THE SURF

Surfing in the British Isles began at Newquay in Cornwall. The identity of the first surfer to actually ride British waves is shrouded in conjecture. Talk to different ol' timers and you'll get different answers. What is established is that surfing became a popular sport in Cornwall when two cultural elements fused.

Firstly, following the catastrophic number of drownings on major West Country beaches (an average of six per beach, per year) the Surf Life Saving Association was established, with trained volunteers being allocated to the many surfing beaches. In later years, some life guards were paid for their hours of duty and guarding is now a recognised surfer's occupation between May and September.

Secondly, whilst the SLSA was spreading around the country, in came the surf music of Jan & Dean and the Beach Boys, and a greater awareness of the growing Californian 'surf culture.' As soon as people realised that it was possible to surf in Cornwall and that the surf wasn't at all bad, surfing was here for good.

Young entrepreneurs set about the task of

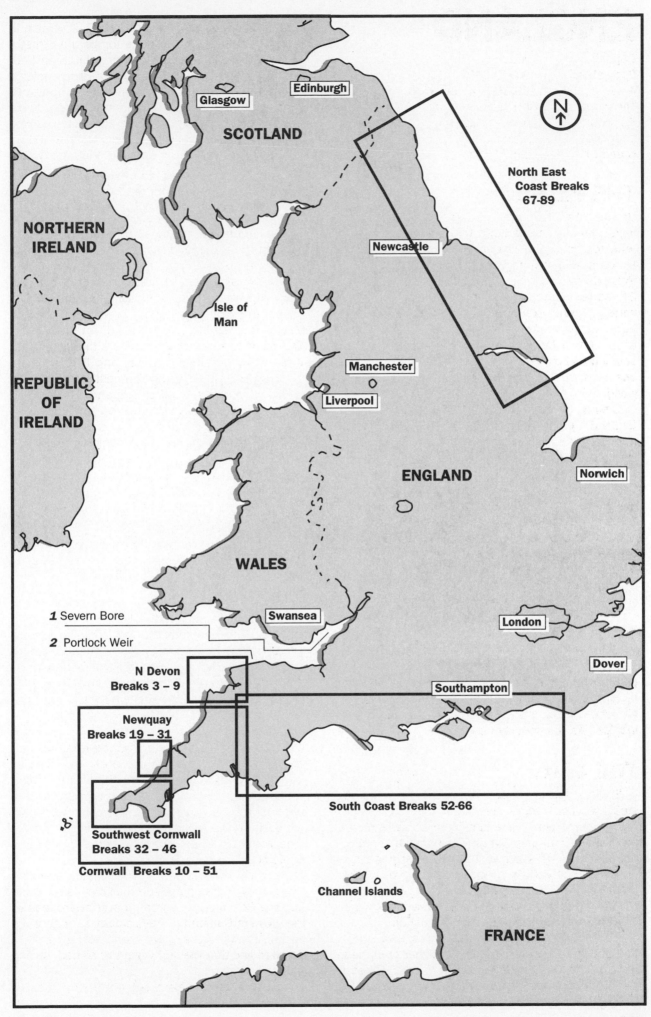

Glasgow

Edinburgh

SCOTLAND

NORTHERN
IRELAND

North East
Coast Breaks
67-89

Newcastle

Isle of
Man

REPUBLIC
OF
IRELAND

Manchester

Liverpool

ENGLAND

Norwich

WALES

1 Severn Bore

2 Portlock Weir

Swansea

London

Dover

N Devon
Breaks 3 – 9

Southampton

Newquay
Breaks 19 – 31

South Coast Breaks 52-66

Southwest Cornwall
Breaks 32 – 46

Cornwall Breaks 10 – 51

Channel Islands

FRANCE

satisfying a demand for wetsuits, surfboards and equipment. Bilbo Surfboards, the first manufacturer in the country, was up and running in the 60s and is still in evidence as the surf shop Bilbo 2000 in Fore Street, Newquay. Technology improved upon the ludicrously heavy, prototype surfboards and the all-year-round surfing wetsuit was perfected. Wetsuit refinements have seen quantum leaps in the surfing population of the UK.

Communications with American, Australian and South African surfers brought magazines, films, ideas, music and more enthusiasm. European and world travel spread the word. New spots were discovered and standards improved. By the 70's, there were a large number of hard-core surfers in Cornwall and a growing number in the emerging areas of Devon and South Wales. Competitions became, and are still, widely popular.

The coast of England can be divided into three broad regions; **THE SOUTHWEST** (Devon, Cornwall), is by far the most popular area with many breaks offering good waves in a variety of conditions. **THE SOUTH COAST** is not as consistent but it can be good if there's a big SW or S swell with winds from the north. **THE EAST COAST** is enjoying growing recognition as an area with consistent, quality waves, but colder air and water temperatures, and severe pollution problems continue to limit the sport's growth there compared to other areas.

Peter Cade

WATER QUALITY

The UK's coastline has sewage problems on a significant scale. This is the cause of intense public debate as a result of the almost complete dependence on tourism along the coast and the fact that a large proportion of the resident population surf, sail or swim off the beaches on a regular year round basis. Water sports enthusiasts have long since claimed that bathing in sewage polluted waters adversely affects their health. The doctors of these coastal communities also acknowledge this risk to health to the extent that a number of GP's have advised all surfers to get hepatitis immunisation.

Over 300 million gallons of sewage (about 2 ½ bucketfuls per person per day) are disposed of in our coastal waters each day! Of 590 significant sea outfalls in the UK (i.e. serving populations of 10,000+), 37% have no treatment, 50% have preliminary treatment (i.e. usually the screening of larger solids), 11% have primary treatment and only 2% have secondary treatment.

England's **Southwest** region has many clean beaches and bathing waters but many popular holiday resorts have hopelessly inadequate sewage disposal systems, especially in summer months when populations swell. Cornwall and Devon have many beaches away from built up areas and if you head to these, you should be surfing in clean waters. Along the **South Coast** clean waters are harder to come by. Heavy coastal development and shipping traffic bring problems of sewage, marine litter, oil and other not so obvious pollutants to the beaches and coastal waters. Generally speaking, the further east up the coast you go, the more polluted the water becomes. Water quality along England's **East Coast** can best be described as 'gnarly.' Waste discharged from steel works, power stations, oil companies, coal mines and sewage outfalls combine to make a highly toxic cocktail – hardly the kind of thing likely to attract surfers to its shores.

TRAVELLING AROUND

TELEPHONING:

Dialling in code:	44
Dialling out code:	010
Operator:	100
Directory Enq:	142
Int. Dir Enq:	153
Int. Operator:	155
Emergency:	999

AIRPORT INFORMATION:

London -

– Heathrow:	081 759 4321
– Gatwick:	0293 28822
– Stansted:	0279 502 380
Manchester:	061 489 3000
Bristol:	027 587 4441
Birmingham:	021 767 5511
Newcastle:	091 286 0966
Plymouth:	0752 707 023

TRAIN INFORMATION:

Information about times etc from London travel stations call:

The London Transport Information	
Line	Tel: 071 222 1234
Kings Cross	Tel: 071 278 2477
Paddington	Tel: 071 262 6767
Victoria	Tel: 071 928 5100

OPENING TIMES:

Banks: Normal banking hours are Mon – Fri, 09.30am – 3.30pm. Some branches stay open slightly longer on weekday afternoons, and open for a few hours on Saturday mornings.

Post Offices: Opening hours are Mon – Fri, 9am – 5.30pm, and 9am – 12.30/1pm on Saturdays.

Shopping Hours: Shops are generally open from 9am – 6pm Mon - Sat. Sunday shopping is in its infancy in the UK.

EMBASSIES AND CONSULATES:

Australian High Commission:

Australia House,
The Strand, London WC2B 4LA
Tel: 071 379 4334

New Zealand High Commission:
New Zealand House,
The Haymarket at Pall Mall,
London SW1Y 4TQ
Tel: 071 930 8422

The United States Embassy:
24 Grosvenor Square,
London W1A 1AE
Tel: 071 499 9000

The Home Office:
Lunar House,
Wellesly Rd,
Croydon, London
Tel: 081 686 0688

The South African Embassy:
Trafalgar Square,
London WC2N 5DP
Tel: 071 930 4488

LONDON

London is Europe's largest city. It also has the biggest airports in Europe and it's here that most travelling surfers begin their European missions.

Three main things will keep you in this surfless zone; 1) Work, 2) Buying a vehicle, 3) Buying a ticket (so one can get out as cheaply and as fast as possible).

Work

Fine for EC nationals, Australians, Kiwis and other Commonwealth peoples who can obtain casual work permits. It's usually easy to find employment in the building or catering trades. Keep an eye out for jobs in *TNT* and *Southern Cross* mags (both free outside many tube stations) and the *Evening Standard*. Australians and New Zealanders have a good reputation for hard work and so will already have one foot in the door. As with everywhere else, use your imagination... London offers countless money making opportunities.

Buying a vehicle

There are several options. Look in *TNT* & *Southern Cross*, or *Loot* and *What Car* magazines. *TNT* and *Southern Cross* often have the best deals as people selling vehicles are often about to leave the country and have to sell fast. Impromptu Antipodean used van lots appear at various semi-permanent park and sell locations, including: Market Rd N7 (Caledonian tube) and Vestry St (near Old Street). People often live here till they sell their vans!

VOLKSWAGEN PARTS: German & Swedish: 843 Harrow Rd NW10 5NW Tel: 081 960 8182. **Car Wreckers:** A1 Metro, Hendon Tel: 081 205 2100.

Buying a Plane, Train or Bus ticket

If you're looking for a cheap flight, and you're prepared to leave at the drop of a hat... look no further than the *Evening Standard*. £60 return to Bilbao (right next to Mundaka), £80 to Lisbon or £80 to the Canary Islands are all realistic prices out of season and these are by far the cheapest and quickest ways of getting to some excellent European surfing destinations. Also look at *Time Out*, *TNT*, *Southern Cross* or in the travel sections of the Sunday newspapers. Here you'll find a wide selection of European and worldwide destinations at the best available prices.

The cheapest form of transport anywhere is the bus. They all leave from Victoria coach station (right by Victoria Tube). For info contact: National Express on 071 730 0202 (for UK), or Eurolines on 071 730 8235 (for Europe). National Express have a strange attitude towards surfboards and check your boards are okay before you set off! If they carry you one way they have to carry you back!

TRAIN TRAVEL offers no real advantages, prices are no cheaper than flights and you could be asked to pay a full fare for your surfboard (especially on the Victoria - Gatwick route). Still, If you're a student or if you plan to travel extensively on the rail networks of Europe, you can get worthwhile deals. Always refuse to pay the surcharge fares initially. Pleading poverty is the easiest way.

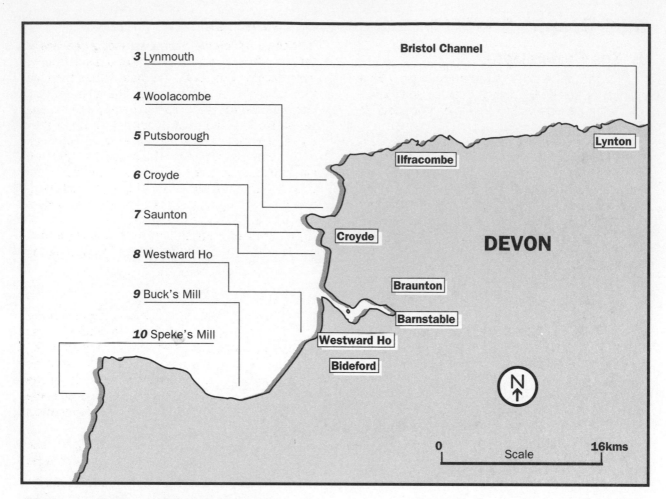

3 Lynmouth
4 Woolacombe
5 Putsborough
6 Croyde
7 Saunton
8 Westward Ho
9 Buck's Mill
10 Speke's Mill

Bristol Channel

Lynton
Ilfracombe
Croyde
DEVON
Braunton
Barnstable
Westward Ho
Bideford

N

0   Scale   16kms

North Devon

North Devon offers high quality and versatile surfing conditions, popular with visiting surfers from the towns and cities further east.

As can be seen on the map, the bulk of the good surf arrives on the west facing beaches between Woolacombe in the north and Westward Ho in the south. It hardly takes great insight to realise that a 4ft swell in conjunction with a light E wind will offer widespread and excellent conditions.

Unfortunately the wind rarely seems to stay light E for all that long! It is for all those days of cross winds, or very small swells or very big swells that this guide is intended.

Not only does the nature of the surf at any one time depend on the swell size and wind direction, it also depends on the sea bed over which it breaks. This is where the tide rears its ugly head.

Tides in this area are extreme and it's important to learn about the best states for various locations. Because of the vast range, there's also a considerable difference in water level between say low spring tide and low neap tide. This affects the quality of some of the low tide breaks. A local tide table costing a few pence is a worthwhile investment. Water depth and therefore wave conditions are likely to change most rapidly at around mid tide.

The tidal flow up and down the Bristol Channel is similar to the current in a huge river – moving eastwards during the flood and westwards during the ebb. The 'push' effect of the incoming tide, by helping a weak swell on its way, can be most important. The only time this 'push theory' is disproved is when new swell arrives in the area during the ebb. That one can catch you out.

Not all the available surf spots have been described. The area between Hartland Point and Duckpool, (actually in Cornwall), is very rocky, possessing some interesting possibilities, especially if you're willing to do some walking.

Broadly speaking, the worst winds are W and NW, although in the summer when the sea is rarely rough, at least these may give rideable waves for the desperate.

Although the climate of the area is far from being 'continental' in nature, it is surprising just how often conditions seem to be calm or offshore before about ten o'clock in the morning during warm summer weather.

Those who get up late tend to miss out on a lot of pleasant summer surf. One thing I've learn't the hard way – if ever the surf is above average and you are free to surf, then go for it. If you optimistically wait around for the conditions to improve, they will almost certainly get worse!

Rick Abbott

Surf Breaks 1 – 9

1. The Severn Bore

At high spring tides a remarkable tidal Bore pushes its way up the Bristol Channel and creates a surfable wave travelling at a speed of about 10 kilometres an hour.

The wave is best caught between Sharpness and Gloucester with the size of the wave being typically waist high.

Spring tides occur when the earth, moon and sun are in line, which is at full and new moon. High spring tides follow when the sun and the moon are overhead at the equator, near to the autumn and spring equinoxes.

The Severn Bore works only 12 times a year and at each time, only one wave is formed. The wave is much easier to catch on a longboard.

2. Porlock Wier

Porlock Wier (in Somerset) can provide some excellent fast and hollow lefthanders when huge swells are closing out most of N. Devon and Cornwall's other breaks.

Best around high tide with S winds. Park in village.

Water Quality: Three pipes discharge raw sewage from 2,500 people at the low water mark.

3. Lynmouth

When swell on the main west facing beaches is 6ft plus, there is a good chance of a rideable sized surf reaching Lynmouth. The best waves here are the fast breaking lefthanders at and after low tide. There are usually three distinct peaks, with the one to the west of the river appearing to be slightly bigger and faster than the other two. There can also be a righthander which breaks into the rivermouth at high tide. Lynmouth faces north and due to the rocks, old swimming pool walls, fish traps and marker poles, is for experienced surfers only. Parking in front of break.

Water Quality: Failed beach! Raw sewage from nearly 5,000 people discharges 110mtrs below the low water mark.

4. Woolacombe

In the longboard days, this was the hub of the Devon surfing scene. Now that the emphasis has shifted to Croyde, Woolacombe is left as a relatively unspoilt and mellow place to surf. The waves will work at any tide but the rocks at the northern end of the main beach can produce some interesting rights above half tide. E winds blow offshore.

Barricane, known locally as Combesgate, can have some nice peaks at and around low tide.

Barricane receives slight protection from N winds, is offshore with an E, and exposed to S winds. Park by the beach.

Water Quality: Passed EC guidelines. Sewage from 11,000 people receives primary and secondary treatment before discharging.

5. Putsborough

Baggy Point protects the southern end of this beach from S or SW winds. The higher the tide, the more protected the waves become. This protection makes Putsborough a worthwhile destination when Croyde and other North Devon breaks are blown out. Putsborough is a popular surfing beach with all types of wave craft being found in the water. Parking and camping by the beach.

Water Quality: Voted best beach in Britain by the MCS for two years running.

6. Croyde

Croyde is certainly the most popular surf spot in North Devon. There are three breaks:

CROYDE REEF is a gnarly right which breaks at high tide over rocks at the north side of the bay, adjacent to the National Trust car park. The swell needs to be pretty meaty for this place to work and when it does the most important feature is the fast, hollow, initial bowl section. This wave breaks in shallow water and is suitable for experienced surfers only.

CROYDE BEACH is one of England's best beach breaks due to the peaky hollow waves it provides. It's consistent and can be surfed at any stage of the tide. The obvious drawback associated with such conditions is crowding, and Croyde beach can get crowded to the point where it becomes dangerous. Be prepared for that... If you're not experienced enough or if you don't like surfing in a crowd then you should head to another beach, especially in summer. East winds blow offshore and the sandbars here are able to hold a bigger swell than Devon's other west facing beaches. Low tide can be particularly hollow and powerful.

CROYDE POINT (DOWNEND) is a righthand point break. In a decent-sized swell with an E wind at low tide you'll be treated to fast take-offs and long walls. Practice caution – the rocks are jagged and the peak has a habit of shifting around. Entry and exit points should be looked at closely. There are gulleys on either side of the point where good timing will save the pain of a damaged board or body.

Water Quality: Bad reports from locals. Macerated sewage from 6,431 people is discharged at the low water mark.

7. Saunton

West facing, Saunton lies at the northern end of three miles of extensive sands, backed by Braunton Burrows. Saunton gets some protection from northerly winds and it's the perfect place for learning surfers and windsurfers due to its length and the slow breaking nature of the waves it receives. Easy parking at the north end of the beach.

Water Quality: Good.

8. Westward Ho

A west facing beach break of average quality, only really surfed by locals from Westward Ho and Bideford. The sands shelve very gently and consequently there are rarely any distinct peaks. Easy parking.

Water Quality: Variable. Sewage from 8,521 people is fine screened and discharged 10mtrs below the low water mark.

9. Buck's Mill

Buck's Mill is an attractive, small village of thatched cottages which overlooks a rock strewn shingle and sand beach. Lefthand waves break along a rocky phalloid called 'The Gore,' on a big swell at around low tide. The break faces N and is one of North Devon's best spots in a S or SW wind. Even in strong SW winds the wave can be surfable. There's a small car park in the village.

Water Quality: Good.

Cornwall

The most consistent, quality surfing conditions in England are to be found in the county of Cornwall. Many surfers from 'up the line' have left work and family to share in a year-round lifestyle that has changed little in the last 20 years. The huge influx of summer surfers to Cornwall has neatly divided the current atmosphere into two distinct seasons. From May to September Cornwall is awash with money, discos, packed surfing breaks, all types of surf craft, hippies, punks, travellers and poseurs. The surf is not usually at its best, lacking the powerful winter groundswells, and the novelty of searching for a parking space to gain access to 2ft waves soon wears a bit thin.

On the coldest mornings in February you will find surfers paddling out all along the coastline for a quick 'blast' before work or a more leisurely session for those with no work to go to. There are out 100 or so surfing beaches in Cornwall and during the long winter season they are virtually deserted. Some of the most dramatic coastline in the British Isles is left exclusively to the Cornish

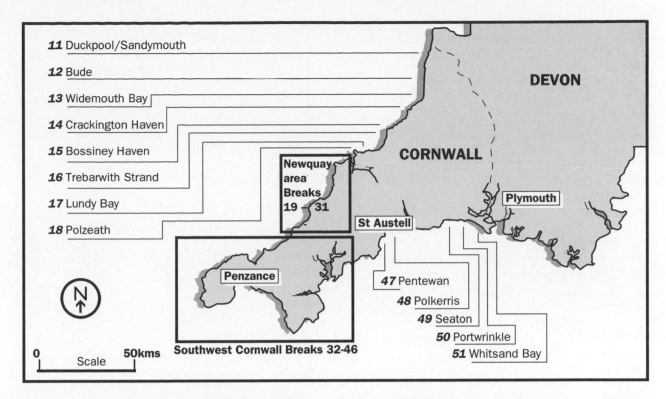

11 Duckpool/Sandymouth
12 Bude
13 Widemouth Bay
14 Crackington Haven
15 Bossiney Haven
16 Trebarwith Strand
17 Lundy Bay
18 Polzeath

DEVON

CORNWALL

Plymouth

Newquay area Breaks 19 – 31

St Austell

Penzance

47 Pentewan
48 Polkerris
49 Seaton
50 Portwrinkle
51 Whitsand Bay

0   Scale   50kms   Southwest Cornwall Breaks 32-46

and the few travellers who have discovered that winter in Cornwall is by far the best surfing season.

Winter waves can reach a rideable 6 – 8ft for days on end. The weather is usually milder than the rest of the British Isles and it is usually possible to find some offshore or sheltered waves as long as reasonable swell is running. There are so many beaches to choose from at this time of year that you may well end up surfing on your own, particularly if it's a weekday and you're away from the towns.

Peter Cade

THE SURF
The North Cornwall Coast

Normally there is plenty of surf on the north coast of Cornwall. Flat spells are not uncommon in the summer but they are not difficult to predict. Anyone who is keen to surf in Cornwall needs to become a part-time meteorologist if they want to avoid a wasted journey. In very general terms, a low pressure system in the mid Atlantic will provide waves two or three days later on the north coast of Cornwall. A prevailing high pressure that covers most of the north Atlantic will eventually flatten all surf. The deeper the low and the faster it moves, the bigger the waves. There are hundreds of variables that combine to thwart wave predictions, but it's essential to grasp the elements of wave generation.

The prevailing winds are from a SW direction so clean conditions are often sought on the few sheltered north facing beaches. Harlyn, Towan, St Agnes and St Ives all have beaches facing north. When the winds blow from the S or E a large number of beaches will provide good surfing conditions. Every beach will have a favourite stage of tide when the sandbanks are better placed for

longer or hollower rides, but these are often impossible to predict as storms and currents constantly move the sand around. Better waves are generally found on low to middle tide, but many beaches may close-out until the water is deeper at high tide. Each year the sandbanks are different and favourite spots can become terrible in a matter of days.

Surf Breaks 10 – 39

10. Speke's Mill

A secluded righthand reef break that can have a rideable wave when everywhere else is flat. See North Devon map.

Water Quality: Good.

11. Duckpool, Sandy Mouth

Faces west and picks up a lot of swell. Popular with all forms of surf craft with the best peaks getting crowded in summer months. Easy parking.

Water Quality: Good.

12. Bude (Crooklets, Summerleaze)

SUMMERLEAZE: Works up to 6ft after which it tends to close-out. A S to SE wind produces clean, offshore conditions. At low tide a lefthand wave can sometimes be had at 'The Barrel' just behind the breakwater. At high tide a righthander can be surfed just off the beach's outdoor swimming pool. Watch out for the rip at low tide by the breakwater on swells above 4ft. Crowded on a good summers day. **CROOKLETS**: Starts to work just after or just before low tide and through till high tide. Rips can be strong at low tide. S to SE winds produce offshore clean waves, which on good days can be surfed to 8ft. At high tide a good shore break forms that's a lot of fun to surf. This break also becomes crowded in the summer months as it's one of the main tourist beaches. Jason/local surfer

Water Quality: Both beaches failed! Sewage from 13,143 people goes through a tidal tank 75mtrs below the low water mark.

13. Widemouth Bay

Beach break that works with S to SE winds up to 6ft. Works all the way through the tide with left and right peaks working all along the beach. Sometimes the wave seems to lack power. No serious rips to speak of – one of the safest beaches in the area. At high tide sometimes a good fun shorebreak can be had, with a bit more power than usual. Easy parking. Jason/local surfer

Water Quality: Good.

14. Crackington Haven

The cliffs of Pencarrow Point rise more than 400 ft above this small sand and shingle beach. It faces W with the spectacular cliffs affording protection against strong winds. On a clean swell a lefthander breaks at low tide off the rocks at the southern end of the beach. Nice village in great Cornish country-side. There's a car park and cafe right on the beach.

Water Quality: Average.

15. Bossiney Haven

Bossiney Haven is a beach surrounded by country steeped in Arthurian legend. Tintagel castle, the Knights of the Round Table and Merlin the Magician are all part of the area's history. The beach faces north and needs a fair sized swell to work. When the swell is there and there's a wind from the S, the waves might not be legendary but they can be good. Access to this beach involves a dangerous descent down a cliff path. Not advised for children or drunks.

Water Quality: Good.

16. Trebarwith Strand

This west facing beach picks up a lot of swell

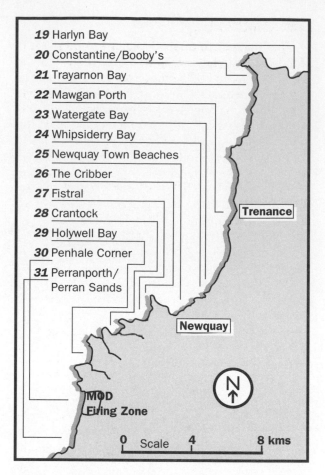

19 Harlyn Bay
20 Constantine/Booby's
21 Trayarnon Bay
22 Mawgan Porth
23 Watergate Bay
24 Whipsiderry Bay
25 Newquay Town Beaches
26 The Cribber
27 Fistral
28 Crantock
29 Holywell Bay
30 Penhale Corner
31 Perranporth/ Perran Sands

Trenance

Newquay

MOD Firing Zone

N

0 Scale 4 8 kms

and the northern end receives good protection from N winds. Low tide is best as the sea covers the whole beach at high. Limited parking by the beach.

Water Quality: Good.

17. Lundy Bay

Lundy Bay is a good spot to check on a big swell when there's a SE, S or SW wind blowing. The ten minute walk from the car park keeps the beach generally free of people. Rights and lefts break over a sand bottom with low to mid tide being best.

Water Quality: Good.

18. Polzeath (Hayle Bay)

A west-facing beach break with a good righthander showing at low tide when there's a clean, decent sized swell. It's a popular beach but is badly affected by anything but a SE, E or NE wind. The righthander is located at the north end of the bay, off Pentire Point headland. There's parking by the beach.

Water Quality: Generally okay but has bad days. Water around the rivermouth is more polluted.

19. Harlyn Bay

This horseshoe shaped bay is a good place to head for when big swells and S or SW winds are blowing out Cornwall's other less protected breaks. All tides are surfable with the incoming tide sometimes increasing the size of the waves substantially. Newtrain Bay, to the east of Harlyn Bay can also have waves worth checking.

Water Quality: Good.

20. Constantine Bay, Booby's Bay

CONSTANTINE BAY is one of the best swell pullers in North Cornwall with two distinct places to surf. In the middle of the bay lefts and rights break on a sand bottom with the waves being best from mid to high tide. At the southern end of the bay, when there's a decent sized, clean swell, a lefthander will break over the reef. Constantine Bay is notorious for strong rips so watch out when surfing here. Its exposed aspect means that any wind not from the east quadrant will ruin the waves. Beginners should only surf here when conditions are small and even then, be careful. Easy parking by the beach.

BOOBY'S BAY, to the north of Constantine, harbours a good but fickle righthand reef break. Ideal conditions are a sizeable clean groundswell, a light NE wind and low to mid tide. The wave is located at the northern end of the bay. Strong rips and dangerous rocks abound.

Water Quality: Good.

21. Treyarnon Bay

Just south of Constantine, Treyarnon is another consistent west facing bay with often above average beach break waves. There can be a left-hander at the southern end of the bay which is surfed at low tide and can get crowded.

Water Quality: No sewage is discharged in this area.

22. Mawgan Porth (Trenace)

A typical west facing beach which needs a light E or calm conditions to make the trip here worthwhile. Lefts breaking into the River Menalhyl are often the best but quality will depend on the state of the sandbars. Low to mid tide is best. Also, just to the south of this beach lies **Beacon Cove**. Conditions required are the same as those at Mawgan Porth but the walk needed keeps this bay crowd free. Park in Trenace.

Water Quality: Failed! Normally OK has bad days.

23. Watergate Bay

Watergate is a popular 2 mile long beach break. On a good day a hundred people can be found in the water but the length of the beach and the number of peaks means it can handle crowds. Watergate faces W-NW and picks up plenty of swell but is badly affected by anything but a SE or E wind. It works on all tides and is surfable to around 6ft, after which the paddle out can be extremely tough.

A car park at the centre of the beach will often be full in high season.

Water Quality: Failed beach! Generally okay but has bad days.

24. Whipsiderry Beach

This beach, which is completely submerged at high tide, can offer good waves when there is a S or SW wind blowing, due to protection received from Porth Island. Low to mid tide is best. Park above the beach, then walk down the steps to the water.

25. Newquay Town Beaches

At low tide the four beaches of **Lusty Glaze, Tolcarne, Great Western** and **Towan** all link up to make up a single mile long stretch of beach break. At high tide each beach becomes its own little cove surrounded by high cliffs. Towan, the most protected of the beaches is a good spot to check on huge swells when there is a S or SW wind. At low tide, lefthanders start to break off the harbour wall. On rare days this can be the best and only rideable wave in Newquay. The rest of the beaches share roughly the same characteristics but they can all become outrageously crowded especially with young grommets and holiday makers learning to surf for the first time. Experienced surfers will only head here when there is no other choice. Park where possible in Newquay.

Water Quality: In peak summer months, 5 million gallons/day of raw sewage from Newquay's entire population goes into the ocean on the north side of the headland between Fistral and Towan. In the prevailing SW winds, Newquay's holiday-goers swim in severely polluted water. The local council and South West Water should be ashamed of the current state of the water at England's premier summer bathing location, but few people want to face the problem.

26. The Cribber

England's big wave spot! Rarely ridden but much talked about by locals, some of which have a board in the shed waiting for the right day. Rips and other obvious dangers associated with this kind of wave make it a venue for only the most experienced surfers. The break is located at the western end of Towan Head.

27. Fistral

Faces northwest, picks up loads of swell and is renowned for peaky, tubing rights and lefts. Low tide provides the fastest and hollowest waves and consequently more experienced surfers will head here at this time. Mid to high is still very surfable with the waves being slower and easier to ride. The northern and the southern ends are the most popular and best parts of the beach. Fistral is the UK's most famous beach break and is home to many large competitions. Good waves and this fame have also made Fistral just about the most crowded surf beach in Britain with the whole place turning into a relative madhouse in the summer season. Big swells thin the crowds out considerably as do the colder months of the year. There's a big car park at the northern end of the beach (often full in summer) and spaces at the southern end.

Water Quality: Depends on wind direction.

28. Crantock Beach

Another good beach break facing northwest. The southern end receives protection from S and SW winds and when the swell is huge, good waves breaking mainly left can be found here. The northern end can also have good waves. The River Gannel runs out here and consequently sand banks are often more pronounced. The waves here also receive some protection from N and NE winds. There's a car park behind the dunes at the northern end and at the southern end, above the beach.

Water Quality: The beach has passed EC guidelines but tests show high levels of faecal coliforms and other pollutants (such as farm run-off) caused by the River Gannel.

29. Holywell Bay

A wide sandy northwest facing beach backed by sand dunes. All tides are surfable with the southern end of the beach receiving some protection from S and SW winds. From the car park it's a 5 – 10 minute walk over the dunes.

Water Quality: The southern end, where the stream meets the sea (where all the kids swim!) can be polluted. The rest of the beach is generally okay.

30. Penhale Corner

The dunes and the beach down to the low water mark, around the northern end of Perran Sands belong to the Ministry of Defence and when the red flags are raised, the area is being used as a firing range and should not be entered. The MOD don't however, own the righthander that peels off Ligger Point. This spot, despite its inaccessibility gets crowded due to the quality and length of the waiting waves. It's better at low tide, will work on just about any swell going and is best with a E or SE wind (also gets some protection from N winds). A useful rip leads out to the peak next to the cliffs. The best way to this break is to walk along the beach via the holiday camp in the middle of the beach.

Water Quality: Although away from built up areas, Penhale Corner seems to trap pollution coming from outfalls to the north and south.

31. Perranporth (Droskyn) and Perran Sands

The lefts breaking at Droskyn (the name given to the wave at the very southern end of the beach) can be good especially at mid tide when long rides are possible.

The peak shifts with the tidal flow so it's good to keep reassessing your position. An E is offshore but it can still work in a S due to protection offered by the headland. Although not particularly dangerous, rocks and rips mean beginners would be better off further along Perran Sands, where good sand bottom lefts and rights can be enjoyed hassle free. There's a car park by the beach in Perranporth.

Water Quality: Failed beach! Sewage from 11,872 people receives maceration and is discharged at the low water mark. This, combined with other pollutants in the river can make water quality very poor.

32. St. Agnes (Trevaunance)

Faces north and can have some good, powerful surf. The bay needs a fair sized swell to break and when it does work the waves break mainly right. All tides are surfable although mid tide is often the best. St. Agnes is a nice town but the waves do get very crowded. Good spot to check on a S or SW wind. There's a small area for parking above the beach. If this is full you'll have to park where possible in St Agnes.

Water Quality: Failed beach! Faecal coliform levels are consistently high and locals report grossly polluted water. Improvements were tried a few years ago by moving the outfall pipe further around the headland (ignoring local fishermen's warnings). This did no good as the sewage simply got pushed back (and is still getting pushed back) through a cave and into the bay!

33. Chapel Porth

The waves breaking at Chapel Porth are more powerful than many of Cornwall's other beaches. At high tide the beach is completely submerged, at low tide it connects up with Porthtowan to the south. Low to mid tides are surfable and often good peaks are produced here. An E or SE wind blows

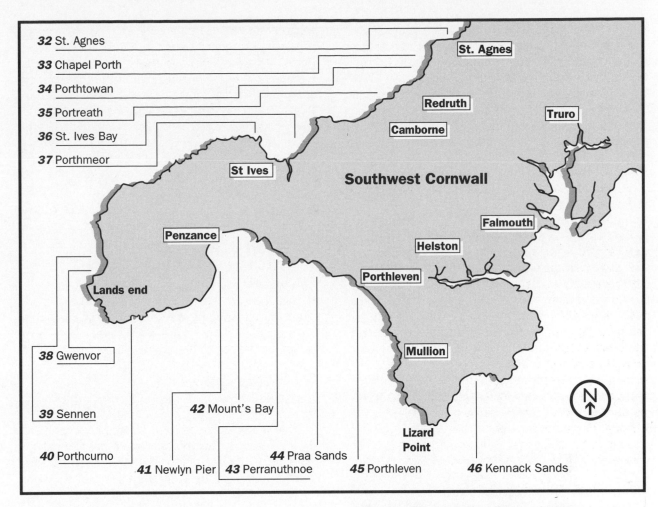

32 St. Agnes
33 Chapel Porth
34 Porthtowan
35 Portreath
36 St. Ives Bay
37 Porthmeor

St. Agnes

Redruth

Truro

Camborne

St Ives

Southwest Cornwall

Falmouth

Penzance

Helston

Porthleven

Lands end

Mullion

38 Gwenvor

39 Sennen

42 Mount's Bay

Lizard
Point

40 Porthcurno

41 Newlyn Pier   43 Perranuthnoe   44 Praa Sands

45 Porthleven   46 Kennack Sands

N

---

offshore. The beach is signposted from St Agnes and there is a National Trust car park by the beach, which is handy.

Water Quality: Variable.

34. Porthtowan

Porthtowan has waves similar to those at Chapel Porth but it's a more popular and crowded place. The waves here can be surfed throughout the tides, with high tide often benefitting by some protection from SW winds (SE winds blow offshore.) Easy parking by the beach.

Water Quality: Varies from good to hideous.

35. Portreath

When there is a decent sized swell the best wave here is a righthander off the harbour wall at the northern end of the beach.

At low tide the rocks make this wave unsurfable, at mid tide the wave becomes surfable but rocks should be carefully noted – high tide is safest.

Beginners should avoid the righthander and surf the beach break waves which are best around mid tide. As with many other Cornish beaches, Portreath gets crowded in the summer months. SE winds blow offshore.

Water quality: Screened sewage from 24,143 people gets discharged at the low water mark. Portreath has its good days but lifeguards often complain of foul waters.

Surf Breaks 36 – 39

Chris South/Freetime Holidays

36. St. Ives Bay

This horseshoe shaped bay has four named areas. **GODREVY**, at the very northeast end of the bay picks up the most swell and works best with an E wind. If the winds are further S, (and depending on how S) you should head progressively around the bay to **CARBIS BAY**, which works on a SW wind. Swell size also dictates which area is best to surf. Carbis Bay will only work on a huge swell, whilst Godrevy picks up just about any swell going.

St Ives Bay is one of Cornwall's best and most popular windsurfing/wave-jumping beaches, however, rips and currents make it suitable for experienced sailors only.

Access is via **GWITHAIN** which is the name of a village near the northeast end of the bay. There's a turn-off south of the village which leads to an extensive car park. **RED RIVER** is a river stained by old iron and tin mine oxides (harmless) and it lies to the north of the car park. Carbis Bay is much nearer to St Ives, with car parking possible near the beach.

Water Quality: Bad and set to get much worse if new sewage disposal plans go ahead.

37. Porthmeor Beach

Faces north and is the beach most surfed by St.

Ives locals. A good beach break that is reasonably consistent and when there's a S or SW wind blowing there can be some good peaks here. Porthmeor is often used as an indicator as to what is available further up or down the coast. If Porthmeor is 1ft then Gwenvor to the south will be 2 – 3ft as will Gwithains to the north. Wave conditions will vary across the beach. Easy parking by the beach.

Water Quality: Good.

38. Gwenvor

One of Cornwall's most spectacular and most consistent beaches – if there's no swell here, then there's no swell anywhere. Faces west and is exposed to all swells and all winds except those coming from E. At the very northern end of the beach a righthand reef/point works best from low to mid tide when the beach is 3 – 6ft. The peaks here shift with the tidal movement and the rips can be strong especially near the righthander. To get there either walk from Sennen, or take a right hand turn down 'Escalls Lane' off the A30, which leads to a small area for parking high above the beach. From here it's a 15 minute walk down some cliff paths.

Water Quality: Excellent.

39. Sennen Cove

Located just to the north of Lands End is Britain's most westerly beach. Sennen in summer can be crowded but for the rest of the year the waves are mostly empty. Like Gwenvor it suffers badly from any winds apart from a SE or E wind and it has waves at all stages of the tide. On average, Gwenvor will be 1 - 2ft bigger than Sennen. Sennen is well signposted and there's a car park by the beach. 'Freetime Surf School' operates from here.

Water Quality: Good. Blue Flag Beach. Macerated sewage from 1,489 people is discharged 130mtrs from the sea wall.

THE SURF
The South Cornwall Coast

Southerly storms in the Bay of Biscay or in the sea area of Finistere produce short-lived but powerful waves on the south facing beaches of Cornwall. An E, N or NW wind will provide the best conditions. Unfortunately, south coast swells are often accompanied with south or westerly winds which drastically reduces the number of 'real' surfing days available.

Ironically, England's premier reef break, Porthleven, is on the South Coast, making the rideable tubes rare jewels indeed. Quite often, a strong SW wind will turn NW for a time – so if a beach faces true south e.g. Portwrinkle, Veryan Bay or Newlyn, the conditions will often clean up very quickly. The South Coast is at its best between January and April when the winter storms take a more southerly track across Europe.   Peter Cade

Surf Breaks 40 – 51

40. Porthcurno

This southeast facing cove can have some good beach break waves when there's a big SW swell and a NW wind. It's a nice spot made nicer when the waves are good. Only works at low tide. There's a large car park by the beach.

Water Quality: Good.

41. Newlyn Pier (The Bone Yard)

When there's a huge swell a righthander can be surfed next to the harbour wall at Newlyn. This wave is sheltered from W or NW gales and can just about handle any Atlantic swell going – worth remembering when Cornwall's other breaks are closing out. Newlyn faces E-SE and works best from mid to high tide. Can get crowded.

Water Quality: Can be badly polluted. Set to improve if plans to pipe waste to Gwithain are approved.

42. Mount's Bay

Eastern Green, Long Rock Beach and **Marazion** provide one of the best windsurfing locations in the UK, with ample parking just off the beaches making rigging up easy. Watch out at Long Rock for rocks just under the surface at high tide. Hire facilities from the Old Station House car park in summer, with a rescue boat on standby.

Water Quality: Can get very weedy after SW storms. Outfall pipe at Long Rock. Water slightly better at Station House but wouldn't advise drinking any! 12 pipes discharge raw sewage from 37,585 people, 11 at low water mark, one 150mtrs below. Faecal coliform levels are high, but perhaps more worrying is the high count of entro-viruses.

43. Perranuthnoe

Faces southwest and works best on a S or SW swell from mid to high tide. Sometimes a good righthander breaks near the rocks at the northwest end of the beach. It doesn't get as crowded as Praa Sands. Good for beginners. Park in village.

Water Quality: Failed beach! Raw sewage from 1,615 people is discharged at the low water mark. Though failed, the quality is only bad on occasions.

44. Praa Sands

One of the most popular beaches in the area, both with surfers and holiday makers. The set up is very similar to Perranuthnoe but Praa picks up a bit more swell. A NW wind is offshore and the northern end receives some protection from W winds by the point, off which a righthander can sometimes break. Best from low to mid tide. The eastern end can have dangerous rips in a big swell.

Water Quality: Generally good.

45. Porthleven

The righthand reef located on the western side of the harbour channel in Porthleven is England's most talked about and respected reef break. Porthleven needs a big SW swell to get it going and a NE wind to clean it up. Under such conditions, clean tubes up to a solid 12ft are tackled by England's more experienced surfers who will always have one eye out for good Porthleven conditions.

Low tide is hollow and dangerously shallow but people do occasionally surf at this time. Mid tide is the most popular, still giving hollow tubes but the danger element is not so high. High tide is surfable but the wave can be affected by backwash – beware of the caves! Porthleven naturally gets crowded. The wave is dangerous enough as it is, crowds add substantially to this danger. More injuries are caused by surfboards and people dropping in than by any other means – remember that! Also watch out for strong rips when it's big. Park where possible in Porthleven.

Water Quality: Failed beach! Raw sewage from 3,852 people gets discharged at the high water mark. Faecal coliform levels are consistently high.

46. Kennack Sands

Two beaches joined at low tide combine to make one of the longest beaches on the eastern side of the Lizard Peninsula. Kennack faces south east and will only have waves on the biggest of swells when there is a NW or N wind. Car park by beach.

Water Quality: Good.

47. Pentewan

About four miles south of St Austell and facing SE, this beach works when there is a huge south coast swell and the winds are blowing from a N or NW direction. The waves can get quite hollow at high tide (when a fast beach break develops) but will break at all stages. There's unlikely to be surf there in the summer because of it's so sheltered.

Water Quality: Average. Not failed but variable.

48. Polkerris

A popular South Coast beach break facing southwest. It needs a big swell to work.

Water Quality: Raw sewage from 57 people is discharged 5mtrs below the low water mark. Although not much sewage is pumped out here, locals often complain of bad water quality.

49. Seaton

Three miles to the east of Looe and facing south, this beach is offshore in a N wind. It only works at low to mid tide and is quite sheltered. If Whitsands Bay is 5ft, expect 2ft waves at Seaton.

Water Quality: The beach can become quite polluted with raw sewage from an outfall at the west of the beach. This is particularly noticeable during strong W winds.

50. Portwrinkle

At the E end of Whitsands Bay. This beach is less exposed than Whitsands so is usually a foot or two smaller. It faces a more southerly direction than Whitsands – so is favoured on big swells when the wind is from the NW. Works on low tide only.

There are a number of rocks that get covered up as the tide moves in so watch your fins! The car park's above the beach and there's a footpath down the cliff.

Water Quality: Raw sewage from 938 people is discharged at the low water mark. Locals report bad pollution on big swells – duckdiving through shit, condoms etc.

51. Whitsand Bay

This four mile long southwest facing beach is much visited by Plymouth-based surfers and it works better at low tide. Tragantle (in the middle of the bay) works quite well at high tide, but access is restricted by the army who seem to know when the surf is good and always close the path for shooting! When working, rips and currents are particularly strong here so beware! No parking near the beach – a 10 minute walk down the road is needed.

Water Quality: Good.

Surf Breaks 52 – 56

Alex Williams

52. Wembury

When there's a big swell, Wembery Bay will have waves at all stages of the tide, with offshores from NW to E. On smaller swells low to mid is best. The best waves of the bay are often the lefts off Blackstone Rocks. The swell here is normally 1 - 2ft smaller than Bantham. A popular place for Plymouth based surfers.

Water Quality: Sewage from 4,383 people receives primary treatment and is discharged 100mtrs below. Faecal coliform levels are often high and seaweed and sewage debris, combined with pollutants in the river can produce a nasty mix.

53. Challaborough

Beach break surf, mid to high tide and lefts off the cliffs when the sand banks are right. Low tide righthand point works to right of beach and can be good. S to NE winds are best although SW or W

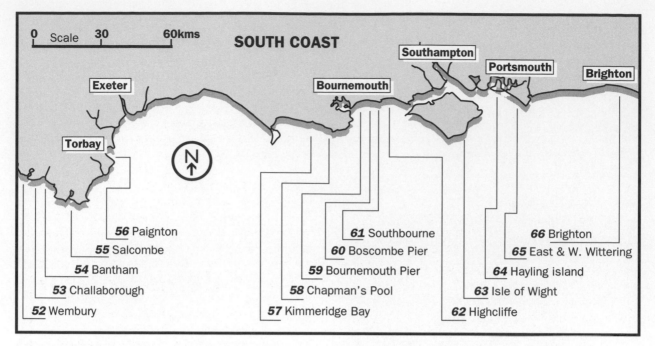

0 Scale 30 60kms

Exeter

Torbay

Southampton

Portsmouth

Brighton

Bournemouth

56 Paignton
55 Salcombe
54 Bantham
53 Challaborough
52 Wembury

61 Southbourne
60 Boscombe Pier
59 Bournemouth Pier
58 Chapman's Pool
57 Kimmeridge Bay

66 Brighton
65 East & W. Wittering
64 Hayling island
63 Isle of Wight
62 Highcliffe

winds will not mess it up too much.

Water Quality: Sometimes good, sometimes bad.

54. Bantham

Facing southwest, Bantham is one of South Devon's best and most consistent beach breaks. All tides are surfable, but on the push the waves are often cleaner with no rip.

Bantham tends to catch the most swell on this part of the coast because of deep water created by the River Avon, this helps to funnel the swell onto the beach.

Rips at Bantham can be strong, especially on the outgoing tide when the river combines with Atlantic swells to create swirling currents. There is a car park, toilets, a village store and pub, a short walk from the beach.

Water Quality: Generally pretty good although water colour can be murky due to silt from the River Avon.

55. Salcombe

Salcombe is located in a heavily protected bay and consequently only works on big winter swells. When the swell is there (only a few times a year), there can be some nice beach break waves that are best at one hour off high tide. Two hours after that an outer bar stops swells coming through.

Salcombe is protected from all winds apart from a SE, and NW winds blow offshore. Watch out for rocks. Easy parking.

Water Quality: Failed beach! Raw sewage from 2,226 people, plus various other pollutants from the Kingsbridge Estuary give cause for concern.

56. Paignton

E or NE winds blow wind swell in from the Channel. When winds turn offshore it will work for a few hours before the swell drops.

Water Quality: Average.

Surf Breaks 57 – 66

Guy Penwarden/Hot Rock Surf Shop

57. Kimmeridge Bay (K. Bay)

Classic reef break, works best two hours before and after high tide. Will hold up to 10 - 12ft surf under the right conditions. Needs a ground swell in the channel. Prone to blow out easily, works best on light N-NE wind.

THE LEDGES: Predominately a lefthander although rights are good as well. A slow breaking, mellow wave can break a mile out to sea on big swells giving long rides. It's a fairly well covered reef though odd rocks do stick out occasionally. Crowded every day, and popular with longboarders.

THE BAY: Predominately a righthander. A very similar wave to Ledges in that it breaks a long way out, but has more power. Occasionally good if it's onshore and big. Located in the middle of the bay. Same bottom conditions as Ledges but never as crowded – an underrated wave!

BROAD BENCH: Another righthander with a short ultra hollow/shallow left, best at 6 – 8ft with a light NE wind. Very powerful and also very shallow. A long wave under ideal conditions. Restricted access Monday to Friday as it's situated in an army firing range. **DO NOT** attempt to surf it if it's off limits! Long walk to get to the break and hardcore locals are very bored with drop in artists!

58. Chapman's Pool

So-called 'secret spot.' Lefthand reef break can be hollow and long, with the odd rock sucking dry! **Cloudbreak**, about a quarter of a mile out to sea, is a long paddle over flat water and could be treacherous due to rip current! You can see another righthand peak as yet unsurfed. It's a long walk to get to it through a nature conservation area and hardcore locals can be unfriendly when you get there. Works in the same conditions as K. Bay.

59. Bournemouth Pier (Kodak Pier)

A very crowded spot with the most popular wave being the peak on the east side of the pier. Can produce excellent surf and there's an incredible rip current on a SE wind. Don't use the pier to paddle out from. Remember, "if you can't paddle out, you shouldn't be out there!" Gath helmets popular due to crowds, drop-ins are inevitable. Car park directly in front of peak – hence the crowds.

Water Quality: Although by no means crystal clear, the waters in the Bournemouth area are generally pretty safe.

60. Boscombe Pier

A carbon copy of Bournemouth Pier but not working quite as well at time of writing. Dredging by local council has made it a bit too deep – hence the crowd at Bournemouth Pier. Worth checking.

61. Southbourne Area

A succession of groynes, going east between Boscombe Pier and Hergistbury Head, can produce excellent hard breaking waves. The groynes pick up more swell than both piers on SW but are prone to the effects of wind. If there's groundswell here then Kimmeridge bay will be going off. Young local crowd and lots of body boarders.

62. Highcliffe Area

Similar to Southbourne area in that it picks up more swell than the piers but it breaks a long way out and rolls for a long way. A slow breaking right-hander is good if it's small at the piers, but there's no protection from the wind here either.

63. Isle of Wight

From **Freshwater** and **Compton Bay** down to **St Catherine's Point** are various SW facing breaks. Swells are most common in winter. Freshwater and Compton get crowded when they're working.

Water Quality: Faecal coliform levels at Compton are pretty low but the presence of other pollutants around the coast warrants further research.

64. Hayling Island

Hayling Island offers some of the best windsurfing conditions on the South Coast. There is only one area of the seafront where windsurfing is permitted (in front of Surf Connection). It is, happily, the best area on the island and has excellent con-ditions throughout the year. For surfing there are two spots, one at the eastern and one at the western end of the seafront.

Hayling Island is also home to the largest windsurfing event in Britain: 'The Round Hayling Marathon' is held annually in September... see windsurfing publications for more details. There are various parking facilities along the seafront and also many guest houses, cafes and restaurants.

Jamie Jamison/Surf Connection

Water Quality: Langstone and Chichester harbours are not suitable for activities involving immersion in the water. Along the seafront it's a bit better but again, do your best not to ingest too much water.

65. East & West Wittering

One of the best surfing locations on the South Coast. The sand and pebble beach stretches for over 4 miles, offers ideal conditions for both surfing and windsurfing and is popular with surfers from as far away as London and Dorset. It has been a favoured venue for more than 20 years.

The Shore Board Surf Club has been resurrected from its recent dormant state. Based in Shore Road, East Wittering, it offers changing facilities, contests and club trips.

Simon Crawford/Shore Boards

66. Brighton Area

SW winds from force 4/5 upwards blowing for 24 hours will produce rideable surf on some good quality beach and reef/chalk beds. S and dead W winds will produce surf but these swells tend to be smaller and diminish at a faster rate. Once a swell has been established (usually by a mid Atlantic low pressure situated near Ireland) the size will increase until the wind either dies or swings around to a W to N direction. During these periods the waves can be at their best – clean and glassy. However, swells don't last long so being aware of the weather chart is vital.

The area is well catered for by local surf shop Oceansports. Call us for a surf check and we're open 7 days a week all year. Tel: 0898 500 456

James and Grant/Oceansports

Water Quality: Very polluted! Keep the toilet roll handy. The local surfers build up immunity to most of the water problems and there's strong support for SAS. The South Coast premier of *Surfers – The Movie* drew the biggest crowd outside Cornwall! with all the profits being donated to SAS. Sewage from 275,000 people receives only screening and is discharged at Portobello.

North Sea

WEATHER CONDITIONS

As the UK is situated beneath a consistently disturbed westerly airflow, its eastern facing coastline experiences offshore conditions for long periods of time, but larger swells only usually develop in the late autumn, winter and early spring months. Required weather patterns are:

1. A deep low pressure system moving east from northern Scotland to south Norway or alternatively moving southeast to Denmark with strong to gale force northerlies developing on its western flank. This produces rough seas and swell in 12 – 24 hrs.

Northerly swells can be huge – 80ft swells in the open sea sent 30ft monsters over the reefs in Dec 1990.

If a mobile ridge of high pressure follows the low, swell will clean up quickly, with dawn katabatic (night wind) glass-offs (Rick Abbott refers to these in his North Devon intro). These are the best conditions to be found on the East Coast in general and swell can last from 1 – 5 days. If the low pressure fills slowly over South Norway it will produce surf for a week at a time.

2. When a deepening low with its associated frontal systems crosses the UK from southwest England to southeast. Scotland, strong to gale force E to SE winds develop south swell with a common wave of 4 – 6ft. In strong winds during winter months 8 - 10ft surf is common but remains messy until after the disturbance has passed and the winds veer SW. These swells last from one to three days due to their short fetch.

3. High pressure over Scandinavia accompanied by Low Pressure over Europe can bring strong

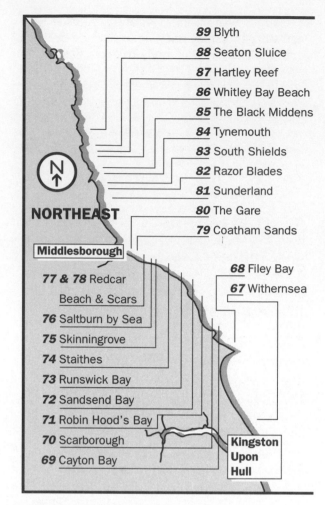

winter northerlies and more big swells, but these tend rarely to glass-off.

SEA TEMPERATURES

The North Sea is at its coldest in Feb/Mar (averaging around 5°C at Scarborough). In the winter of 1991 the sea temperature fell to 2.5°C, therefore a winter wetsuit with a hood is advised from November onwards as ice-cream headaches are a problem to some surfers. The North Sea is at its warmest in September, averaging around 14°C. A 3mm suit should keep you comfortable. In both 1990 and 1991, temperatures reached 17°C on hot sunny days.

D.R. Hindley F.R. Met. Soc./Killerby Park

GEOLOGY & WATER QUALITY

An important factor influencing the quality of surf along this stretch of coastline is the local geology. Horizontally bedded Jurassic sedimentary rock reefs accompanied by wave action has produced extensive wave cut platforms stretching seaward from the bases of high, rugged cliffs. Locally these wave cut platforms are called 'scars' and in clean groundswells can produce excellent waves. Such breaks usually work from low to mid tide, with the water becoming too deep at higher stages. It is easy to get cut off by the especially strong tides, so be careful! The region also has its fair share of good quality beach breaks.

Sadly sewage from most of our seaside towns and villages simply ends up in the sea by way of outfall pipes, fouling many of our breaks. Other pollution is of an industrial nature – Teeside is heavily industrialised and the River Tees remains a convenient dump for industrial waste, causing unknown damage to the river and to coastal waters. **The cold we can accept and even enjoy, but something can and should be done about local marine pollution!**

Nick Noble/Saltburn Surf Shop

Surf Breaks 67 – 89

67. Withernsea

Faces east-northeast and is just one point of access to a long sand and shingle beach. Due to the way N swells push down the coast the lefts are often best. Parking by the beach.

Water Quality: Average. Sewrage from 12,000, with primary treatment at the low water mark.

68. Filey Bay

If there's a big swell, and Cayton bay is blown out by north winds then Filey bay can have good waves due to protection from Filey Brigg.

Water Quality: Passed NRA tests but failed by an independent study conducted by the Robens Institute and Greenpeace.

69. Cayton Bay

THE POINT is the most dangerous of the three, but renowned for being one of the longest lefts on the East Coast. The waves break around the point, and no matter how messy it is, tend to clean themselves up. Good from 6 - 15ft. When working, the point is Cayton Bay's best wave.

THE PUMP HOUSE area is again partially covered with rocks. Surfable at mid to high tide in about a 3 - 5ft swell. Any bigger and a strong rip develops between the rocks. The wave can be long but on a bad day close-outs occur.

THE BUNKERS is characterised by a horse-shoe shaped sandbank making both lefts and rights very good. One of the best beach breaks for miles.

Water Quality: Average.

John Hindley/Killerby Park

70. Scarborough (S & N Bay)

South beach faces east and can have a good left off the east pier when there's a big swell working on all tides. North beach faces north-northwest and can have a righthander breaking off the headland when there's a good swell. Sand and rock bottom. Both beaches are often surfed (by friendly locals).

Water Quality: Screened sewage from 93,750 people is discharged 1.5km below the low water mark. Water quality can be awful. Robens/ Greenpeace study failed both beaches.

71. Robin Hood's Bay

Faces east, sand and shingle beach break waves.

Water Quality: Average.

Sandsend to The Gare

Between Teesmouth and Whitby lies approximately 25 miles of coastline with some of the sharpest contrasts one could imagine. To the north lies the industrial and urban sprawl of Teeside – 'Steel River' as it was once known. Steel and more recently chemical industries dominate much of the landscape. To the south the North Yorkshire Moors National Park meets the sea with impressive cliffs. Small fishing villages give access to the surfing breaks and the scenery in this part of the region is magnificent. Facilities for surfing in the region amount to a surf shop and hire business located in the Saltburn pier car park.

Nick Noble & Gary Rogers/
Saltburn Mobile Surf Shop

72. Sandsend Bay

A large open bay facing northeast with several notable breaks. At the bottom of Lythebank (A174) there is a car park through stone arches. Park here to surf a break called **Caves** – a lefthander which peels off a well formed scar under the cliffs. It works on a N swell around half tide and it's one of the only places along this coastline that offers shelter from a strong westerly wind. On a decent sized swell it will produce a good 4 - 5ft fun wave, and can be a popular place due to the shelter it receives. **Sandsend Beach** is the best beach break in the area, in my opinion. Peaks along the beach work from low to three quarters tide but close-out at high. Whitby has a beach which picks up similar swell to Sandsend though is not often surfed. There's car parking above the beach alongside the road giving good views and access to the surf.

Water Quality: Sewage from 450, raw at LWM.

73. Runswick Bay

When there's a big N swell running and other breaks along the coast are too big, here's the place to head for. There are several reef breaks and a beach break in the middle of the bay. On the north side of the bay an unpredictable but impressive lefthander breaks off the **Cobble Dump** – the name indicating the nature of the bottom. This break works through most stages of the tide but is rarely surfed. On the south side of the bay there are three righthand reef breaks, the **innermost reef** is well protected from big N swells (when Saltburn is breaking at 8 - 10ft you can expect 5 - 6ft here) and rides can be very long with a fairly easy paddle out in front of the Yacht House. The **middle reef** is likely to be a few feet bigger in size and the **outer reef**, out from Kettleness gets the full force of any big N swell. Rideable surf of 15ft+ can break out there! The three righthand breaks work from low to mid tide. Runswick Bay is a picturesque place and is one of my own favourite surf spots when it's on. There's a car park at the north end of the bay.

Water Quality: Not too bad except for sea debris. Raw sewage from 480 people is discharged at the low water mark.

74. Staithes

Staithes is home to some of the best reef breaks in the Northeast. When there's a good N swell running and the tide is low there are three obvious breaks as you look out to sea from the village.

The first is off the scar lying to the north of the Harbour – a well formed peak which breaks with impressive force and then peels left. Access is over the Harbour wall below the Cowbar cliffs and then out across the scar – watch out for rocks beneath the surface of the water, this is not the best of sea bottoms!

The next break is off the head of the large scar lying to the south of the Harbour. Further away, but again a quality peak breaking left.

The third and best break is **The Cove** breaking off the south side of the scar in close proximity. Arguably one of the best breaks in Britain. The take-off is very critical and if you make it you're in for a fast hollow wall with lots of power. All the Staithes breaks work from low to mid tide with the waves crashing up against the cliffs at higher stages of the tide. On weekends it can get packed.

Water Quality: Failed beach! Raw sewage from 4,000 people is discharged at the low water mark.

75. Skinningrove

There are two beaches here, one to the north of the jetty and one to the south. Both beaches face northeast and are exposed to swell from the N through to the SE. The southern and smaller of the two beaches is sheltered to some extent from a W (cross shore) wind by a large stone jetty, though it only works from low to mid tide (waves bounce off the earth cliffs at higher stages). To the south of **Skinningrove Beck** lies the long **Hummersea Scar** and a right breaks off the Skinningrove end of the scar; again a low to mid tide break only. Park in Skinningrove.

Water Quality: Failed beach! Raw sewage from 7,700 people is discharged at the low water mark.

76. Saltburn by the Sea

Certainly the most popular surfing beach in the Northeast. To be honest Saltburn beach is not that good a break. Being a flat beach, waves tend to lose power a long way from the shore. However, there is a point break at the south end of the beach off the huge scar lying beneath **Huntcliff**. The wave is a fast and powerful righthander when it's working.

Water Quality: One problem – a sewage outfall 'throws out' on the south beach headland, worst on a SE wind. Saltburn Gill and Saltburn East both failed badly. Raw sewage from a combined total of 20,650 people is discharged via 2 outfalls at the low water mark.

77. Redcar to Saltburn

A three mile long north east facing beach where waves can be found at most points of access when there's swell from the NW to SE. Accessible at any point by walking some 50 - 100 yards over the 'Stray' (the dunes).

78. Redcar Scars and Beach

Good waves can be found off the scars which lie off Redcar. People occasionally surf off the inside scars outside **Denny's Garage** and outside **Lovetts Amusements**. As yet I have not heard of anyone surfing the outer scars. Swell comes from the north through to southeast and there's a car park above the beach.

Water Quality: Not too bad except near the lifeboat station which has failed! Screened sewage from 35,000 people is discharged 1599mtrs below the low water mark.

79. Coatham Sands

Approximately 2 miles of sandy beach, backed by dunes stretching from South Gare to West Scar off Redcar. The beach faces north-northeast and picks up swell from N through to SE. Access is only practical at the Redcar.

Water Quality: Raw sewage from 1,200 people is discharged 25mtrs below.

80. The Gare

Actually just inside the mouth of the River Tees on the south bank about 300 yards upstream from the light house. Works only on a SE or E swell of a moderate size and above. Swell wraps round the headland producing a very fast, hollow righthander breaking over a man-made boulder dump. Best from low to mid tide, but can be dangerous due to the nature of the bottom and pollution! A world class wave at its best. Access is from Redcar along the Warrenby road and on past British Steel out to the headland; park by the light house compound gates and walk over the grass bank to check it out.

Water Quality: Waste from ICI, British Steel and other industries ends up in the river, which is especially bad on the incoming tide, with onshore winds. Failed beach! Macerated seawge from a combined total of 59,800 people is discharged via 2 pipes at the low water mark and 25mtrs below.

Sunderland – Pease Bay Surf Breaks 81 – 89

Gabriel Davies (young Geordie surfer, member of the English surfing team, member of *Foam at the Mouth Surf Club* run by his father Peter, Tynemouth, 091 257 0853.)

81. Sunderland to South Shields

There are some sheltered breaks for the heavy winter storms – **Cats and Dogs** by Roker Pier, **Sunderland** and the beach at **Whitburn**.

82. Razor Blades, Whitburn

Three lefthand reefs produce good but fickle waves around mid to high tide. Access is across a firing range to the cliff path and is restricted, particularly at weekends.

Water Quality: Failed beach! (Whitburn). Raw sewage at low water mark.

83. South Shields Beach

Beach break with waves of varying quality. Local surfers tend to surf in the middle of the beach in front of the Life Guard Station. Better waves may be had at the south end next to the cliff.

Water Quality: Not too bad at Sandhaven – failed badly in the inner harbour.

84. Tynemouth

Tynemouth is the centre of surfing on Tyneside. Autumn, winter or early spring is the best time for waves. Tynemouth has three main breaks which are within walking distance of each other.

LONG SANDS is the main beach and has the most reliable waves. It's a fairly average beach break with the best waves breaking near the outdoor pool on the south side of the bay, best at high tide. The point is occasionally a bigger and better option. King Edward's Bay is a sheltered beach overlooked by Tynemouth Priory.

EDDIE'S, to the locals, is generally best at low tide and depending on the swell direction and sandbanks – can be better than adjacent Long Sands. To find out about what's going on, call in at

Sandy's Surf Shop in Front Street, the only specialist shop for many miles.

Water Quality: How can it be anything but horrendous!

85. The Black Middens

The good news is that this is one of the best waves on the East Coast. The bad news is that it is polluted and seldom works. The Black Middens is sited at the mouth of the River Tyne on the north bank. The two piers built out to sea to protect shipping from winter storms clean up the waves. A lefthand barrel breaks over a boulder reef but unfortunately needs large swells to get between the piers. Conditions are best from low to mid tide, better on the incoming. It can be seen from the coastguard's cottages or Lord Collingwood's monument.

86. Whitley Bay Beach

Only surfed in storm conditions when it's more sheltered than Long Sands. Best at mid to high tide with quality sandbanks at times. Park at the cafe towards the north end of the beach.

Water Quality: Average.

87. Hartley Reef

An excellent reef break that needs a well lined up N swell and light offshores, rideable at mid to high tide – very fickle but worth checking, just in case. Picks up two feet or more than the Tynemouth beaches.

Take the coast road (A193 North) past St Mary's Lighthouse and at Hartley roundabout take the turn to the sea. Some two hundred yards away there's a car park which overlooks the break. Take the path to the right and there are steps in the cliff to the beach.

88. Seaton Sluice to Blyth

Southern beaches are rarely surfed. Blyth at the north end of the bay is more popular. The peaks are of varying quality but it does offer shelter from the large swells.

Water Quality: Seaton – failed.
Blyth – not failed but poor water quality.

89. Blyth, Bamburgh, Pease Bay

Further north from Blyth the coastline is rarely surfed but the beautiful and historic coastline with its reefs and beaches offers great potential. When the conditions are right the whole East Coast works and there is not much incentive to leave the popular breaks. Some spots are known at **Newbiggin, Alnmouth, Beadnell** and **Sea Houses**. You will be guaranteed no crowds. The further north you go the clearer the water. It's great fun surfing with the seals at Bamburgh. Take the turn in the village to the beach. **Holy Island**, has a fabled left, which few have ridden. The next recognised surf spot is **Pease Bay**, across the Scottish border.

THE CHANNEL ISLANDS

THE PEOPLE

Although the Channel Islands are much closer to France than to England, they represent one of the oldest parts of the Queen's realms, for her predecessors ruled them as part of the Duchy of Normandy long before they became kings of England. In 1066 the Duke of Normandy conquered England and became King William I. 100 years later, King John lost Normandy but the French failed to seize the islands for themselves.

Some centuries later, on the 28th of June 1940, the Germans invaded and occupied the islands, establishing their only hold over British soil during World War II. Over their four year stay, the Germans turned the islands into fortresses, building towers and burrowing tunnels filled with hideouts, bunkers and hospitals. Today, French and German influences remain much in evidence, both in road names and language as well as crumbling reminders of darker war-torn days.

Although still attached to Britain, both Jersey and Guernsey have their own independent governments, their own currencies (though English pounds can still be used) and much lower taxation than in Britain. This, combined with a favourable climate and fine coastal scenery has attracted a considerable number of investors, retired people and holiday makers to the islands.

THE LAND

Impressive rocky coasts, fine golden beaches and lush green interiors attract thousands of tourists every summer, giving opportunities for many of the islanders to make a living from looking after visitors' needs. The other chief occupation is agriculture. Jersey and Guernsey cows are famous, for they reputedly produce better cream in more volume than any other breed. Farms are generally small, and for centuries the farmers have spread seaweed on their land as fertilizer. Early tomatoes, potatoes, fruit and flowers are all produced for the English market.

Over 2000 hours of sunshine a year give the Channel Islands a kinder climate than England. Spring and Autumn produce consistent swells.

TRAVELLING AROUND

Airport: 3.5 miles SW of St Peter Port. Tel: 0481 37424.

Buses: Like Jersey, Guernsey has a reliable, efficient bus service; main terminal at Picquet House, St Peter Port. Tel: 0481 724677

Tourist Office: PO Box 23, Whiterock, St Peter Port Tel: 0481 723555

Guernsey

Capital:	St. Peter Port
Area:	78km (30mls)
Population:	55,000
Languages:	English, French

Guernsey, the most westerly of the Channel Islands and the second largest (ten miles by eight), is surrounded by beaches and offshore reefs. It's situated roughly 20 miles to the west of the Cherbourg Peninsula and 70 miles south of Weymouth, on the northern side of the Bay of St Malo. It's exposed to any swells that come up the Channel.

Access to all the bays is simply a matter of using the coast road. All the bays have parking facilities and most have beach side cafes or beach kiosks. Despite one of our surf breaks being nicknamed 'pooh pooh's', this refers to one of the island's many land drainage pipes situated near the break and not a sewer pipe.

Windsurfers will find many other bays on the island most of which provide access for the determined sailor, except for the south coast which is cliffs. The locations mentioned are the most popular for both launching and social sailing; if you must sail on your own, be warned the tides around the Channel Islands are amongst the most powerful in the world and it's best not to venture too far outside bays without taking advice.

Guernsey is not the most consistent surf spot on the globe. If you live here and watch the weather and tides you will occasionally get some excellent waves, but arrive here for a two week holiday, hell bent on surfing every day, and you could be disappointed. The travelling windsurfer or someone looking to take up windsurfing for the first time is more likely to spend time on the water.

Chris Mason/Nautifun Windsurf Shop and School.

Surf Breaks 1 – 8

Chris Mason/Nautifun Windsurf Shop & School

1. Vazon Bay
The Beach Break

The centre of Guernsey's surfing; predominantly a righthander breaking from the centre of the bay diagonally towards the land drainage pipe. Usually at its best from half tide up to the start of the backwash (caused by waves hitting the wall), which makes surfing impossible. Occasionally excellent just before the tide becomes too high.

The Reef

LEFT: When the tide is too high for the beach, the left on the reef starts to break. It can offer an exhilarating drop with a fast occasionally spitting section. Increase your adrenalin by a confrontation with Nipple Rock smack in the middle of the reef.

RIGHT: This wave needs a spring tide to cover the bigger rocks sufficiently. Better than the left, and provides a sucking take-off followed by a longish ride into the shallows. The right only works up to about 6ft when it walls across to join...

T'OTHER SIDE: The other side of the reef comes into its own on a big swell when the beach and the reef are closing out. It can provide long rights from the reef diagonally across the beach. There is no doubt that when everything gels this break can be classic. Lack of strong rips make this a groovy ride.

CENTRES, POOH POOH'S, PIPELINE: A wave breaks over sand, with a peak that can be ridden left or right. The rides are usually short, very fast and break predominantly right. Rarer, equally fast and hollow lefts also wind across the beach into one of the ubiquitous land drainage pipes.

FUNBOARDING: Vazon is the wave–sailor's paradise, where the surf often isn't powerful enough for pure surfing and when the wind blows from anywhere between SE and NW, excellent wave jumping conditions prevail. Down the line wave-riding can be excellent with winds between S and SW, but whatever the direction the wind becomes gusty near the sea wall when the tide comes in.

2. Perelle Bay

DOM HUE: The jewel in the crown of Guernsey surf, including a variety of waves at mid to high tide and the big wave spot of the Island. Far out to sea, and very rocky surfing, Perelle is generally left to the 'experts' and can be a daunting prospect.

THE PEAK: This big right breaks a long way out in the centre of Perelle Bay and is reached from the Islet of Dom Hue. The peak is very shifty and on a big day it's hard to suss the take-off point. To get there you have to pass two excellent breaks behind the island so it's not surfed much. See below.

THE LEFT This is the wave that's ridden most at Perelle. It generally picks up more swell than other breaks on the island. Because it is 300 yards out to sea, it can suffer if the wind is blowing, but provides the best shaped and longest rideable left

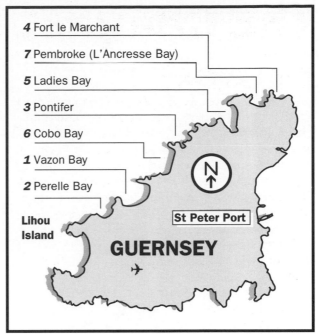

on the islands. Breaking off or around a rocky outcrop, one can catch long walling waves well into the shallows. Best on a smaller tide, it can hold a swell up to 10ft. Due to the rocks and position, this is only for the most experienced surfers. Get caught on a big day and the rip can wash you to the other side of the Island. On a small day you can lose a fin on the rocks below the surface as the tide recedes.

THE RIGHT: Probably the best wave on Guernsey, which breaks on a big swell, with a large tide. A sucking take-off, right next to a group of rocks, propels you onto a powerful pealing wave, over a couple of large rocks which emerge as the tide drops. A long ride, pedal down from start to finish. Don't get caught on the inside.

3. Portinfer

A popular surfing bay which picks up more swell than Vazon, offering a consistent half tide break. At half tide a peak in the centre provides lefts and rights. As the tide drops the waves break more powerfully on the northern headland to provide a right across the narrow part of the bay. On a small tide, a respectable left can be found breaking off the rocks just below the Port

4. Fort le Marchant

A difficult rock reef break wrapping around a headland, and throwing just off the rocks with a shoulder walling up into deep water. This wave wraps through 90 degrees. When everywhere else is totally huge, and blown out, head for here and watch probably the best wave on the island break.

WINDSURFING

Guernsey is very popular with windsurfers as well as having a large indigenous windsurfing population. The best places to learn are Ladies Bay or Cobo Bay. There are schools located at both of these beaches, run by RYA qualified instructors.

5. Ladies Bay (Grand Havre)

Ladies Bay offers experienced boardsailors the fun of the open sea and beginners the security of a sheltered bay. A horse–shoe shaped bay facing west provides the safest windsurfing in Guernsey. It's a regular venue for both racing and speed events. Due to the shape of the bay, sailing can be excellent here on any wind direction. The flattest water, speed sailing type days are best when the wind is between NE and SE, but whatever the direction, conditions can be found to suit most abilities – except for the out and out wavehead.

6. Cobo Bay

Predominantly flat water and sheltered. This beach is situated in front of a busy section of coast road. The beach here is extremely popular during the summer, and access for rigging and launching your own gear is very limited, which contributes to it being more popular for the windsurfing school than for the experienced windsurfer.

7. Pembroke (L'Ancresse Bay)

Another sheltered bay popular with windsurfers, less than a mile from Ladies Bay but facing north, if the conditions are good, i.e. if wind is between NW and E, racing is held here. If the wind blows from between SE and W the venue is moved to Ladies Bay which can provide better conditions. Pembroke Bay has been used twice to host the Mistral European Championships.

8. Herm

The island of Herm is located 3 miles off St Peter Port, across a busy stretch of water called Little Russell. Once a year the Guernsey Boardsailing Association organise a weekend in Herm consisting of a race across the Russell through incredibly strong tides, and dodging incoming passenger ferries, yachts, hydrofoils and all kinds of sea going traffic. (Don't sail across to Herm without some form of boat cover.) Over the weekend, racing takes place outside of Herm harbour consisting of a slalom course, depending on the conditions and usually a race around the island. A great social weekend open to visiting sailors. The island itself is picturesque in the extreme as there are no cars on the island and transport either *a pied* or on the back of a donkey, or tractor. The first ferry over from Guernsey is the milk boat which is a special low price, but you've got to get up at sparrow fart to catch it! There's an island to the south west of Herm called Jethou which is privately owned and not open to the public.

Jersey

Capital:	St Helier
Area:	115km (45mls)
Population:	85,000
Languages:	English, French

Jersey is roughly rectangular in shape (five miles by nine) and is the largest and most southerly of the Channel Islands. Nearly all of the island's surf can be found along the west coast, with the spectacular St Ouen's Bay providing five miles of beach and reef break waves (restricted during summer months). Windsurfing is also very popular and one can find many beaches where good conditions will suit all levels. Access to all the breaks is easy and like Guernsey, water quality is generally very good.

Surf Breaks 1 – 9

Steve Wilkinson/Freedom Surf Shop

1. St Brelade's Bay

St Brelade's bay is a popular tourist beach with flat water windsurfing found here throughout the year. Waves will only appear on very big swells when Jersey's west facing breaks are either closing out or are just too big for the average surfer. The waves are best from low to mid on the incoming tide with the best peaks usually found by the pier. North to east winds blow offshore and crowds will be found here when it's working.

2. Petit Port

Petit Port is Jersey's spectacular big wave break and is only suitable for very competent surfers. It breaks both left and right with the righthander providing the real quality rides with heavy and hollow waves up to 15ft. The waves here are surfable throughout the tides but the lower the tide gets, the hollower and more dangerous the wave becomes. It breaks over a rock bottom and is best with an easterly wind. To get out, jump off the slipway and a rip will take you out to the line-up. Timing is crucial with mistakes being extremely dangerous! There's a car park next to the slipway.

TRAVELLING AROUND

Airport: 4 miles west of St Helier Tel:46111
Buses: Jersey has a cheap, efficient bus service; main terminal at St Helier. Tel: 0534 21201
Tourist Office:
Liberation Square, St Helier
Tel: 0534 24779 (information)
Tel: 0534 31958 (accomodation)
General Hospital:
Gloucester St, St Helier
Tel: 0534 71000
Emergency:
Police: 0532 75511, Ambulance: 0534 72222

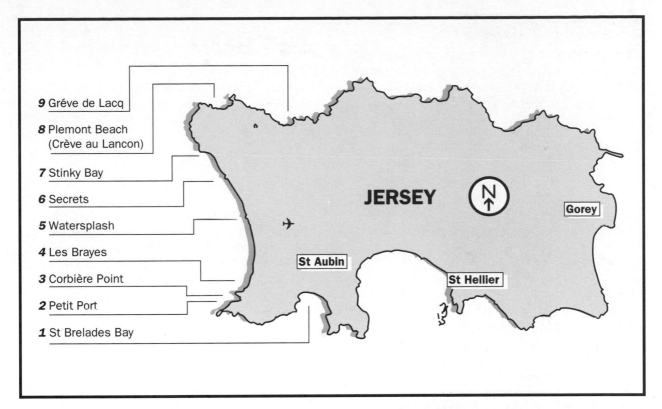

Map labels:

9 Gréve de Lacq
8 Plemont Beach (Crève au Lancon)
7 Stinky Bay
6 Secrets
5 Watersplash
4 Les Brayes
3 Corbière Point
2 Petit Port
1 St Brelades Bay

JERSEY

N

Gorey

St Aubin

St Hellier

3. Corbière Reef

Corbière reef only starts to work when the swell reaches 15ft. Needless to say it's only ever been surfed by a handful of very experienced locals and as a travelling surfer it's unlikely that you will arrive with the equipment needed to tackle this break. However, if you do decide to surf this reef ask the locals for advice which they will be more than happy to provide. Access is the same as Petit Port.

4. Les Brayes

A medium to big wave spot which is best surfed with an E to SE wind. The waves here can pack a punch even though it's only a sand bottom. Low to mid on the dropping tide is best and there's a rip that always runs from south to north. On a good day the waves here can be excellent.

5. Watersplash

If there's no swell at the Watersplash then there's no swell anywhere. This consistency, and the good quality of the beach break peaks, makes this spot easily the most popular break on the island. All tides are surfable with low tide providing the fastest and hollowest waves which are best with an easterly wind. Watch out for rocks at low tide and beware of rips when it's big.

6. Secrets

Not secret any more, this break can have some near perfect waves when there's a clean swell with an easterly wind blowing. The main wave is a righthander which gives long tubey rides which remain surfable up to a good 10ft. There's also a left which starts to work when the swell reaches 4ft. The waves here have the quality of a reef break even though they break over sand.

7. Stinky Bay

Located at the very northern end of St Ouen's Bay is a break that will work only on a very low tide. A left breaks over rocks and works like a point giving excellent rides when conditions are favourable. South winds are best and when working it will always be crowded. The name Stinky Bay comes from the smell produced by rotting seaweed in the gulley where you paddle out to the waves.

8. Plemont Beach (Creve au Lancon)

Only on big swells with a south wind and at low tide will one find worthwhile waves here. When these conditions are present it can be rewarding with good waves in beautiful surroundings.

9. Gréve de Lacq

A few times a year, normally in winter when the swells are huge, a visit to this little north facing beach can be a good move. Under such conditions one will find some good quality righthand barrels.

FRANCE

Capital:	Paris
Population:	56,160,000
Area:	543,965km²
Time:	GMT+1 (summer time GMT+2)
Religion:	Roman Catholic, Protestant & Muslim minorities
Languages :	French (Breton & Basque also spoken)
Currency:	French Franc (FF)

THE PEOPLE

As with all of Europe, the human history of France is an immense topic. The first people were believed to have been part of the 'Mousterian' civilisation. They were hunters, cave dwellers and painters whose archeological remains have been found around the Dordogne. As the northern ice cap receded after the ice age, an agricultural and pastoral society developed (c 1500 BC).

The Gauls were their Iron age descendants and there were around 15 million of them when the Romans invaded in 52BC. The social and cultural contortions since then have been many and varied and a succession of outrageous characters have asserted their place in the history. Charles Martel (The Hammer) won the mantel of defender of Western Christianity with a victory against the Muslim tide sweeping through Spain in 732. His successors included Pepin the Short, Charlemange, William the Conqueror, and many other luminaries including Joan of Arc and Louis XIV, both of whom influenced French civilisation greatly.

The region of France has been invaded by a long succession of expansionist societies (starting with the Francs themselves), yet it has maintained one of Europe' s strongest individual cultures, placed centrally between some tough neighbours. French cultural influence extends through The Mediterranean, Africa, Indo-China and The Pacific. The language is sheer music, and remains the centrepiece of French culture. The Gallic style of communication is unique and thoroughly physical. The French capacity for arts and cuisine needs no explanation and the general feeling in France is one of cultural vibrancy in all areas.

THE LAND

Western Europe's largest state contains within its boarders an incredible diversity. The North Coast faces La Manche (The English channel), The West, the Atlantic. The South is separated from Spain and Africa by the Pyrenees and the Med, and the eastern boarders are Italy, Switzerland, Germany, Luxemourg and Belgium. A high inland plateau, the Massif Central, steps up to the Alps.

The climate is quite different in the various regions. Whilst The North experiences similar rainfall and temperatures to southern England, as one heads south to the Med, temperatures rise and rainfall drops. The West Coast is strongly influenced by the Atlantic and the Pyrynees. During summer the North Atlantic feeds remarkably warm water along the coast and regular dawn winds tend to blow offshore, the result of consistent high pressure over the South West. In winter, the east wind is freezing, coming from snow covered Central Europe. Snow falls on the beaches on rare occasions, but summers are long and mellow. To balance the intensity of winter, a sympathetic blend of physical conditions for all water sports can be found, from April to October, on all Atlantic coasts.

THE SURF

In 1956, Hollywood scriptwriter Peter Viertel was in to Biarritz to shoot a film adaptation of the Hemingway novel *The Sun also Rises*. He was amazed by the waves on la Côte Basque and arranged for a friend to send a surfboard from California. But he was a strict beginner and shared his apprenticeship on the board with a couple of Biarritz locals, Georges Henebutte and Joel de Rosnay. His wife, the actress Deborah Kerr, became the patroness of France's first surf club, The Waikiki.

The following year, Viertel came back to Biarritz with more boards and the sport's numbers had grown. In his absence Hennebutte, Philippe Barland and Jaques Rott had begun to make longboards which today one can find housed in the museum. So began the history of surfing in France.

A lot of waves were surfed between Guéthary and Hossegor in that era by Billy Hamilton, Keith Paull and Mark Markinson, on location to shoot *A Wave Of Change*, a film by Greg MacGillivary and Jim Freeman. In the summer of '68, Paul Witzig was on the Côte Basque with his camera; the cast of his film included Nat Young and Wayne. The seting for the principal scenes of *Evolution* was La Barre, which that year became the site of France's first international competition, when a young Wayne Lynch battled it out with the legendary Nat in big, hollow waves.

Until the early 80's, surfing in France remained a marginal sport. The Lacanau Pro, was created in 1979, and the World Amateur Championships happened in 1980. From that moment surfing gained considerable recognition and a generation of French surfers was born who were. More interested in the radicality of manoeuvres and competition results than going on surf 'holidays.' The surfers of the 60's, who never went anywhere without five or

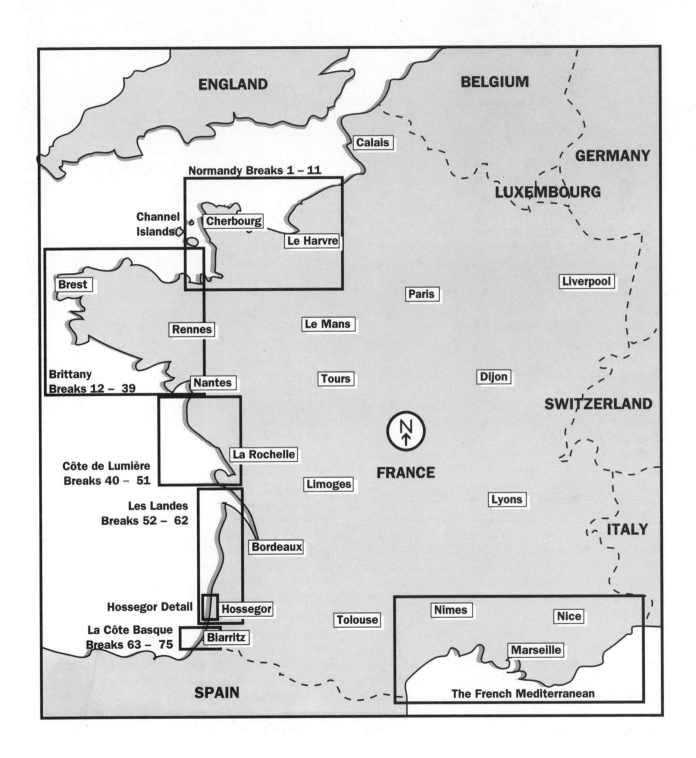

ENGLAND

BELGIUM

GERMANY

Calais

LUXEMBOURG

Normandy Breaks 1 – 11

Channel
Islands

Cherbourg

Le Harvre

Liverpool

Brest

Paris

Le Mans

Rennes

Tours

Dijon

SWITZERLAND

Brittany
Breaks 12 – 39

Nantes

La Rochelle

N

Côte de Lumière
Breaks 40 – 51

Limoges

FRANCE

Les Landes
Breaks 52 – 62

Lyons

ITALY

Bordeaux

Hossegor Detail

Hossegor

Tolouse

Nimes

Nice

La Côte Basque
Breaks 63 – 75

Biarritz

Marseille

SPAIN

The French Mediterranean

six in a car, were surpassed by a generation of individualists. At the same time France experienced a boom in all the glisse (sliding) sports like skateboarding, surfing, snowboarding, windsurfing etc. This created the basis for a strong market. The competitions became more important and *Surf Session* was born as a monthly magazine. Hossegor and Biarritz became new competition venues, surf started to be shown more and more on TV and in the press. And, of course, the best surfers found sponsors to keep them surfing, whilst remaining amateurs.

Today with the competitions at Lacanau, Hossegor and Biarritz, France is one of the most important stops on the new A.S.P World Tour. Each year during August, all the pro's are there and it is both a wonderful festival and a superb lesson for young French surfers to see their home breaks become the scene of controlled, radical surfing.

Two camps have emerged amongst the fans – pro-Curren and pro-Elkerton. Comparisons are useless but since they are both married to French girls, heavy betting went down over who would win the 1990 world championships.

Sadly, the question we still ask is when will we find a Frenchman in the top 30. Vetea David, although Tahitian, is an adopted Frenchman by the locals of the Côte Basque. But you can't really compare him with, say Jean-Loup Poupinel, the Hossegor surfer and champion of Europe in 1989. Tahiti is not France and surfing conditions there are totally different from France, where cold winter conditions make it difficult to be as relaxed as in summer.

Certainly the cold was not a problem for Welshman Carwynn Williams when he beat Damien Hardman at the Rip Curl Pro Hossegor, in 1988, in powerful surf. But Carwynn is not French. Like many British, he's not afraid of travelling. He rose to international level after trips to Hawaii and Australia and there's no doubt about what is missing from French surfing – having the courage to try to be the best somewhere else other than at home. One of those who has taken the risk of travelling each winter to Hawaii is Thierry Domenech. He's been doing it for years and now has a certain knowledge of the North Shore and a good technique in big waves.

France really has very few surfers. Today they number between 15,000 and 20,000, and France has only one pro surfer – Sebastian St Jean, who will be competing on the A.S.P. Tour for the first time this year ('92). At the André Malraux college in Biarritz, surfing has been introduced as a sporting option. The French Surf Federation now has a national technical director and French surfers are accepted as high level athletes at home.

The inauguration of a European Pro-Am circuit modelled on the lines of the A.S.P. can only encourage the growth of future champions.

Whilst many aspects of French surfing today may lag behind Australia or America, French board design is at a high standard. Local shapers like J.P. Stark and Barland continue to produce quality sticks and with the permanent local influence of figures like Maurice Cole and Tom Curren, the quality is rising all the time. The South West is the centre of the European surfing industry and the Quiksilver and Rip Curl factories are the largest single European surf organisations.

The surf breaks in France fall into five main regions. In the **Normandy** region between Calais and St Malo, surf happens in the winter months, believe it or not!

Once in **Brittany**, west of St Malo, swell starts to become consistent. A wide variety of breaks collect surf from the north and west and the heavily indented coastline offers multiple choices. Brittany is an extremely popular windsurf location, due to frequent summer wind and warm water conditions. Infinite inlets provide good surf conditions even in strong west winds and several breaks have gained notoriety as spectacular spots, including Quiberon, La Torche and La Palue.

From St Nazaire south, the coast offers excellent surf potential on the islands, beaches and points.

The River **Gironde** marks a psychological and physical line dividing North France from 'The South'. From Pointe de Grave the coast stretches in an almost uninterrupted line to Boucau. **Acquitaine,** as the region is known, shares with the **La Côte Basque** the honour of being France's best and most popular surf locations. Lacanau and Hossegor are both extremely popular contest and recreational spots offering reef-like power on a sand bottom. The sheer immensity of the beach and huge number of peaks spread the surf population around and it's safe to say that except for a few weeks per year, crowds are not a problem.

South of the River L'Adour and you're in the French Basque country, the birthplace of French and European surf sports. A handful of world class reefs, jetties and beaches surround Biarritz, providing superb waves all year round.

The Mediterranean gets surf in winter and is gaining popularity as an unlikely surf spot. Conditions are not as consistent as the Atlantic but if you strike it right, you could be pleasantly surprised. Corsica also falls under French juristiction and like Sardinia, gets good surf in the right conditions during winter.

The French have accepted the old spirit of surfing and more than the excitement of competitions, surfing appeals as a sport which brings people close to nature.

Today, the spots are more crowded in the summer than they've ever been but one still wouldn't compare it to California. You can still find yourself in the water with good waves, offshore winds and only a couple of friends around. France's surfers are rapidly becoming aware of that privilege.

Gibus de Soultrait/Surf Session

TRAVELLING AROUND

VISAS

Holders of EC passports DO NOT need a visa for a stay of up to 90 days. All other passport holders should check what is required with your nearest French Embassy or Consulate. All Embassies are listed in the Paris section.

French visas from London:
French Consulate
29/31 Wright's Lane
London W8
Tel: 071 937 1202

TELEPHONING

Dialling out code   : 19
              (then wait for a tone)
Country code   : 33
Operator   : 10
International Operator : 19 33 11
Directory information   : 12
Emergency   : 17 Police
                   : 18 Ambulance

FERRIES

By far the most popular method of travelling to France from the UK is by car passenger ferry. Brittany Ferries offers the best routes. The overnight crossings (which are usually cheaper) from Plymouth – Roscoff, and Portsmouth – St Malo can leave you rested and ready to hit the water in Brittany within a few hours. Prices vary throughout the year with the peak season running from mid July to the beginning of September. Off peak prices can be very reasonable if you're a group travelling in a campervan. For information contact Brittany Ferries in Plymouth Tel: 0752 221321, or Portsmouth Tel: 0705 827701.

Another option worth investigating if finances are low is the Dover - Calais route. Several companies ply the route with ferries leaving regularly throughout the day and night. It's the shortest and therefore the cheapest (especially from midnight to dawn) way of getting across the Channel, although it does add quite a few hours to your driving time.

DRIVING

French roads are some of the best in the world. For long distances you will nearly always have the choice between the high speed Péage (which can work out quite expensive) or some very good A roads. The route south from the ferry terminals in Roscoff and St Malo to Hossegor is pretty direct and takes about 10 hours if you drive without stopping.

Two main rules of the road are to drive on the right hand side of the road and always give way to traffic coming from the right (unless there're are signs to the contrary). Petrol prices are on par with the UK and one must carry your vehicles registration and insurance documents with you.

TRAINS

Like French roads, the French national train network (SNCF) has a reputation for efficiency and speed.

Naturally they're not cheap but student discounts and other deals can make it an attractive option. The T.G.V (France's new hi-speed train) now runs from Paris to Bayonne and can be an excellent way to get to the coast from the north.

HEALTH & INSURANCE

EC citizens can receive medical treatment if they possess an E111 form. These are obtainable from DHSS offices but they will only cover part of your bill so therefore regular travel insurance is a good idea. Non EC members should definitely take out comprehensive travel insurance.

PUBLIC HOLIDAYS

1, January
Easter Sunday
Easter Monday
Ascension day
              (40 days after Easter)
Pentecost   (7th Sunday
     after Easter, Plus the Monday)
1, May   (Labour Day)
8, May   (VE day)
14, July   (Bastille day)
15, August   (Assumption of the
                             Virgin Mary)
1, November   (all Saints day)
25, December

WATER QUALITY

The French Atlantic is a vast and relatively lightly-populated coast, therefore problems of water quality present themselves at specific spots near major river mouths, ports and towns. The English Channel is obviously not the cleanest sea in the world but some spots are OK.

Normandy and Brittany have a similar aquatic environment to Cornwall. Clean water exists away from the main population centres. Les Landes and La Côte Basque reflect the same situation.The French have on average a higher standard of sewage disposal then many other European states. Problems still exist as evidenced by the CWI chart in the Water Quality Appendices, but like in Portugal, beaches are well maintained in summer time. Flotsam on the beaches in winter grows to astounding proportions, with plastic bottles the biggest nuisance. Locals report huge swirling offshore islands of bottles and much waving of hands towards Spain goes on, but the truth is that these are international issues which won't be solved simply by pointing fingers.

The Surfrider Foundation has founded its European Headquarters in Biarritz, presided over by Tom Curren and Maurice Cole.

Already they have highlighted problems associated with the River Adour and other information is coming to light all the time. The Clean Water Initiative results from last summer's water tests suggest that the future may see some intense debate in coastal towns about the issue of sewage disposal priorities. The news is not all bad, but truthfully, it's not that good either. Any information regarding water quality at any breaks would be gratefully received by Surfrider or the CWI.

Some FRENCH language

Surf Speak

Bad waves...........mauvais vagues
bay...............................La baia
beach ....La plage
Big...........................gros/grand
bottom ....le fond
coast ....côte
deep ....profond
drop ....la chute
East.................................l'este
fibreglass.................fibre/résine
fins...............................l'aileron
flat......................entendu/plat
good waves...........bonnes vagues
good wind ....bon vent
high tide ....marée haut
high pressure ....haut pression
hollow..............................creux
in front..........................devant
late ....tard
left ....gauche
lip ....levre
low pressure ....basse pression
low tide ....marée basse
map ....carte géographique
near.................................prés
north................................nord
outside........................en dehors
peak.................................cime
point ....pointe
reef ....r´cif
resign..............................résine
right.................................droit
rip ....courant
rivermouth..............emboucheure
rocks.................................rocher
sand ....sable
sandbank ....banc de sable
set ....set
shallow......................peu profond
slow...................................lent
small ....petit
south ....sud
surfboard ....planche
swell ....thoule
the weather ....le temps
thick lipped........................lippu
prediction ....prevision
wall ....mur
water ....eau
waves...................vagues/onde
wax...................................cire
weather report ....bulletin
.......................météorologique
west.................................ouest
wetsuit.....................combination
wind ....vent

Useful words

all...................................tout
after.................................après
before ....avant
because ....parce que
behind ....derrière
boat ....bateau
cheap ....bon marché
cold ....froid
condoms ....preservatifs
dangerous ....dangereux
everybody ....tout le monde
fast ....vite
fire ....le feu
God ....Dieu
good ....bon
here ici
high ....haute
hot ....chaud
like ....comme
little ....petit
lost ....perdu
many ....beacoup de
near ....prés
no ....non
old ....vieux
please ....s'il vous plait
rain ....pluie
slow...................................lent
snow ....neige
soon ....bientot
thank you ....merci
thunder ....tonnerre
under ....sous
very ....trés
well...........................bien/bon
when ....quand
why?..........................pourquoi?
with ....avec
without ....sans
yes ....oui

Useful phrases

good morning...................bonjour
Good afternoon.................bonjour
Good evening..................bonsoir
Good night......................bon nuit
I'm sorry/pardon ....
.................Pardon/excusez-moi
I don't speak.....Je ne parle pas...
Do you speak?.......Parlez-vous...?
My name is..........Je m'appelle...
I come from... ....Je viens de...
Where is/are...? ....Oú est?/
..................................oú sont...?
Can I have...? ..puis-je avoir de...?

I would like ....je voudrais
How do you say...? ....comment
....on dit...?
What time is it?.........quelle heure
....est il?
How much? ....combien de?
How many? ....combien?
Could you tell me...?..pouvez-vous
.................................me dire...?

Public signs & notices

Open ....ouvert
closed...............................fermé
entrance ....entrée
exit ....sortie
free...............................gratuit
occupied ....occupé
ladies ....medames
gentlemen ....messieurs
lavatory..................toilettes/WC
forbidden..........................interdit
no parking ....stationement interdit
no smoking ....defence de fumer
out of order ....cassé/
...........Ne marche pas/en panne
I understand ....Je comprends
I want ....Je veux
I don't understand.....................
..................Je ne comprends pas
I don't know ....Je ne sais pas
I don't want ....Je ne veux pas
Let's go ....Allons-y
See you soon ....A bientôt

Shops and places

bank...............................banque
bakery.....................boulangerie
chemist ....pharmacie
fish shop...................poissonerie
library.....................bibliothèque
market ....marché
newsagent ......papeterie/buraliste
travel agent.......agence de voyage

Restaurant

bill..................................addition
boiled ....bouilli
bottle...............................bouteille
breakfast ....petit déjeuner
cup ....tasse
dinner ....diner
drink.................................boisson
fork ....fourchette
fried ....frit
glass.................................verre
knife.................................couteau
lunch ....déjeuner

plate ....assiette
roasted...........................roti
sandwich ....sandwich
spoon ....cuillèr(e)
table ....table
tip ....pourboire
waiter ....serveur

Drink

beer ....biére/pression
coffee - black.......................café
　　　-white..............café au lait
ice...............................glace
juice.............................jus
tea ....thé
water ....eau
wine -red ....vin rouge
　　- white ....vin blanc

Food

apple ....pomme
avocado.........................avocat
banana.........................banane
beans ....haricots
beef ....boeuf
biscuit ....biscuit
bread ....pain
butter..........................beurre
cabbage.........................choux
carrot ....carotte
cauliflower ....choux-fleur
cheese ....fromage
chicken ....poulet
cream ....crème
cucumber.....................concombre
egg ....oeuf
fish............................poisson
garlic..........................ail
grapes..........................raisin
ham ....jambon
ice cream.......................glace
lamb...........................agneau
lemon ....citron
lentils ....lentille(s)
margarine ....margarine
marmalade/jam ....confiture
milk ....lait
mushrooms ....champignon(s)
mussels ....moules
mustard ....moutarde
oil ....huile
olives ....olives
onion...........................oignon
orange..........................orange
peach ....pêche
pear...........................poire
pepper(veg) ......poivron vert/rouge

pepper(table) ....poivre
pork ....porc
potato ....pomme de terre
rice ....riz
salad ....salade
salt ....sel
sauce ....sauce
sausage ....saucisses
shrimps ....crevette
soup ....soupe/potage
spinich ....epinards
strawberries ....fraises
sugar ....sucre
toast ....toast/tartine
vegetables ....légumes
vinegar ....vinaigre
yoghurt ....yahourt

Numbers

one...............................un
two.............................deux
three............................trois
four............................quatre
five.............................cinq
six..............................six
seven...........................sept
eight ....huit
nine ....neuf
ten ....dix
eleven ....onze
twelve..........................douze
thirteen ....treize
fourteen.......................quatorze
fifteen ....quinze
sixteen ....seize
seventeen ....dix-sept
eighteen........................dix-huit
twenty ....vingt
thirty...........................trente
fourty ....quarante
fifty ....cinquante
sixty............................soisante
seventy....................soisante-dix
eighty ....quatre-vingt
ninety ....quatre-vingt-dix
one hundred......................cent
one thousand ....mille

Days of the week

Monday ....lundi
Tuesday ....mardi
Wednesday....................mercredi
Thursday ....jeudi
Friday...........................vendredi
Saturday..........................samedi
Sunday ....dimanche

Mechanic words &

phrases

oil ....huile
petrol..........................essence
puncture........................crevaison
Something is wrong with.............
.........Quelque chose ne va pas...
the engine............dans le moteur
the clutch.........dans l'embrayage
the gearbox ....
............dans la boîte de vitesses
the breaks ....aux freins
the steering.............à la direction
the suspension ....à la suspension
My car...has broken down............
............Ma voiture...est en panne
...has run out of gas.........n'a plus
.... d'essence
...is...kms from here....................
....se trouve à...km d'ici
Can you...? ....Pouvez-vous...?
...tow the car to a garage.............
...remorquer la voiture à un garage
...repair the car...réparer la voiture
When will it be ready? ....
.......Pour quand sera-t-elle prête?
How much will it cost?................
.........................Quel sera le coût
.........................del la réparation?
I don't have sufficient cash..........
.........Je n'ai pas assez de liquide
Will you accept a credit card? ....
......Acceptez-vous carte de credit?

Other phrases

Give me a kiss........Embasse-moi
Would you like a drink?...............
....Veux tu quelque chose à boire?
Do you want to go for dinner? ......
Est-ce que tu veux diner avec moi?
You have beautiful eyes ....
...........Tu as de très beaux yeux .
Your eyes are like the moon ....
......Tes yeux ressemble à la lune
I love you ....Je t'aime
Do you love me? ....Tu m'aime?
Do you like my "stick"?...............
.....Est-ce que t'aims mon "stick"?
I'm trying to chat you up ....
..........J'essaies de to faire la cour
What are you doing after dinner?
Qu'est ce que tu fais ce soir après
　　　　　　　　　　　　diner?
What's your telephone no? ....
.....T'as un numéro de telephone?
Are you going out tonight? ....
........................Tu sors ce soir?
Where?................................Ou?

PARIS

Paris is the capital of France and one of Europe's most enchanting cities, unfortunately though, like London it's landlocked. You could end up there for a vast number of reasons, and it's always fun travelling through. Unfortunately, Paris is one of the costliest areas in the world to live. The city is laid out in zones (known as arrondisments) which start with central Paris and spiral outwards, clockwise.

A ring road (la Périphérique) runs around the city proper and it most definitely pays to be on the case when turning off.

AIR TRAVEL
The main airports are; **Roissy –** **Charles de Gualle Tel: 48 62 22 80** which is 23km NE of Paris, and; **Orly Sud Tel: 48 84 32 10** located 12km south. These airports service all main international air routes.

TRAIN TRAVEL
S.N.C.F
There are several major national and international train stations. Gare De l'est, Gare Austerlitz.
Metro The paris metro is excellent and also cheap.
T.G.V Leaves Paris for the south and takes four hours to arrive in Bayonne.

DRIVING
Parisians drive on the right hand side of the road very fast! The best way to handle it is to go with it. The main road south is the N.10 via Tours, Poitier and Bordeaux. The A.10 is the Péage or toll road, which makes for a very fast trip but also greater cost and a deprived view of the country.

Telephone: Paris area code: 1
EMBASSIES/CONSULATES
UK
16 Rue d'Anjou, 8e
Tel: 42 96 87 19
US
2 Av Gabriel, 8e Tel: 42 96 12 02
AUS
4 Rue Jean-Ray, 15e
Tel: 45 75 62 00
NZ
7 Rue Léonard-de-Vinci, 16e
Tel: 45 00 24 11
ACCOMMODATION: See the *Rough Guide to France*

Normandy

Normandy shares the English Channel (La Manche) and receives direct W or SW swells which occur most frequently in the winter months. The Cherbourg peninsula is the most popular area in the region with at least 200-300 locals. The most exposed breaks pick up quite regular swells and could surprise with their quality.

Tides and currents are exceptionally strong here and waves are usually bigger on higher tides when currents are strongest.

Cherbourg itself is not the most exciting town in France but you get off the ferries from Southampton, Portsmouth, Poole and Rosslare here, and if the crossing is rough you could be in head-high waves within half an hour. Alternatively the Cherbourg peninsula is approximately 350km from Paris, and if you're stuck there and want a surf it could be a good place to head for.

Normandy is more renowned as a sailing site but surfing is currently gaining a strong following. The growth of local clubs and other organisations reflects this.

Surf Breaks 1 – 10

1. Cap Gris Nez

Not strictly in Normandy but one of the best spots in the north. Works in a straight W swell with S to E winds. Avoid low tide. Other known spots are **Wimeraux** and **Wissant**.

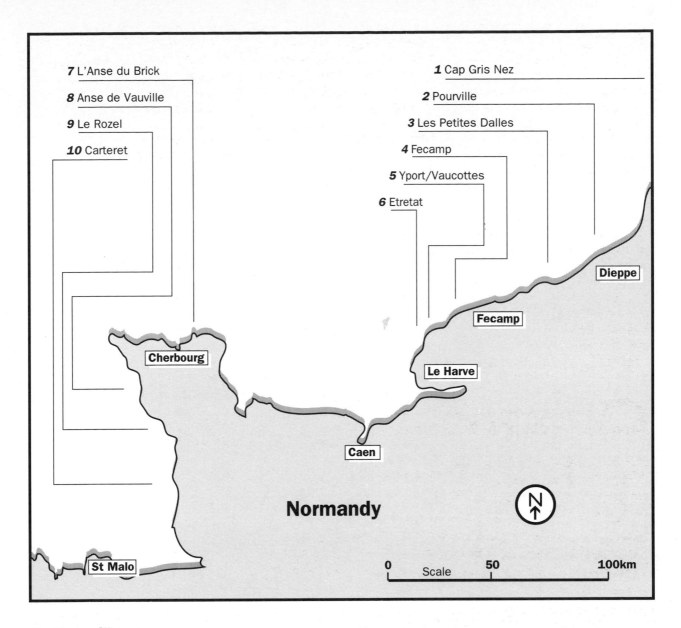

The map shows the Normandy coast with the following surf spots labelled:

7 L'Anse du Brick
8 Anse de Vauville
9 Le Rozel
10 Carteret

1 Cap Gris Nez
2 Pourville
3 Les Petites Dalles
4 Fecamp
5 Yport/Vaucottes
6 Etretat

Dieppe
Fecamp
Cherbourg
Le Harve
Caen
St Malo

Normandy

N

0   Scale   50   100km

2. Pourville

Just east of Dieppe, a beach break faces NNW and picks up waves in a strong W swell.

3. Les Petites Dalles

Between Dieppe and Fecamp, a series of west facing waves work in NE winds at high tide.

4. Fecamp

A popular spot with wave-sailors which holds swell up to 6ft.

5. Yport/Vaucottes

Ten kms southwest of Fecamp you'll find more good lefts and rights. Currents are very strong here.

6. Etretat

Thirty kms from Le Harve, set amongst magnificent scenery, at the foot of 'L'Aiquille Creuse' (a series of beautiful cliff formations), you'll find the most publicised spot in Normandy.

Waves break left over a steep reef bottom and swells in winter can be consistent. On a rising tide the shore break can be particularly heavy. Off-

shores are from the E to NE.
Water Quality: Excellent.

7. L'Anse du Brick

Very good rights and lefts break on reefs 12km east of Cherbourg. A popular spot, especially in S winds or when W swell is closing out other more exposed breaks.

8. Anse de Vauville

Fifteen kms of beach face W into the Atlantic and pick up as much swell as many Cornish beaches. The most northerly spot is Vauville and from here south you'll find numerous peaks, best at **Siouville** and **Les Cous Cous.**

9. Le Rozel

Three peaks, the most powerful waves in the area work best in an E wind with W swell.

10. Carteret

A popular spot that's well signposted with good access. Another popular wave-sailing spot with rights and lefts over a sand bottom.

Brittany

Coastal Brittany is known as 'Amour,' or 'the country near the sea.' The coast is heavily indented by swell action and the most typical and energetic seascapes are found on the western tip. Rugged cliffs, islands, rocks and reefs give the surroundings a grim feel, reflected in many local names – The Channel of Great Fear (Fromveur), The Bay of the Dead (Baie des Trépassés), etc...

On the north coast tides of up to 40ft have been measured. Swell can also be savage and the huge number of inlets can allow surf in almost every wind. Brittany holds enormous unexplored potential which is only just beginning to be discovered.

Surf Breaks 11 – 39

11. Cap Frehel/Plevenon

Red, grey and black cliffs rise vertically to a height of 70mtrs, fringed with reefs which break some heavy swells. From the top of the lighthouse you can get a good swell check and on a clear day you can see the Channel Islands.

12. Les Sables d'Or

Beach breaks to the west of Cap Frehal work in huge conditions. It's a popular spot for bodyboarders and beginners, and is well protected from W winds.

13. Beg Légeur

At the mouth of the river of the same name you'll find some of the gnarliest waves in the region in an E wind. It's 10km west of Lannion.

14. Primel – Tregastel

In a NW swell and SE winds good waves break at high tide over a sand and rock bottom. At low tide check **St Jean de Doigt** to the east.

15. Dossen

If you land at Roscoff, less than 10km from the ferry terminal you'll find a beautiful beach town facing west that's one of the most consistent spots in Brittany. W to NW is the only really bad wind.

16. Lampaul Ploudalmezeau

One beach in a sea of rocks, popular with wave sailors, holds surf up to 6ft. You'll find other waves in the area if you look. Named spots have been omitted out of sensitivity to local feeling, but if you consider this coast receives as much NW swell as Cornish breaks, the possibility of numerous unsurfed waves lingers in the mind.

17. Anse des Blancs Sablons/ Le Conquet

Sand and rock bottom rights and lefts in a big swell and SE winds.

18. Trégana

Various spots near Brest break in S swells. A left breaks off rocks here onto sand, best on the incoming tide.

19. Talbosse

Remained for a long time a secret spot – just before Petit Minou. Waves break for 200mtrs over rocks and sand. At high tide a tubey right and left; at low tide the right becomes extremely hollow due to the strong current pushing out of the harbour from Brest. Water quality is variable.

20. Pointe du Petit Minou (Little Pussy Point)

A low to mid tide break in front of the lighthouse at Finistere.

21 – 24 Presqu'Ile de Crozon (The Crozon Peninsula)

21. Pointe du Toulinget

A beautiful southwest facing beach on the northwest tip of the peninsula. Can get big in winter with a savage shore break. Strong currents, better on the incoming tide.

22. Anse de Dinan

A beautifully protected bay faces WSW and is a great place to head in big swells. Located between Crozon and Camaret and works on all tides. A righthand point breaks west of Dinan with a savage reputation.

23. Pointe de 'Lost March'

One of several excellent righthand points breaks over a sand-fringed bottom at high tide.

24. La Palue

La Palue features strongly in the annals of Brittany surf. Holds big swells (3mtrs+) and generally gets plenty over the winter. Other protected beaches receive good swell when everywhere else is huge. They can be found on the south of the peninsula.

25. Baie de Dournenez

Three strips of beach and rocks which get straight W swell, south of the Crozon Peninsula. To the west of Dournenez a fickle right point called **Pointe de Leydé** works in big swells.

26. Baie des Trepassés/ Pointe du Raz

An extremely heavy setting for a surf – one little beach crowded by steep rocks, exposed to all W swell, providing excellent tubey surf in winds from NE to S.

Baie des Trepassés means 'Bay of the Dead,' a name given to mark the bodies of dead sailors wrecked on its reefs.

Low

pressure

means

THURSDAY 2200

HIGH

LOW

HIGH

High

surf....

Photo: Eric Chauché

. . .in

Europe

Photo: Tim Rainger

the Celts

Carwyn Williams, 5 times European champion

Photo: Phil Holden

Skirza,

North Sea,

Scotland

Photo: Alex Williams

Freshwater West, Dyfed, Wales

Photo: Phil Holden

Matt Stephens, South Gower Reef

Photo: Phil Holden

Thurso East, Scotland

Photo: Alex Williams

Durness, Scotland

Photo: Alex Williams

Freswick Bay,

North Sea,

Scotland

Photo: Alex Williams

Kilcummin, Ireland

Photo: Phil Holden

the Celts

2

Secret spot, Wales

Photo: Phil Holden

Freebooter's castle,
Caithness, Scotland

Photo: Tim Rainger/
Low Pressure

Easky Right, Co Sligo,
Ireland

Photo: Tim Rainger/
Low Pressure

Hunts Bay, Wales

Photo: Phil Holden

Neil Harris, Thurso East, Scotland

Photo: Alex Williams

Bantham, South Devon

Photo: Alex Williams

Porthleven, South West Cornwall

Photo: Simon McComb

Porthleven,

English surf

at it's best

Photo: Peter Cade

Downend Point, North Devon

Photo: Rick Abbott

Fistral, New

Photo: Phil H

Little Fistral, Newquay

Photo: Chris Power

Rudy,

Porthme

St Ives

Photo: Alex

Towan Beach,
Newquay

Photo: Peter Cade

Gwithian, Cornwall

Under threat

from sewage

Photo: Simon McComb

Kimmeridge Bay, Dorset

Photo: Phil Holden

Porthtowan,

Bad lands

Croyde Bay, North Devon

Photo: Phil Holden

Photo: Phil Holden

England

Avalanche

Photo: Eric Chauché

Tom Curren at home, Les Cavaliers

Photo: Tim McKenna

France

canau

oto: Tim McKenna

Boucau

Photo: Eric Chauché

Brittany

Photo: Alex Williams

Guethary

Photo: Eric Chauché

Hossegor

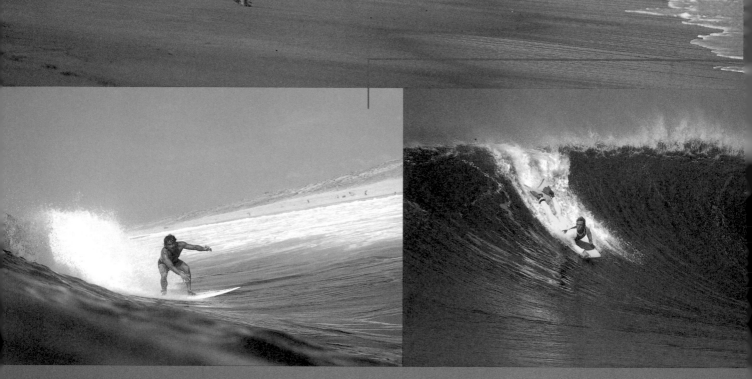

Mr X, Dawn Patrol

Photo: Simon McComb

La Graviére

Photo: Eric Chauché

Maurice, Mongrels

Photo: Eric Chauché

Sebastien St Jean, La Piste

Photo: Eric Chauché

Le Nord

Photo: Eric Chauché

Lucky traveller,
Les Estagnots

Photo: Simon McComb

Jean Poupinel, V.V.F.

Photo: Eric Chauché

Cou Nou

Photo: Eric Chauché

Hossegor

perfection

Photo: Eric Chauché

Capbreton

Photo: Eric Chauché

Ioseba Iriondo,

Playa de Gros

Photo: F Muñoz/Surfer Rule

Pantin, Galicia

Photo: F Muñoz/Surfer Rule

Eneko Acero,

Tapia de Casariego

Photo: F Muñoz/Surfer Rule

Spain

Bodyboarding has exploded in Spain during the last five years. The standard is becoming exceptional. Meñakoz

Photo: Jakue

Andikortxea/

Tres 60

Mundaka

Photo: F Muñoz/Surfer Rule

Polluted perfection, Punta Galea

Photo: Javier Amezaga/ Tres 60

Sunny Garcia, adopted

son, Seland Pro, 1990

Photo: F Muñoz/Surfer Rule

Salinas, Asturias

Photo: F Muñoz/Surfer Rule

Jorge Imbert, Sopelana

Photo: F Muñoz/Surfer Rule

It's the same
scene everywhere
in the world

Photo: F Muñoz/
Surfer Rule

Doniños , Galicia

Photo: Chris Power

Paddling out, Mundaka

Photo: F Muñoz/Surfer Rule

J Amatriain,

praying to Huey

Photo: F Muñoz/Surfer Rule

Meñakoz

Photo: Javier Amezaga/Tres 60

Portugal

1

Espinho, Jetty View

Photo: Joåo Valente/
Surf Portugal

Supertubos

Photo: Tim McKenna

Semente Factory,
Ribamar

Photo: Eric Chauché

Rodrigo Heredia

Pedra Branca

Photo: Joåo Valente/

Surf Portugal

The Big Wave crew

Photo: Joåo Valente/
Surf Portugal

Miguel Ruivo,

Coxos

Photo: Surf Portugal

Portugal

2

Parked boat, Cascais

Photo: João Valente/Surf Portugal

Secret spot

Photo: João Valente/Surf Portugal

Supertubos

Photo: Eric Charché

Alvaro Costa, Ferral

Photo: Tim Raniger/Low Pressure

Carcavelos

Photo: João Valente/Surf Portugal

Bento,

Costa Caparica

Photo: Luis Quinta/

Surf Portugal

São Pedro do Estoril

Photo: João Valente/Surf Portugal

the Canary

1

Las Palmas
de Gran Canaria

Photo: Tim Rainger/
Low Pressure

Spanish Left, one of
Europe's best waves,
threatened by tourist
development!

Photo: Peter Cade

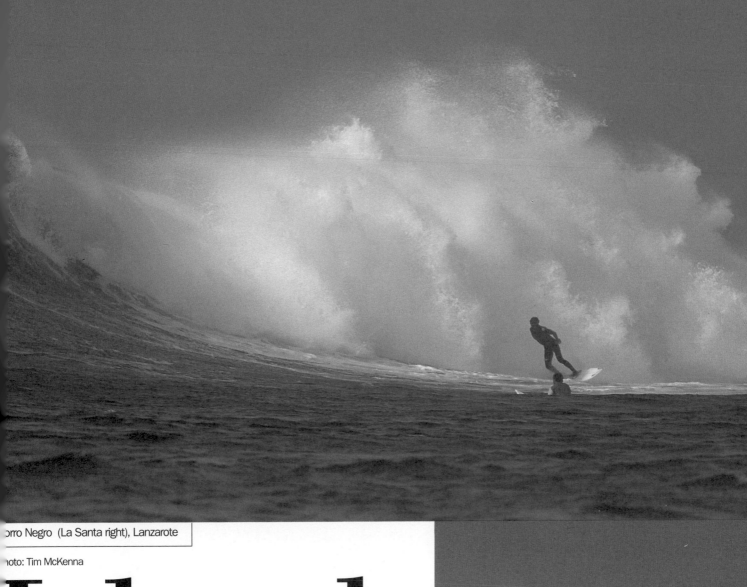

Porro Negro (La Santa right), Lanzarote

Photo: Tim McKenna

Islands

Mast high waves are a common occurence, North Shore, Fuerteventura

Photo: Phil Holden

Reefs equals cuts

Photo: Eric Chauché

Gabriel Davies,
Boca del Abajo, Lanzarote

Photo: Chris Power

Cotillo,

Fuerteventura

Photo: Alex Williams

La Santa Left, Lanzarote

Photo: Eric Chauché

Majanicho, Fuerteventura

Photo: Alex Williams

2 The

North Shore, Fuerteventura

Photo: Raider Waveski UK

The Canary Islands are

clean compared to the

rest of Europe

Secret spot, Lanzarote

Photo: Alex Williams

Photo: Tim Rainger/Low Pressure

Village left, La Santa, Lanzarote

Photo: Chris Power

Canary Islands

Cotillo, Fuerteventura Photo: Phil Holden

Italy

Varazze

Photos:

Luca Garibaldi

The Clean Water Initiative

"If I'm not part of the solution, I'm part of the problem"

Patagonia

Photos: Tim Rainger

A universal problem, Playa la Arena

Photo: Borja Peñeñori/ Tres 60

Beach rubbish, Seaton

Photo: Peter Cade

The Clean Water Initiative is a European water testing program with global interest

J L Poupinel, Lanzarote   Photo: Eric Charché

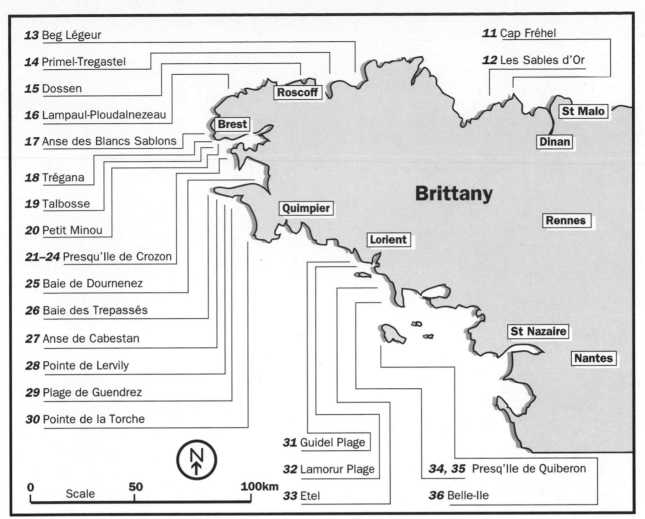

Map labels:

13 Beg Légeur
14 Primel-Tregastel
15 Dossen
16 Lampaul-Ploudalnezeau
17 Anse des Blancs Sablons
18 Trégana
19 Talbosse
20 Petit Minou
21–24 Presqu'Ile de Crozon
25 Baie de Dournenez
26 Baie des Trepassés
27 Anse de Cabestan
28 Pointe de Lervily
29 Plage de Guendrez
30 Pointe de la Torche

11 Cap Fréhel
12 Les Sables d'Or

Roscoff
Brest
Quimpier
Lorient
Brittany
Rennes
St Malo
Dinan
St Nazaire
Nantes

N

0   Scale   50   100km

31 Guidel Plage
32 Lamorur Plage
33 Etel
34, 35 Presq'Ile de Quiberon
36 Belle-Ile

27. Anse de Cabestan

SW and big W swell gets in here with rights and lefts and wicked tubes, best in winter. A heavily localised spot.

28. Pointe de Lervily

Long righthand point south of Audierne provides savage surf on all tides.

29. Plage de Guendrez

Faces south west. Beach waves work in similar swells with the best peaks generally at the northern and southern tips.

30. Pointe de la Torche

The most famous spot in Brittany, well known by surf enthusiasts of all persuasions.

The area is rich in wind and waves with a distinctly surfey vibe.

Several spots include;

PENHORS: The northern tip of the Baie d'Audierne usually has bigger swell than further south.

TRONOEN: A couple of hundred metres north of the rock waves break over sand with less crowding.

POINTE DE LA TORCHE: Various peaks break right and left near the rocks. Rideable in big surf.

PORZ CARN: Further south of La Torche – can get hollower and gnarlier.

ANSE DE LESCONIL; This beach gets good when La Torche gets too huge or in S swell.

31. Guidel Plage

Three breaks east of L'Orient: **Le Fort Bloque** has good lefts and rights to 6ft. **Le Loch** offers beach breaks and **Bas Pouldu** has more stable banks which form over sand in similar conditions. There are other breaks in the area that await the determined.

32. Larmor Plage

L'Orient town beach faces S and needs a decent swell to pump.

33. Etel

An infamous bar at the river was long considered unsurfable. Strong currents produce tubey surf. Dropping tide is notably heavy.

Presqu'Ile de Quiberon (The Quiberon Peninsula)

34. Penthievre

The road runs along this long west facing beach giving fine views of the surf. It receives untold swell but suffers from common onshore winds.

35. Port Blanc, Port Ru, Port Bara

Three spots below the cliffs set amongst some of the nicest scenery in France. These breaks could be the best spots in Brittany but become ridiculously crowded in summer.

PORT BLANC, is a heavy lefthander breaks right in front of a big rock and can tube for 50mtrs. If you can't surf, don't go out!

PORT RU is another heavy tube with a steep take-off.

PORT BARA is another lefthand wave which gets more crowded than its neighbours due to its more lenient disposition.

36. Belle-Ile

The largest of the Breton islands pumps! One spot at the river mouth at **Port de Donnant** has a good reputation for quality surf without the crowds. The rest of the island needs exploring.

37. Rade de Croisic

Another Côte Savage. Beach breaks favouring lefts.

38. La Govelle

Another underrated break can hold surf to well over head height. Check for rocks at low tide.

39. Sainte Marguerite

A long righthand point break that is a good spot to head for in big swells, best at high tide. Offshores are from the N to E.

Côte de Lumière

This region extends south of the Loire River at St Nazare to Royan at the mouth of the Gironde. Surfing is very popular here and like further south, many fine beach breaks can be surfed without crowds. The islands provide an interesting diversion though it is at places like Les Sables d'Olonne that competitive surfing has begun to flourish north of the Gironde.

Surf Breaks 40 – 51

40. Ile de Noirmoutier

Several stretches of west facing beach and some interesting reefs pick up good swell.

41. Le Club

Lefts and rights on the sands north of St Gilles Croix de Vie.

42. La Suzaie

Left and right reef with a strong reputation holds surf up to 10ft, and is considered one of the best breaks in the region. It's located north of Sauveterre.

43. Sauveterre

In the middle of the forest of d'Olonne, a road

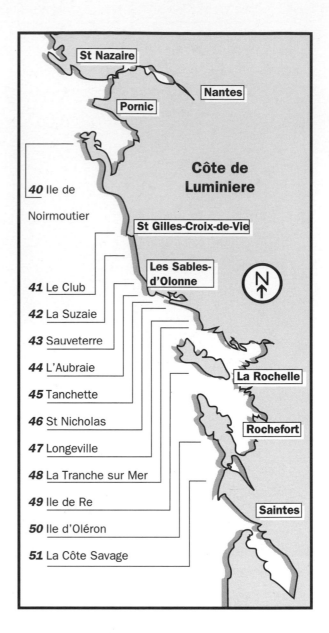

leads to an excellent uncrowded spot on the coast. At high tide a powerful sand bar does the business.

44. L'Aubraie

Just north of La Chaume, good right and lefts break over sand and rock. Different peaks work depending on tide and swell – all can be good with a powerful shorebreak to boot. Another break with a long history.

45. Tanchette

Not the most consistent beach, but it can get good and the Europeans were held here in 1987. Nice long lefts break fast and hollow at low tide. Popular with grommets from the local schools.

46. St Nicholas

Near Parcs de la Grange, long lefts often above head height.

47. Longeville

Various spots: **La Plage**, is unreliable but can get good, **Bud Bud**, the happening break at high tide. Thick peaks break both ways.

48. La Tranche Sur Mer

Various peaks that are good for beginners set in a relaxed atmosphere.

49. Ile de Re

A beach break at la Couvade has a consistent reputation. The potential on this little island is excellent. Follow the road to the north tip.

50. Ile d'Oléron

Access is over the toll road. Crowding on the island can be a nightmare in summer. There are various spots:

CHASSIRON; An exposed rocky lefthand point under the lighthouse is a consistent swell puller but maxes out easily. East-northeast is offshore. **St Denis** has long lefts working at high tide in big swells. **Los Trois Pierres** is a very popular beach break. Tubey rights and lefts break close to the shore up to 6 - 8ft. **La Cotinière** offers lefts and rights on rock reefs in front of the village. **Vert Bois/La Grand Plage** is one of the finest spots on the island. Vert Bois lies at the northern end of 10km of beach backed by pines. If you want to escape the crowds in summer, walk down it!

51. La Côte Savage

Fifteen kms of excellent beach breaks north of Royan suggest the beginning of the Landes Coast. Currents flowing out of the mouth of the Gironde are both strong and dirty.

Acquitaine

"Landes (Celt: Landa) Heath, moor, wasteland; (p1) dunes, barren tracts."

Acquitaine is the name loosely given to the coastal and forest areas stretching south from the mouth of the Gironde to the Adour river at Bayonne.

Before Napoleonic times this was a swampy place of little economic value. Napoleon set about draining the land and planting pines behind the sand dunes which extended for 200km in an almost unbroken line of west-facing Côte Savage.

Whilst no longer a moor, the region remains thinly populated; a flat expanse of forests, straight roads and small towns, fringed by the raging Atlantic.

Swell develops from lows forming almost anywhere in the North Atlantic or Bay of Biscay, and whilst Les Landes is really one huge beach with few major variations, the regularity of sand banks and consistent offshore conditions produce surf of extreme quality. Names like Lacanau and Hossegor are now well known world wide. The waves breaking in front of the podium for the Rip Curl Pro, Landes in 1991 looked more Hawaiian than European; Backdoor-like rights were consistently swallowing surfers and sometimes spitting them back out.

Between Point de Grave and Boucau some of the world's best beach surf, breaks in isolation for most of the year. Many foreigners have already made the pilgrimage and they regularly stay for longer than they planned. Two of the best known are Gary Elkerton and Maurice Cole, both surfers with a strong appetite for ferocious waves. That speaks volumes.

In summer time, the landscape transforms into a chaotic holiday resort exhibiting some of the best characteristics of French culture. Forget the myth that there's no surf in summer. It mightn't be as consistent as in winter but can be just as good! That there are two A.S.P. events on this one stretch of coast in August is proof of both energetic public participation and good waves. The ambience on the beaches exudes fun and freedom and even in winter, whilst cold, the quality and consistency of surf make it a quality destination.

WATER QUALITY

This is a sparsely populated region for 8 months of the year. During that period the water quality is pretty good. Summer time sees some disturbing evidence of faecal contamination but the currents are strong and well macerated sewage disperses quite rapidly. There are few bad spots.

Surf Breaks 52 – 62

52. – 55. La Gironde

The region loosely known as Acquitaine, can be divided into two regions, La Gironde and Les Landes.

Between Pointe de Grave and Cap Feret at the mouth of the Arachon Basin, the Côte Landes begins. Several breaks receive swell in similar conditions (W swell, E wind, changing banks etc) The most popular spots are **Soulac, Hourtin, Carcans, Lacanau and Grand Crohot**. Little distinguishes these from dozens of other unnamed spots. Buy a map and open your eyes to possibility. The coast is backed by Bordeaux and a rich wine producing region steeped in history. Unfortunately the water flowing from the Gironde is of suspicious quality.

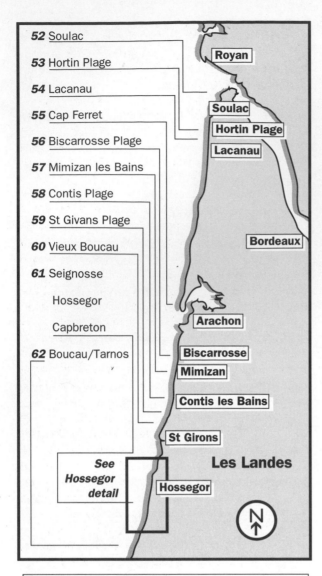

52 Soulac
53 Hortin Plage
54 Lacanau
55 Cap Ferret
56 Biscarrosse Plage
57 Mimizan les Bains
58 Contis Plage
59 St Givans Plage
60 Vieux Boucau
61 Seignosse
   Hossegor
   Capbreton
62 Boucau/Tarnos

Royan
Soulac
Hortin Plage
Lacanau
Bordeaux
Arachon
Biscarrosse
Mimizan
Contis les Bains
St Girons
See Hossegor detail
Hossegor
Les Landes
N

56. – 62. Les Landes

From Pointe d'Arachon south, most of the coast until Hossegor is almost identical. A few water flows interrupt the sand banks with interesting results but essentially one beach stretches for aproximately 250kms. Some bars are stable in position but don't always work. It needs constant reconnaisance. The main spots are **La Salie, Biscarrosse, Mimizan, Contis, St Girons, Vieux Boucau, Port D'Albret, Hossegor/Capbreton and Boucau.** Each of these towns are only random points along a largely empty coastline. A keen walker would find vast numbers of unsurfed peaks between these key destinations.

Hossegor is certainly the most renowned of them all and this is for a couple of particular reasons. A finger of extremely deep water points to Hossegor. The 'Fosse de Capbreton' is the signature of the River Ardour on the ocean bottom, a deep scar formed over thousands of years of powerful water flow. Napoleon diverted this major river, re-routing it to Bayonne in efforts to build a safer port away from the violent waves on this tempestuous ten km stretch. An unusually grand vision has had spectacular results for the surfing community. The known spots start north of Le Penon and Les Bourdaines and reach south of the river at Capbreton.

All have individual characteristics which can change daily. the atmosphere at these towns is extremly relaxed. The night life is consistently good which matches the high standard of food and wine. Particularly in summer the coast becomes a writhing mass of young suntanned bodies playing in the surf. Go see for yourself.

TRAVELLING AROUND

Accommodation: Camping is a favoured and easy option in summer. Consistent fine weather and open space make even beach sleeping easy and accepted. Most rental accommodation has to be booked one year ahead for summer rentals. There are very few hotels and hostels at any time!

FOOD: As everywhere else in France, all the little towns have good restaurants and usually Hypermarchés.

DRIVING: The roads are generally excellent, much of them amongst pine trees. The roads around and through the beach towns operate on holiday logic and patience is urged.

La Côte Basque

This area stretching from Les Cavaliers at the mouth of L'Ardour to Hendaye on the Spanish border, can be considered the cradle of surfing on the European continent. It's a span of coast now rich in surf and surf culture and the sport is increasing in popularity yearly. Unlike the long beach farther north, the Basque coast is the home of some excellent reefs and one fabulous point. The Basque people are proud of their individuality like in the Spanish territory of the same name, and although many spots are close to some well populated towns, crowds for most of the year remain minimal. For many years the Basque coast, like Les Landes, has been a lure for travellers. The resident population includes some of the most experienced surfers, including the likes of Jeff Hackman and Tom Curren. Their influence is having a marked effect on the aspirations and standards of young locals.

Competitive surfing began here in 1968 and has continued to flourish. Biarritz is in effect the surf capital though better waves can be found at several other spots. 'Localism' can be potent, especially in the summer months as everywhere else – the French deserve respect. In the last few years some unnecessarily ugly incidents between travellers and locals are proof of increasing tensions. With so many breaks in the area, this seems unnecessary but there's always someone who thinks they're lord of everything they survey. Not true. Get it?

A good percentage of France's surfing industry is based here including the Quiksilver plant and the surf magazine *Surf Session*.

La Côte Basque is one of Europe's most enjoyable destinations for a combination of aquatic and social factors.

63. La Barre

At the river mouth there used to be a superb, much photographed wave known as La Barre. Unfortunately in 1973 the jetty was extended and the wave was no more.

64. – 66. Les Cavaliers

Cavaliers is a stretch of sands just south of the River L'Adour and is the place surfers chose to go, as the waves here can be excellent with tubey rights and lefts up to 10ft. The beach is very popular, with crowding a problem during the peak months from July to September. For the rest of the year it's less busy. The beach is signposted and there is a large area for parking in front of the waves. Between here and Anglet various peaks break in different conditions. Most popular are **Les Dunes, L'Ocean, La Madregue, Les Corsaires, Marinella, Les Sables d'Or,** and **La Piscine.**

62. Boucau Tarnos/Le Metro/ La Dique

The Berlin Wall of French surf divides the Côte Basque from Les Landes. Le Boucau was much better but the sands have moved and it is not as good. Surfers from the Biarritz area say that once past the river L'Adour you are already in the North. This however, has little effect on the good quality of the lefthander that breaks along the jetty wall next to the river. The wave breaks over a sand bottom so its characteristics and its quality do change throughout the seasons but it often works well giving a powerful fast tube when the swell is big enough. Best at low-mid tide up to 12ft. There is easy parking by the jetty.

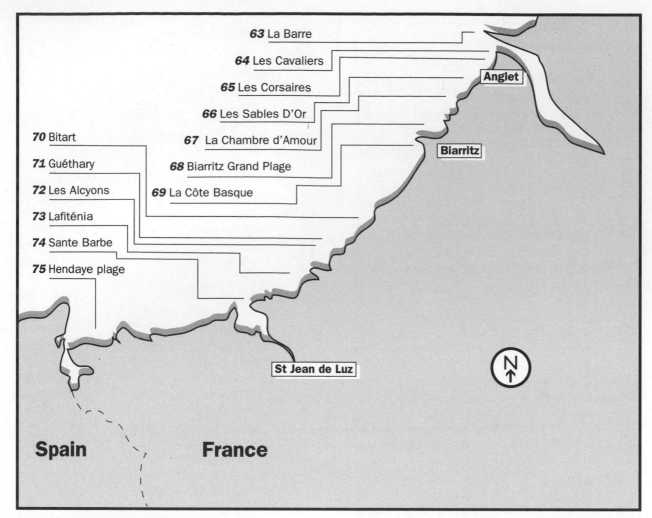

Map labels:
- 63 La Barre
- 64 Les Cavaliers
- 65 Les Corsaires
- 66 Les Sables D'Or
- 67 La Chambre d'Amour
- 68 Biarritz Grand Plage
- 69 La Côte Basque
- 70 Bitart
- 71 Guéthary
- 72 Les Alcyons
- 73 Lafiténia
- 74 Sante Barbe
- 75 Hendaye plage

Anglet

Biarritz

St Jean de Luz

N

Spain   France

67. Anglet/Chambre D'Amour

Two lovers drowned here and now its a spot popular with tourists. A legendary beach, hollow and tubey. There are some excellent quality beach break waves along this part of the coast. Several large rock jetties help to stabilise the sandbanks, ensuring consistent peaks with good tubes. It is along this stretch of coast that one may come across the large travelling entourage of foreign surfers and good times are had both in the water and in the bars. The waves are best at mid tide up to 10ft. Chambre d'Amour is located in the town of Anglet and there is a large area for parking in front of the waves.

68. – 69. Biarritz

The surf capital of Europe is home to various peaks which work at different tidal states, generally less powerful than Anglet or Guethary. **LA GRAND PLAGE, LA COTE BASQUE, LA MOUSSE, MARBELLA, MILADY BORA BORA, EDUOARD VII.**

Biarritz is an expensive town and perhaps not the best place to hang out for long periods. None of the main beaches of La Côte Basque are particularly clean in summer (see appendicies for CWI results), but Biarritz is unique and always a lively place to party.

TRAVELLING ARROUND

ACCOMMODATION: Auberge de la jeunesse, Route des Vignes, Anglet
Tel: 5963 8649

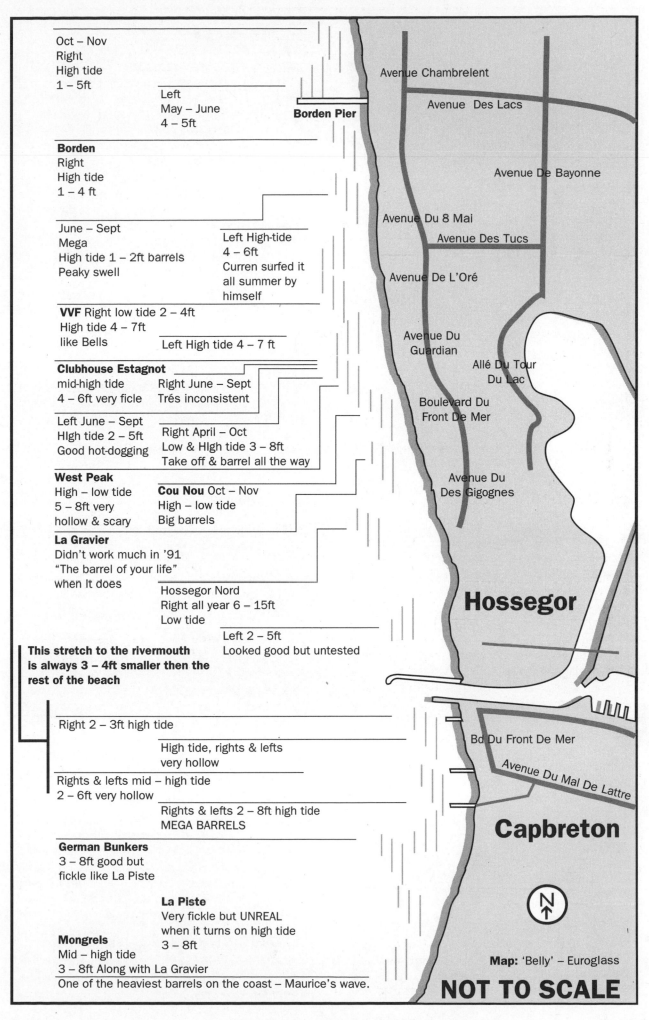

Oct – Nov
Right
High tide
1 – 5ft

Left
May – June
4 – 5ft

Borden Pier

Borden
Right
High tide
1 – 4 ft

June – Sept
Mega
High tide 1 – 2ft barrels
Peaky swell

Left High-tide
4 – 6ft
Curren surfed it
all summer by
himself

VVF Right low tide 2 – 4ft
High tide 4 – 7ft
like Bells

Left High tide 4 – 7 ft

Clubhouse Estagnot
mid-high tide   Right June – Sept
4 – 6ft very ficle   Trés inconsistent

Left June – Sept   Right April – Oct
HIgh tide 2 – 5ft   Low & HIgh tide 3 – 8ft
Good hot-dogging   Take off & barrel all the way

West Peak
High – low tide   **Cou Nou** Oct – Nov
5 – 8ft very   High – low tide
hollow & scary   Big barrels

La Gravier
Didn't work much in '91
"The barrel of your life"
when It does

Hossegor Nord
Right all year 6 – 15ft
Low tide

Left 2 – 5ft
Looked good but untested

**This stretch to the rivermouth
is always 3 – 4ft smaller then the
rest of the beach**

Right 2 – 3ft high tide

High tide, rights & lefts
very hollow

Rights & lefts mid – high tide
2 – 6ft very hollow

Rights & lefts 2 – 8ft high tide
MEGA BARRELS

German Bunkers
3 – 8ft good but
fickle like La Piste

La Piste
Very fickle but UNREAL
when it turns on high tide
3 – 8ft

Mongrels
Mid – high tide
3 – 8ft Along with La Gravier
One of the heaviest barrels on the coast – Maurice's wave.

Avenue Chambrelent

Avenue Des Lacs

Avenue De Bayonne

Avenue Du 8 Mai

Avenue Des Tucs

Avenue De L'Oré

Avenue Du
Guardian

Allé Du Tour
Du Lac

Boulevard Du
Front De Mer

Avenue Du
Des Gigognes

Hossegor

Bd Du Front De Mer

Avenue Du Mal De Lattre

Capbreton

Map: 'Belly' – Euroglass

NOT TO SCALE

70. Bidart

Bidart has some decent waves and when it's working well, can prove to be a good alternative to the over crowded beaches of Biarritz. It gets big in winter with a powerful shore break. Waves are good up to 6ft but be careful of scattered rocks in the water. There's easy parking by the beach.

71. Guéthary

Guéthary has been compared to Sunset with rideable waves from 3 – 10ft. It's here that surfing was first introduced to France and since then it has attracted surfers from all four corners of the world. It breaks both right and left over a rock bottom, with the righthander being the real quality side, giving rides up to 400mtrs when the outside and inside sections connect.

Tides are important here, with the outside best from mid to high tide and the inside being best from low – mid tide. The size of the waves is often deceiving when viewed from the land. Always add a couple of feet to your estimations. Beware of sea urchins and crowds. Park where possible in Guéthary.

Water Quality: Avoid the sewer pipe just south of the harbour.

72. Les Alcyons

This excellent lefthander breaks over a shallow rock bottom, throwing out mean lips with steep take-offs. It's definitely not a beginners wave. The break faces west-northwest and is located just a few hundred metres south of Guéthary, with the best time to surf being around mid-tide.

Like Guéthary, Alcyons can hold some of the Atlantic's biggest swells with makeable waves up to 12 - 15ft. At this point, the normal crowds one finds here thin out considerably, with only a few of the hardcore locals still out. Booties are a must and it's a popular spot for wave-riding windsurfers. Follow the sign in Guéthary that says "Plage et Port." It leads down a very short but steep hill to an area for parking. The wave is at the end of the road. A mega left called **Avalanche** works up to 7 mtrs. It's rarely surfed, being a long way out to sea – reserved for an insane few.

73. Lafitenia

A superb righthander that breaks as a point, giving perfect long walls as it wraps around the headland. Beneath the sea is a rocky plateau, guaranteeing the take off zone up to 12ft, and in rare conditions up to 15ft. It breaks on all tides, with low tide giving a more tubey ride, especially on the inside.

Like all world class waves, crowds are a sure thing. Lafitenia is no exception. Non locals, especially foreigners are not welcomed. Take the road heading south out of Guéthary for about 1km. Take a right turn by a blue sign that says "Acotz & St Jean-de-Luz." You will come to a signpost with many beaches listed. Head towards Inter Plage. It is right there. There's a large area for parking above the break and a small sign saying "Lafitenia."

74. St Jean de Luz /St. Barbe

The large bay of St Jean-de-Luz shelters two excellent breaks. Both need a big swell and only work at low tide. The first breaks in the entrance on the north side of the port giving rights and lefts with preference to the right. The other, known as St.-Barbe is a right breaking over a slab of rock inside the N entrance of the bay. This wave, can give some great tubes and is surfable up to 8ft. When they work, both spots get crowded. Park where possible in St. Jean-de-Luz. There are other reefs between here and Hendaye.

75. Hendaye Plage

Hendaye, the last beach before Spain, faces north and stretches for 3kms. The western end, just near the Bidassoa River often has the best sandbanks and, although it's usually smaller than the rest of the beach, the protection it receives against W and NW winds makes it well worth a look. The beach is good on all tides up to 8ft with regular crowds and lots of Spanish surfers. There's easy parking by the beach.

The French Mediterranean

The French Mediterranean coast must rate as the most hyped-up stretch of coast anywhere on the planet. From the docks of Marseille to the glitz in Cannes, most of the coastline is ludicrously crowded and the ocean feels the pain – the water is often opaque by the more crowded resorts.

Contrary to much popular belief, Coastal Provence and the Côte d'Azur do receive surf, most often in a Mistral (SE wind). The coastline is irregular offering the choice of optimum wind and swell conditions. Whilst windsurfing has long been popular in the area, surfing has only had a following for four or five years. Consequently the coast is still being discovered.

The popular spots start in **The Camarg**e at **Saintes-Maries-de-la-Mer** and include **Sausset-les-Pins, Marseille (Plage du Prado), Baie de Cassis, St Cur/Les Lecques, Cap Saint Louis, Ile de Bendor, Bandol, Sanary Sur Mer, Brutal Beach, La Seyne (Les Sablettes), Cannes, Isle de Sainte, Marquerite, Antibes and Nice**.

Corsica, like Sardinia would surprise many with its versitality and consistency. The problems of water pollution, which are pressing on the mainland diminish on the Islands and the pace mellows somewhat.

TRAVELLING AROUND

Trains: The Ventimiglia line folows the coast from Marseille to Menton.
Buses: On this stretch are a nightmare.
Boats: Marseille (Bassin de la Joliette) to Corsica, Sardinia and Algiers.
Planes: Airport de Mariqnane (Marseille)
　　　　　　　　　　　　　Tel: 42 78 2100
British Airways　　　　　Tel: 91 54 9292
Hospital:　　　　　　　Tel: 91 90 6114

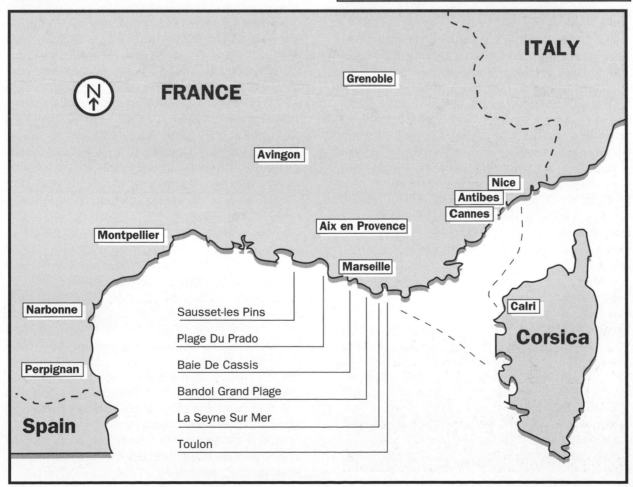

SPAIN

Capital:	Madrid
Population:	38,810,000
Area:	504,782km²
Time:	GMT+1 (summer time GMT+2)
Religion:	Roman Catholic
Languages:	Spanish (Castilian), Catalan, Basque, Gallego
Currency:	Pesetas (ptas)

THE PEOPLE

Spain occupies the majority of the Iberian peninsula. The Balearic Islands in the Mediterranean and the Canaries off the African coast also fall under its jurisdiction.

For 700 years after the fall of Rome, Spain was Islamic, until reconquered by violent Christian crusaders who more often resembed bandits than missionaries in their hunt for loot. The final conflict was won by Ferdinand and Isabella and the Catholic Crown became the inspiration behind the 'reconquista' at home and the 'conquistadores' who carved out an empire for Spain in the New World. Spain's Catholic Kings had been the only European monarchs willing to back Columbus's venture to sail westwards to India and, fortunately for the coffers of the Spanish treasury, the Aztec and Inca civilizations of America lay in the way. From an early age, Spain was a beach-orientated nation – the inhabitants watching frantically for the treasure ships on the horizon and hoping that they had not been captured by English pirates.

Hapsburg Spain of the 16th and 17th centuries dominated European events – stridently Catholic, dogmatic and conservative, she was both the victim and the propagator of countless wars and conspiracies. She then sank into obscurity for a couple of centuries, until the outbreak of the Spanish Civil War when liberals worldwide arrived to fight the Fascists led by General Franco. Franco triumphed, thanks to some timely help from Hitler. He managed to avoid Hitler's fate by refusing to return the favour during the Second World War.

After Franco's death in 1975, the monarchy was restored, and today Spain has a democratically elected socialist government. Since joining the European Community in 1986, one of Europe's least developed economies is catching up, with a spectacular growth rate in recent years.

From national monuments to local churches, Spain's rich heritage is a prominent part of the Spanish way of life. Vestiges of Islam, the Medieval Age, the Golden Age, and the Civil War years combine in a country that produced the Jesuits, Cervantes, Cortes, Franco, and Picasso. The modern blend is uniquely Spanish and persistently enjoyable.

THE LAND

The country consists mainly of a broad central plateau, sloping to the south and east, crossed by a series of mountain ranges and river valleys. The chief mountain ranges are the Pyrenees, the Picos de Europa, Sierra de Guadarrama and the Sierra Nevada (location for many famous spaghetti westerns). The chief rivers are the Tagus, the Duero, the Ebro, the Guadiana and the Guadalquivir.

Spain's climate is diverse and often at odds with other places lying at the same latitudes. The Northwest (Galicia) projects far into the Atlantic and lies at the same latitude as Marseilles, yet is much wetter, with a climate more similar to Cornwall or Brittany than southern France. The Southeast is excessively dry and torrid, irrigation being necessary for cultivation. The great central tableland, owing to its elevation, is bleak and arid, alternating between brilliant sunshine and cold winds.

Northern Spain is the coldest, wettest and windiest part of country. Weather patterns moving in from the Atlantic shed their moisture on the coast and along the mountains that separate the North from the rest of the mainland. This colder, wetter climate does have its benefits; it's the main reason why the North has escaped the fate of such places as the Costa del Sol and the Costa Brava.

The North Coast is also the most exposed to swells from the NW with big W swells also providing waves. If there is a W, SW or big S swell then the west facing breaks in Galicia can have the only sizable waves. If the swell is from the S or SW then Southern Spain has rideable surf which, although not consistent, can be enjoyable due to the bonus of winter sun.

Tides affect all of Spain's breaks with few peaks remaining surfable for long. At most banks, tide table books are provided free of charge. These are vital and should be sought out at the beginning of any surf trip to Spain.

THE SURF

Although Asturians and Cantabrians dispute where surfing began on the Iberian Peninsula, the truth is that it came to Spain through France, from Biarritz to be more precise, at the beginning of 60's and almost simultaneously spread into both regions, after moving rapidly through the País Vasco (Euskadi). Surfing arrived in the Canaries around the same time but not from the European continent – It was Australian and North American travelling surfers who introduced it there.

By the mid 70's, the País Vasco could already boast of supremacy in quantity and quality of practising surfers on its beaches: Zarautz

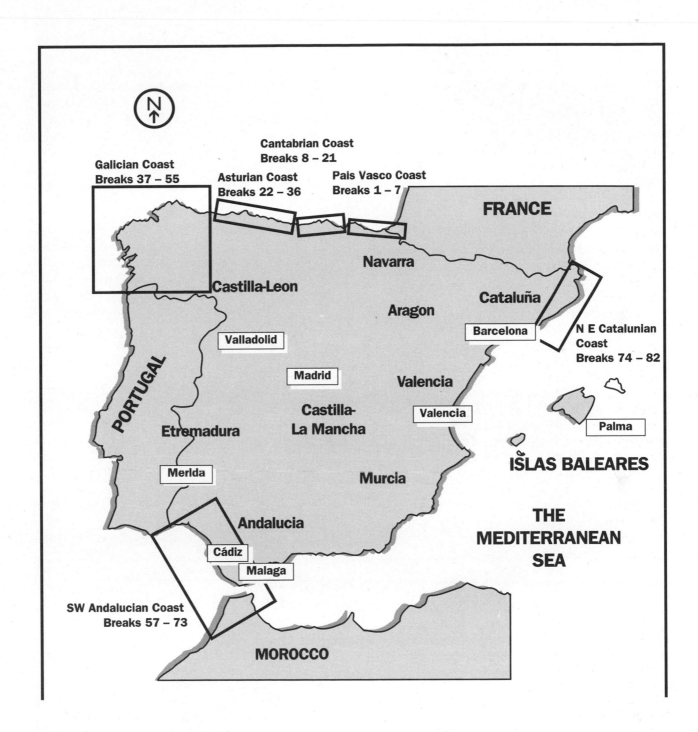

Galician Coast
Breaks 37 – 55

Cantabrian Coast
Breaks 8 – 21

Asturian Coast
Breaks 22 – 36

Pais Vasco Coast
Breaks 1 – 7

FRANCE

Navarra

Castilla-Leon

Cataluña

Aragon

Barcelona

N E Catalunian
Coast
Breaks 74 – 82

PORTUGAL

Valladolid

Madrid

Valencia

Castilla-
La Mancha

Valencia

Palma

Etremadura

ISLAS BALEARES

Merlda

Murcia

THE
MEDITERRANEAN
SEA

Andalucia

Cádiz

Malaga

SW Andalucian Coast
Breaks 57 – 73

MOROCCO

(Guipúzcoa), Bakio and Sopelana (Vizcaya) were considered to be surfing 'meccas' and surfers like Raúl Dourdil, Estanis Escauriaza, Jon Susaeta and Gonzalo Gandarias stood out compared to others in different regions. By the beginning of the 80's, surfing had expanded all along the North Coast, from the País Vasco to Galicia and even (though in small numbers) down to the coasts around Cádiz, from Puerto de Santa Maria to Tarifa.

By 1987 various surf shops, clothes labels, wetsuits, boards and accessories were readily available and *Tres 60* emerged as the first specialised Spanish surf magazine. Within a few months, and from then on, the market rocketed and the number of surfers and surf shops multiplied rapidly across the whole Peninsula.

Today, even though the País Vasco and the Canaries continue to set the pace, surfing is practised on all the coasts and even in the Mediterranean, in the provinces of Málaga, Valencia and Cataluña. In the last two years the phenomenon of bodyboarding has appeared. The sport exploded over one summer to the extent that in a few months the number of bodyboarders amply surpassed that of surfers, it being a much easier sport to learn.

Due to the good quality of some of the waves in the north of the Peninsula, these coasts are frequently visited by Australian, French, South African and British surfers during the autumn months when powerful swells from the NW arrive, created by the storms just off the west of Ireland and lined up by the SW winds that are so common at that time of year. The majority of surfers come to Mundaka, an already legendary wave, and then they move along the North Coast on their trip towards Portugal. The British surfers like to go to the Canaries during the winter months, in search of winter waves, sun and warm water, escaping from the cold of the British coasts.

Javier Amezaga/*Tres 60 Magazine*

WATER QUALITY

The pollution problem is now drastic in Spain. In the Canaries an association has already been formed, fighting in defence of the coasts (ADES) but on the Peninsula there's still no such body.

The pollution on the Basque coast is especially intense. Even though the 70's Nuclear Centre of Lemóniz will never be functional because of pressure from the Basque people, the Port of Bilbao is a collection point of toxic waste for all of Europe. The expansion of this port will further contribute to our coastal deterioration. All the surrounding area of the Port of Bilbao has a strong dose of contamination and it's precisely in this area where there are the greatest number of surfers. To the west is Playa de la Arena, which has good waves but swimming is not recommended by the authorities due to the contamination from the oil refinery right next to the beach. The situation on the east of the port is no better. On the beach of Ereaga, bathing is prohibited because of pollution. On the beaches of La Salvaje and Sopelana (once home to very clean waters) bathing was discouraged for a great part of the summer of '91. From Meñakoz on, the waters are cleaner but residues dumped by ships stain the rocks with tar. One can say that the only clean wave in all of Vizcaya is Mundaka.

In Guipúzcoa the situation is slightly better as industry is scarce. Even so, at Playa de Gros (in San Sebastián, where the majority of surfers from Guipúzcoa practise), swimming is not recommended because of the contaminated residues in the River Urumea which opens into the sea at that location. The beaches Orio, Zarautz, Deba and Zumaya are somewhat cleaner but during the summer period they always reveal elevated levels of pollution resulting from the unpurified residues of a busy tourist industry. In general, the situation is not very encouraging.

Javier Amezaga/*Tres 60 Magazine*

TRAVELLING AROUND

Holders of passports (valid for the entire period of the visit) issued by the governments of EEC, USA, Canada, do not need a visa to visit Spain and the Canary Islands. Australians and New Zealanders are supposed to get a visa in advance although, for stays of a month or less, entry permits can be issued on arrival – for this you'll need to have a ticket out of the country and proof that you can support yourself. In reality the authorities often don't even stamp your passport!

Flying

Flying to Spain is possible from just about every airport in Europe and prices can be very reasonable. Bilbao in Northern Spain is the most popular and often the cheapest destination if you plan to surf Spain's northern coasts. Málaga can also be ridiculously cheap to fly to, especially in winter months when it can be worth checking out Tarifa and the breaks around Cádiz, or going to Morocco for good winter swells and warm weather.

Madrid airport – Tel: 91 408 5200. Other airport information is listed regionally.

Ferries

One of the best ways of getting to Spain's north coast is by ferry. Brittany Ferries operates a twice weekly 24 hour ferry from Plymouth to Santander. For information contact Brittany Ferries at: Millbay Docks, Plymouth PL1 3EW. Tel: 0752 221 321. Or Santander. Tel: 34 42 214 500. It can be quite expensive in summer but once again, the advantage of being able to take a vehicle can mean your expenses, once there, will be greatly reduced. Ferries also leave from Cádiz in Southwest Spain to the Canary Islands (see the Canary Islands chapter for more info).

Driving

Spain's roads have improved tremendously over the past few years, making life for the motorist much easier. However, Northern Spain is mountainous with winding single roads making journey times often a lot longer than expected, especially in summer. Take your time, enjoy the often spectacular scenery and be patient with the many lorries which seem to move at a snail's pace. Most foreign driver's licences are honoured in Spain – including EC, US and Canadian ones – but an international driver's licence is an easy way to put your mind at rest. If you're bringing your own car you must have a 'green card' from your insurers, and a bail bond or extra coverage for legal costs is also worth having. As in the rest of continental Europe you drive on the right with petrol prices being similar to Britain and France. Spain has some good toll roads which vary in price and on some routes, they can save a considerable amount of time. Lastly, it's well worth being extremely careful about leaving your vehicle unattended. Unfortunately, Spain, like many other countries in the world, suffers from car and campervan break-ins.

Health and Living

As an EC country, Spain has reciprocal health agreements with other member states. To take advantage, you'll need form E111, available from most major post offices. However some form of travel insurance is still necessary, and of course only EC citizens are covered. Local doctors may not be too pleased with the E111, and in many parts Spanish public health care still lags behind much of northern Europe. With insurance you'll be able to claim back medical expenses, and it will also cover your baggage or tickets in case of theft or loss.

Telephoning

Dialling in code: 34 (then omit 1st 0 of area code.)

Dialling out code: 07 (wait for high pitched tone.)

Operator: 003

International Operator: 008

Emergency Services: 091

Embassies and Consulates

UK
c/ Fernando el Santo, 16
Madrid
Tel: 91 4l9 0200 /419 1528

US
c/ Serrano, 75
Madrid
Tel: 91 276 3400 / 276 3600

AUS
Paseo de la Castellana, l43
Madrid
Tel: 91 279 8501 / 279 8504

NZ
Nearest NZ embassy: Paris
Tel: 331 500 2411

Opening Times

BANKS (Bancos): Opening hours are 08.30 – 16.30 Monday to Thursday; 08.30 – 14.00 on Fridays; 08.30 – 13.00 on Saturdays. From June to September, Monday to Friday, 08.30 – 14.00. Saturday closed.

POST OFFICES (Correos): Normal hours are 08.00 – 12.00 noon, and from 17.00 – 19.30, Monday to Friday. Larger ones are open on Saturday mornings.

SHOPS (Tiendas): Shops are open from 09.00 – 13.00 or 13.30 and from 15.00 or 15.30 – 19.30 or 20.00, Monday to Friday. Some shops open on Saturdays and one or two on Sunday mornings.

Public Holidays

1, January	New Year's Day
6, January	Epiphany
Variable	Good Friday
Variable	Easter Sunday
Variable	Easter Monday
1, May	May Day/ Labour Day
Early or mid June	Corpus Christi
24, June	Día de San Juan
25, July	Día de Santiago
15, August	Assumption of the Virgin
12, October	National day
1, November	All Saints
6, December	Día de la Constitución
8, December	Immaculate Conception
25, December	Christmas Day

some SPANISH language

Surf Speak

big ....grande
beach ....playa
bottom ....fondo
break ....rompiente
cliff ....acantilado
coast ....costa
current/rip ....corriente
cutback.........................cutback
drop ....caida
fin.................................aleta
grommett .... grommett
high tide ....marea alta
help! ....¡socorro!
island............................. isla
lava...............................lava
left...........................izquierda
low tide.....................marea baja
offshore .... viento terral
reef.............................arrecife
right ....derecha
rivermouth ....boca de ria
rock ....rocas
sand ....arena
shallow ....poco profundo
sheltered ....abrigado
small ....pequeño
surfboard .... plancha de surf
swell ...marea de fondo/marejada
water ....agua
waves ....olas
wax ....cera
north ....norte
south...........................sur
east..............................este
west ....oeste

Useful Words

all.................................todo
before ....antes
because.........................porque
behind ....detrás
boat ....barco
cold .... frío
everybody.............todo el mundo
fast...............................rápido
fire................................fuego
food ....comida
God ....Dios
good............ bueno, buena, bien
good bye ....adiós
hello ....hola
here ....aquí
high ....alto
hot ....caliente, calor
how many? ....¿cuántos?
how much? ....¿cuánto es?

left............................izquierda
lightning.....................relámpago
like ....como
little............................pequeño
lost ....perdido
many ....muchos
near ....cerca
no ....no
old ....viejo
over ....sobre
please ....por favor
rain ....lluvia
right ....derecha
slow ....lento/despacio
snow ....nieve
soon ....pronto
thank you.......................gracias
thunder ....trueno
under ....debajo
up ....arriba
very .... muy
well ....bien
when?.....................¿cuándo?
why ....¿por qué?
with ....con
without..........................sin
yes ....sí

Useful Phrases

Good morning ....Buenos días
Good day ....Buenos días
Good afternoon .... Buenas tardes
Good night...........Buenas noches
I'm sorry ....Lo siento/
....Perdona
I don't speak.. ....No hablo..
Do you speak?..........¿Hablas?...
My name is................Me llamo...
I come from ....Soy de....
Excuse me ....Perdón
Where is/are ....¿Dónde está/
....están?
Can I have? ....Puedo tener
How do you say?.¿Cómo se dice?

Public signs & notices

open ....abierto
closed ....cerrado
entrance ....entrada
way out..........................salida
free ....libre
occupied........................ocupado
ladies ....señoras
gentlemen.............. caballeros
toilet.....................lavabo/aseo
private ....privado
forbidden ....prohibido

no parking ....no aparcar
no smoking ....no fumar

Shops & places

bakery ....panadería
chemist ....farmácia
cinema ....cine
fishmonger ....pescadería
grocer.......................comestibles
library ....bíblioteca
market ....mercado
police office ....reten
post office ....correos
quay............................muelle
shop ....tienda
stationer ....papelería
view point............punto de vista

Restaurants

bill ....cuenta
bottle ....botella
breakfast ....desayuno
cup ....taza
dinner ....cena
drink............................bebida
fork.............................tenedor
glass ....vaso
knife ....cuchillo
lunch...........comida del mediodía
plate ....plato
cup ....taza
sandwich......................bocadillo
spoon ....cuchara
table ....mesa
tip ....bote
waiter..........................camarero

Drink

beer ....cerveza
coffee – black ....cafe sólo
       – white........cafe con leche
ice ....hielo
juice ....zumo
tea ....té
water ....agua
wine ....vino

Food

apple ....manzana
avocado........................aguacate
banana..........................platano
beans ....judías
beef.............................ternera
biscuit ....galleta
bread...........................pan
butter...........................mantequilla
cabbage ....col

124

carrot...........................zanahorria
cauliflower ....coliflor
cheese..........................queso
chicken ....pollo
cream ....nata
cucumber .... pepino
egg................................huevo
fish...............................pescado
garlic.............................ajo
grapes...........................uvas
ham .... jamón
icecream ....helado
lamb ....cordero
lemon............................límon
lentils ....lentejas
marmelade ....confitura
milk...............................leche
mushrooms ....champiñones
mussels ....mejillones
mustard.........................mostaza
oil ....aceite
olives............................aceitunas
onion ....cebolla
orange...........................naranja
peach ....melocotón
pear..............................pera
pepper(veg)....................pimiento
pepper(table) ....pimienta
pork ....cerdo
potato ....patata
salad ....ensalada
salt...............................sal
sauce............................salsa
sausage ....salchicha
shrimps ....gambas
spinach ....espinacas
strawberries ....fresas
sugar ....azúcar
toast..............................tostada
vegetables ....legumbres
vinegar..........................vinagre
yoghurt ....yogur

Countries

Scotland ....Escocia
Ireland............................Irlanda
Wales ....Gales
England ....Inglaterra
Channel Islands   Islas Normandas
France ....Francia
Spain ....España
Canary Islands ......Islas Canarias
Portugal..........................Portugal
Azores ....Islas Azores
Italy................................Italia
Germany.........................Alemania
Switzerland......................Suiza

Numbers

one ....uno, una, un
two ....dos
three ....tres
four ....cuatro
five ....cinco
six................................seis
seven ....siete
eight ....ocho
nine...............................nueve
ten ....diez
eleven ....once
twelve ....doce
thirteen ....trece
fourteen ....catorce
fifteen.............................quince
sixteen ....dieciséis
seventeen ....diecisiete
eighteen ....dieciocho
nineteen ....diecinueve
twenty ....veinte
twenty one ....veintiuno
twenty two......................veintidos
thirty..............................trenta
forty ....cuarenta
fifty................................cinquenta
sixty ....sesenta
seventy ....setenta
eighty ....ochenta
ninety ....noventa
one hundred ....cien
two hundred ....dos cientas
five hundred ....quinientas
one thousand ....mil
one million ....un millón

Days of the week

Monday ....lunes
Tuesday ....martes
Wednesday ....miercoles
Thursday ....jueves
Friday.............................viernes
Saturday.........................sábado
Sunday ....domingo

Months

January ....enero
February..........................febrero
March..............................marzo
April ....abril
May.................................mayo
June ....junio
July .... julio
August.............................agosto
September...................septiembre
October ....octubre
November ....noviembre
December ....diciembre

Measures of time

minute ....minuto
hour................................hora
day ....día
week ....semana
month ....mes
year................................año
decade ....década
century ....siglo

Mechanic words & phrases

oil ....aceite
petrol.............................gasolina
puncture.........................pinchazo
Something is wrong with...?.........
...........Hay algún percance en...?
the engine......................el motor
the clutch.................el embrague
the gearbox .....la caja de cambios
the breaks ....los frenos
the steering ....la dirección
the suspension ....la suspensión
My car...has broken down ....
...........Mi coche...se ha averiado
...has run out of gas...................
.........se ha quedado sin gasolina
...is...kms from here ....
...................está a...km de aqui
Can you...?.................¿Podría...?
...tow the car to a garage
...remolcar el coche al garage
...repair the car ....
...........................reparar el coche
When will it be ready? ....
...................¿Cuándo estará listo?
How much will it cost?................
.......................¿Cuánto costará?
I don't have sufficient cash..........
............No tengo suficiente dinero
Will you accept credit cards? ....
.....¿Aceptaría tarjetas de credito?

Other phrases

Give me a kiss ......Dáme un beso.
Would you like a drink? ....
...................¿Quieres tomar algo?
Will you put oil on my back? ....
.......................¿Puedes ponerme
...................aceite en laespalda?
Do you want to go for dinner? ....
................¿Quieres salir a cenar?
You have beautiful eyes. ....
...........Tienes los ojos preciosos.
Your eyes are like the moon ....
...........Tus ojos son como la luna.
I love you. ....Te quiero.
Do you love me?......¿Me quieres?
Do you like my "stick"? ....
...................¿Te gusta mi "stick"?
Are you trying to chat me up? ....
........¿Me estás intentando ligar?
It doesn't smell nice ....
...........................No huele bien
Where is the doctor?...................
.............¿Dónde está et medico?

125

Pais Vasco

The País Vasco (Euskadi) province is made up of three smaller states of Guipúzcoa (Gipuzkoa), Vizcaya (Biscaia) covering the coast and Alava inland. The landscape is extremely mountainous and incredibly green with highways winding in and out of valleys. Small villages and several big cities house a population of independently-minded and unique people, who have their own language – Euskera, the origins of which remain a mystery.

Surf spots along the coast are set amongst some truly spectacular country. The pleasures of surfing in such places, plus the excellent quality of many of it's breaks has led many young Basque people to take up surfing. Some of these breaks have been omitted at the request of local people due to the large numbers of foreign surfers who end up in this area.

EARLY DAYS

In the early 1970s a small group of surfing pioneers was formed: Iñigo Letamendia from Guipúzcoa, Raúl Dourdil from Bakio (now working with ADES in Tenerife), José Manuel Merodio and Carlos Beraza from Cantabria. They were called the 'Tanganazo Boys.' They lived the surfing lifestyle – long hair, running shoes, good music, surf and girls. With their suits and ties banished to the wardrobe and the world at their feet, their aim was to find a way to lead the life they loved and still earn a living. Making boards seemed to be the answer. Santa Marina Surfboards was the first board factory in Spain, started up by Merodio.

By the mid 70's the surfing population had grown to some 100-200 people, all well known to each other. Iñigo Letamendia started up Geronimo Surfboards with an American called Jay, and an artist called Txema Elexpuru who gave the boards the personal touches. Shortly after, Gonzalo Campa 'Zalo' joined up with Iñigo. They also started a surf shop in Zarautz. Between them, they shared the workload of the factory in Cantabria and the surf shop in Zarautz on a 15 day haul each. Later, Gonzalo decided it was easier to just stay in one place and kept the business in Cantabria while Iñigo did the same in Zarautz.

Some years after, Miguel Azpiroz, alias 'Pajarua,' started the first surf shop in San Sebastián (Donostia). The surfboard that he'd hung on his shop sign only lasted for two days – some surfer, keen on waves and short on cash, may still be having a good time on it! It was around this time that the name 'Pukas' appeared. The word literally means hole but it's also the name given to a type of shell which has holes in it to make neckleces. From then on, surfboards have been made non-stop and by now Pukas is the biggest and most well-known surf-related trademark in Spain.

GUIPUZCOA
Surf Breaks 1 – 3
Juan Pedro Sansinenea/Rip Curl Spain

1. San Sebastián (Donostia)

San Sebastián has three surfing beaches. **Playa de Gros** is the most consistent and most popular, giving good sand bottom waves from 1 - 8ft. The waves are surfable on all tides though at high tide the peaks become less numerous (and more crowded) and can be affected by backwash. S, SE and SW winds are best. The other two beaches are called **La Concha** and **Ondarreta**, and when Playa de Gros is closing out there can be good waves here. La Concha has a right and Onderreta a left, breaking off the wall. These breaks can be surfed with any wind apart from a N or NE. All the beaches get crowded and La Concha is the most suitable for beginners. Access for Playa de Gros is easy, there's a free parking lot on the right. La Concha and Ondarreta are not so accessible, park where possible.

Water Quality: Playa de Gros is clean in winter, but in summer it's the complete opposite, with contamination often reaching extreme levels! Concha and Onderreta aren't as bad...apparently.

TRAVELLING AROUND

Area Code:	Guipúzcoa – 94, Vizcaya – 94
Tourist Office:	Miramar, esquina a Andia
	20004 San Sebastián
	Tel: 943 426 282/261 755
Airport:	San Sebastián Tel: 943 642 240
	Bilbao – Tel: 94 453 1350
Railway Station:	San Sebastián
	Tel: 943 283 089 / 283 599
	Bilbao – Tel: 94 423 8623

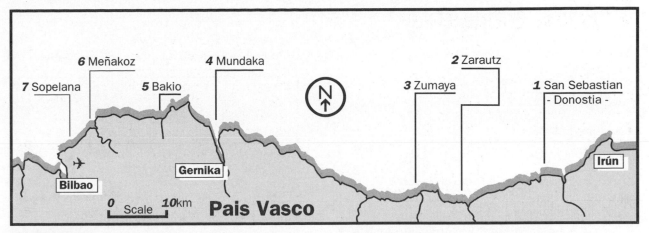

Pais Vasco

2. Zarautz

Zarautz has a long stretch of north facing sands giving some decent beach break waves. Surfing is big in Zarautz with this popularity spurred on by the ASP world tour which often takes place here. Zarautz can offer a novelty to the surfer, at high tide the street and bar lights along the promonade provide enough light to be able to surf at night – the waves work on any tide up to around 8ft - 10ft but when it does get big it can be very tough to paddle out. Park where possible near the beach.

Water Quality: A polluted river runs out to sea at the eastern end of the beach.

3. Zumaya (Zumaia)

Zumaya itself is not one of the Basque coast's most attractive towns. The beach lies next to a harbour mouth and the banks created can be good, giving peaky waves on all tides up to 8ft. Gets crowded. Park on the road towards the harbour.

Water quality: No info available.

VIZCAYA
Surf Breaks 4 – 7
Alejandro Nebrada/Banana Surf Shop

4. Mundaka (Mundacca)

Mundaka is supposedly Europe's longest left, certainly one the hollowest and probably the most famous. Swells break over a consistent sand bar formed by the currents at the mouth of the River Guernika. The paddle out to the peak is made easy by the river flow and excellent waves can be ridden from 2 - 14ft. It faces north, is well protected from the west wind, best from low to mid tide.

Today, the wave is well known throughout the world and is visited by surfers from many countries. There are only a few real locals and among the pioneers of this wave are Carlos Beraza, Txema Elexpuru, Manel and Rafa Fiochi, Stanis Escauriaza, Tatono Garaizabal, Jon Susaeta, Pato Morenes, Raúl Dourdil, Kike Nebrada, Manolo Robles and Marcelo Puente. Parking is usually difficult since the village is small and the streets are narrow. The local police tolerate camper-vans in the town centre as long as strict rules are adhered to. Nudity and bathing in public are uncool. Low profile is good profile. If you end up an inmate of 'The Cave' – good luck. At all costs avoid having to unblock any drains. It's a ghoulish sight! The cave aside, Mundaka is a cool place to hang when there's surf. When it's flat, most life focuses on entertainment. The bars go off but even more fun can be had at Guernika – Friday and Saturday nights (especially in summer) are madness on a grand scale. Street life reigns supreme.

Water Quality: The water is some of the cleanest in the País Vasco and the surrounding area is a nature reserve.

5. Bakio (Baquio)

Beach break facing west-northwest. The sand banks are constantly shifting according to the currents originating from the two rivers that open on either side of the beach. For this reason, one can surf Bakio from 2 - 6ft with very good waves, or, one can wait for two months without a decent peak breaking at all. There's a high level of surfing amongst the locals who are protective of their waves. It's easy to park by the beach, despite the urban chaos and the crowds that arrive here during the summer months.

Water Quality: During summer, when the town's population swells, water quality can be very bad.

6. Meñakoz

A powerful righthander of good quality with a critical take-off, which breaks up to 15ft. It faces north and is highly dependent on the swell direction. If the wind is from the W or NW, the wave heaves up towards the rocks, demanding respect. If the swell comes from the N then the waves will be hollower and more approachable. It's rocky bottom allows surfing from mid to high tide. There's no parking or services by the break and the last kilometre of dirt track is pretty rough, with surfers and fishermen the only people using it.

Water Quality: Minimal contamination.

7. Sopelana

An open 2km long northwest facing beach divided into three areas: **La Salvaje**, **Larrabasterra** and **El Sitio**. On all there are good sand bottom waves that break well from 2 - 10ft. Good waves on all tides. Their proximity to big towns make them very crowded in July and August but for the rest of the year there's a good surfing atmosphere. Easy parking and good facilities.

Water Quality: The quality of the water is acceptable except in the summer months. The problems of contamination in the summer of '91 were caused by the break down of a residual water collector. In Sopelana, like in Meñakoz, the influence of industrial contamination is minimal.

Cantabria

In 1963 Cantabria was the cradle for surfing in Spain. Jesús Fiochi ordered a surfboard from the Barland workshop in Bayonne and his first surf was at the 'Primera Playa' of Playa del Sardinero.

Right from the start, a group of swimmers and scuba-divers used to accompany Jesús on his surfing safaris, armed with plywood boards with rounded tips. They then realised that proper boards were available in Bayonne (Jesús had rubbed out the trade mark from his board and had claimed that he had ordered it from Australia!) and they promptly bought a 'Barland' each. They formed two groups, consisting of some 12 surfers in total.

Soon, one of these pioneers, Jose Manuel Merodio, began crafting boards – at first for himself and then for his friends as well. In 1969 he labelled these first boards 'MB Surfboards.' At the beginning of the 70's, he moved to Loredo, then to Somo, and started a legendary trade mark and surfboard factory under the name 'Santa Marina.' This factory gave birth to much of Cantabria's surf culture.

Until the mid 70's all the surfers came from Santander, except for a small nucleus in San Vicente that had been around since 1970. Under the influence of these guys who continually showed up at Playa de los Locos, a group was formed by the locals from the city of Torrelavega. Within 5 years and right through to the early 80's, this group dominated the surfing competitions in Cantabria. Now, at the beginning of the 90's, there are locals from practically all the beaches of the area. Somo, along side El Sardinero and Los Locos are considered the best spots of the region.

The most pleasant time to surf here is in the summer but swells are inconsistent, not normally reaching above 4ft. The ideal time for waves is October and November since the water and air temperatures are still bearable and swells coming from the NW are powerful and consistent. In a big W swell the waves are especially good at beaches like Los Locos, Liencres and Somo. When the swells come from the N, they can bring good waves to places like Ajo and Noja.

In winter the waves are as good as in autumn but the water temperature is 9°- 13°C and the air temperature is similar, so even on good days many people think twice. Although with spring comes warmer weather, the surf is unpredictable; there could be good swells or one could wait for months with mushy seas coming from the N or NE.

Gonzalo Campa Villegas/Xpeedin' Surf Shop

TRAVELLING AROUND

Area Code:	942
Tourist Office:	Plaza Porticada, 1
	39001 Santander
	Tel: 942 310 708 /
	310 756
Airport:	Santander -
	Tel: 942 251 004
Railway Station:	Santander –
	Tel: 942 210 288
American Express:	Viajes Attair
	c/ Lealtad, 24
	Santander
	Tel: 942 311 700

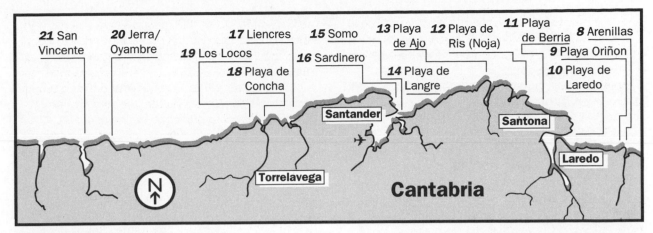

Surf Breaks 8 – 21
Gonzalo Campa Villegas/Xpeedin' Surf Shop

8. Playa de Arenillas

This is the beach at Islares and it extends as far as the eastern side of the rivermouth of Oriñon. The wave breaks left with little force. It can stand a NE wind but those coming from the S are better. It can be caught from 2ft and above and works at low tide. Close to the rocks there's a current (useful for experienced surfers, dangerous for beginners) that helps you get out the back. This place is protected from swells from the N and NW and consequently needs a big swell.

Water Quality: Good.

9. Playa de Oriñon

The western continuation of Playa de Arenillas. A sandbank produces fast tubey lefthanders that work well with winds from the S, W and NW if they're not too strong. It's even more protected than Arenillas, and needs a big swell for the waves to get in. It breaks at 3ft and above in autumn, winter and spring. When there are waves, it gets more crowded than Arenillas surfers come from nearby Santander. Park in the village.

Water Quality: Good.

10. Playa de Laredo

The busy seaside town of Laredo can be a good place to check out when there's a big N swell. The bay stretches around from a northeasterly direction to a northwesterly direction and is good in winter, with the best peaks generally located in the centre of the beach. The waves are surfable on all tides, although swells rise above 4ft plus and low tide can be very dumpy. The best winds are from the S and SW although winds from the W and NW are no bother if they're light. Good frm 2 - 7ft. Crowding is rarely a problem. Easy parking by the beach.

Water Quality: Good.

11. Playa de Berria

Various peaks giving both lefts and rights which work all along a long beach, depending on the swell size and the tide. Normally on high tide the central area goes off while at low tide it's the ends of the beach that are working, although the banks shift a lot. It faces north picking up swells coming from the NW and the N. It's a beach for summer and autumn that closes out when the waves reach 7 - 8ft. S winds are offshore. It is 3kms from Santoña and there are places to park all along the beach.

Water Quality: Good.

12. Playa del Ris (Noja)

This beach is in the village of Noja to the west of the peninsula which separates it from Playa del Trengandin. It faces north although it's protected from NW swells by the cape of Ajo. A left and right peak breaks in the centre of the beach. The righthander is the better quality ride, giving powerful and hollow waves, especially in the first section. It's a beach for autumn, winter and spring. It works best from mid to high tide from 2 - 7ft. It can stand winds from the NE and from the W and NW if they aren't too strong. There aren't any locals here but there's a big group who come regularly in summer on vacation.

Water Quality: Good.

13. Playa de Ajo

Playa de Ajo has some fair rights and lefts breaking over a sand bottom. The beach faces NW picking up a lot of swell and is best surfed from low to mid tide up to 6ft. Ajo is a small but busy seaside town, consequently the beach gets crowded during summer months. Parking by beach.

Water Quality: Excellent.

14. Playa de Langre

Playa de Langre is protected against W and NW winds by high sheer faced cliffs. The setting for a surf here is impressive. A good lefthander breaks in the centre of the beach at low to mid tide up to 6 - 8ft with offshores coming from the E and S. Rarely surfed because the eastern end is a nudist beach. Parking on top of the cliff. A path down the cliffs that leads to the centre of the beach.

Water Quality: Excellent.

15. Playa de Somo

Playa de Somo stretches round from a northerly to a westerly direction. The beach is long with numerous, consistent peaks breaking onto seasonally shifting sandbanks. The waves are good on all tides from 1 - 10ft. Favourable winds are from the S and E. Because of its proximity to the Cantabrian capital, Santander, and the existence of a ferry every 20 minutes, this beach gets the most crowded in all of Cantabria, with 200 – 300 surfers concentrating here in summer. Nevertheless, the locals are open and tolerant, and incidents in the water are very rare. In winter it's much calmer. There is a car park in the centre of the beach.

Water Quality: Good.

16. Santander
(Playa del Sardinero)

When there's a big swell, with strong W or SW winds, then Sardinero can be a worthwhile spot to check out. Otherwise it is very missable. A far better idea is to make the short trip to the breaks east or west of Santander. In winter it's usually very crowded with 100 – 200 surfers in the water. One catches waves at mid to high tide if it is less than 3ft. In summer it's forbidden to surf and it is difficult to even find a place to lay down a towel. Parking all along the beach.

Water Quality: Good.

17. Liencres Area

The coast around Liencres offers a number of good right and left, sand and rock reef breaks. The area faces west to northwest and consequently picks up a lot of swell, with different peaks breaking throughout the tides. Along with Los Locos, this is the biggest and most consistent spot in Cantabria. The long beach is separated in the eastern area into various sections by rocks. At high tide, here you'll find the best and most crowded peaks. The western area is bigger and has dangerous lateral currents which form sand banks. From low to mid tide and with winds from the S the quality improves a lot. From the village of Liencres, head for Dunas de Liencres where there's a bar and a large area for parking.

Water Quality: Excellent.

18. Playa de Concha

If Los Locos is blown out by strong NW or W winds then the western end of Playa de Concha is the place to head for. A large headland separating the two beaches offers good protection against these winds, without blocking out all of the swell. The beach faces north and is best at mid tide from 2 - 8ft. Crowds can get big here and the water does get polluted. At low tide a sand bar is formed in the rivermouth of San Martín, but surfers need to go in with anticontamination equipment! Easy parking by the beach.

Water Quality: The water is very polluted with all sorts of industrial residues, especially bisulfitic bleaches from the paper mills. In August 1992 the tipping will cease (we hope).

19. Los Locos

Los Locos has some of the best beach break waves in Spain! Catch it on a clean 6ft swell and you'll see why! The waves peak perfectly, giving long, fast, hollow barrels that are makable right down the line. When the waves are between 4 - 8ft a right hand point, off the rocks at the eastern side of the beach starts to work. Like the beach break, it can also have fast, perfect barrels, with rides up to 150mtrs in length. The beach faces northwest, works on all tides and, naturally, it gets crowded. It's the only beach in summer that is well situated for the dominating winds that come from the NE. At high tide it needs 6ft+ in order to break and it gets dangerous on the shore because the beach disappears. The beach is signposted from Saunces and there's an area for parking above the beach.

Water Quality: In spite of its proximity to La Concha, the water quality is excellent.

20. Playa de la Jerra
(Playa de Oyambre)

Playa de la Jerra (which is not marked on most maps) is located at the very left hand side of Playa de Oyambre. The big plus for this beach is that it faces SE and still picks up a lot of swell, making it an ideal alternative to San Vicente. The wind will nearly always be good for one of them. The waves here are best at mid tide and are good from 2-8ft. Unlike San Vicente, crowds are negligible here. In Oyambre, towards the river, quite a bit more swell gets in. There's one or two small spots to park next to the road above the beach. If these are taken, then you'll have to park at Playa de Oyambre and walk.

Water Quality: Excellent.

21. San Vicente (Playa de Meron)

On the eastern side of the Ría de San Vicente, there's a very good sandbank. This bank gives off a consistent peak which breaks both left and right. Of the two, the left is generally the better, being a longer faster ride that can tube, especially at low tide. Facing northwest, the break picks up a lot of swell and it can get quite busy with a lot of surfers staying for the weekend in a campsite right next to the beach. The wave is good from 2 - 8ft and there's an energy-saving channel to the left of the peak. The rivermouth only breaks in a big swell. It's signposted from San Vicente. Easy parking in front of the wave.

Water Quality: Good.

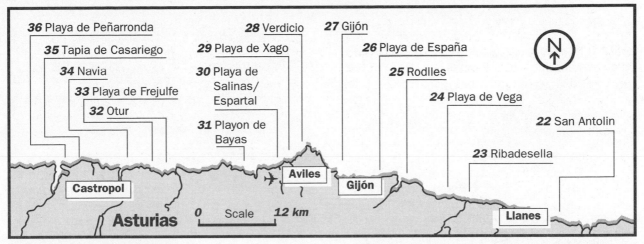

36 Playa de Peñarronda
35 Tapia de Casariego
34 Navia
33 Playa de Frejulfe
32 Otur
28 Verdicio
29 Playa de Xago
30 Playa de Salinas/ Espartal
31 Playon de Bayas
27 Gijón
26 Playa de España
25 Rodiles
24 Playa de Vega
22 San Antolin
23 Ribadesella

Castropol
Aviles
Gijón
Llanes
Asturias
0 Scale 12 km

Asturias

Asturias has a coastline of approximately 483kms. You can find a great many beaches, reefs, points and rivermouths – all of good quality. Asturias is considered a natural paradise. Its climate is oceanic and moderate, and it's green landscapes offer mild and agreeable temperatures.

The region is full of contrasts – ocean, forests, mountains, flora and fauna combine to create vistas that are difficult to describe. The people are strong and hardy, yet simple and friendly.

Surfing started in Asturias in the 60's. I personally have experienced its whole evolution as I began surfing when I was only eight years old. It was in Tapia de Casariego and in Gijón (and later in El Espartal) where the first surfers began to appear in the sea.

During the 70's the 'Federación Española de Surf' (Spanish Surf Federation) was created, springing from different clubs in Asturias, Cantabria, Vizcaya and Guipúzcoa. In Asturias two clubs were in charge of promoting the sport and organizing competitions. The contests held by 'Club de Surf Bajamar' in Tapia and by 'Grupo Cultural Covadonga' in Gijón, were both recognised venues on the Spanish circuit. These clubs were the foundation stone for Asturian surfing, and there were good relations between them. Good surfers emerged and I wish I could describe the atmosphere that surrounded those championships. I will never forget those days – they were the best! I don't mean they're bad now, but times change!

Some years later, this thriving club scene was forgotten. The clubs in Asturias were dissolved, the Federation disappeared, yet the numbers of surfers continued to grow. It was left to the surf shops to organize championships on a local level.

In 1989 a new surf club formed: 'Club Picante – Playa de Tapia', again organizing contests (local, regional and international). The Tapia ProAm now attracts surfers from all over Europe and the rest of the world.

I've divided the Asturian coast from east to west:
1. EAST COAST: There is not much to talk about regarding the surf in this area – few good waves and even though there are a lot of beaches, they tend to be closed (i.e. coves) and have deep waters. As far as tourists go, this is the most crowded area in the region.
2. CENTRAL COAST: In this area of the coast there are heavily populated cities (Aviles, Gijón) and industrial areas which make the water the most contaminated of the region. Gijón is the most popular surfing nucleus. Within a 40km radius there are some popular breaks like Rodiles, Gijón, Espartal and Salinas, many others are only known by the locals.
3. WESTERN COAST: This is the wildest and least crowded area in Asturias. As far as the surf goes, we say that the surfing capital of the western coast is Tapia de Casariego. It's a fishing village, small but charming, and it has a lot of surfing charisma. Personally, I consider it the best area to surf.

Use this information in the true spirit of surfing. We hope that your discovery of new breaks won't mean they become exploited and polluted, rather, enjoy and protect them – a mission for us all.

Diego Méndez/Picante Surf Shop

TRAVELLING AROUND

Area Code: 985

Tourist Office: Marqués de San Esteban, 1
33206 Gijón
Tel: 985 346 046

Railway Station: Oviedo
Tel: 985 243 364

EASTERN COAST
Surf Breaks 22 – 24
Diego Méndez/Picante Surf Shop

22. Playa de San Antolin

Faces northeast with a sand and boulder bottom, and a rock bottom on the right side of the beach. Holds a lot of swell, will work on all tides and is best with a SW to SE wind. It's easy to see, since the road passes just above it but it's not normal to see a lot of people surfing here, although when conditions are good, you can have a good time. There's a parking lot just above the beach and another by the beach itself.

Water Quality: Clean.

23. Ribadesella

A fishing village that, during the summer vacations, is a popular tourist destination. Its beach faces north-northeast, which makes it very sheltered from all winds, except those coming from the N. It has a surfing tradition so you'll always find people in the water, especially in summer (in winter only on classic days). Various breaks and peaks can hold quite a lot of swell both at high and low tide.

Water Quality: Good.

24. Playa de Vega

Faces northeast. Sand bottom which is variable like all sand beaches. Good rights and lefts in small swell, so we call it a summer beach since this is when it's full of people. Not many surfers here. Turn off the main road towards La Vega.

Water Quality: One of the most polluted beaches on the Asturian coast, due to the little creek that flows into it which is used to wash flourite from the mines upstream. Bad news!

CENTRAL COAST
Surf Breaks 25 – 31

25. Rodiles

This is a wave that's produced at the mouth of the River Villaviciosa. To the west of the beach a sand bank gives some perfect lefthanders (powerful, hollow, long etc.) best at low tide. At high tide on the eastern side of the beach, there are further good peaks, with rights usually better than the than lefts. It's a very famous wave and also the best in Asturias but due to this, there is a 'localism' factor to contend with. The place is a paradise and when the conditions are perfect, (climate, waves) it can be hallucinegenic! Good camping, bars etc.

Water Quality: Rodiles is considered a natural reserve by the Principality of Asturias. It's clean, without any polluting additives.

26. Playa de España

This beach faces north, so favourable winds come from the SW and SE. Its bottom is sand and flat rocks, best at mid tide. Good waves break close to the shore. Since it's close to the city of Gijón crowds are common but it's a pretty beach, surrounded by trees and green countryside. Parking by the beach.

Water Quality: Clean.

27. Gijón

Like all cities where surfing is practised, there exists a massive urban surf scene. Three spots are the most important, in a 5km radius.

PLAYA DE SAN LORENZO: This is the most crowded, since it's right inside the city. All along the beach various different peaks are formed over a sand bottom. They work on all tides (although at high they can suffer from backwash). At low tide, on the right side of the beach, the rights over a sand and rock bottom can be a lot of fun.

EL MONGOL: Close to Playa San Lorenzo, going east, a good option in a big swell. A long and powerful wave breaks right here over a rock bottom (depending on the tides, you might have to dodge the rocks) and when there's a lot of swell it doesn't get crowded.

PEÑARRUBIA: On the eastern outskirts of Gijón you'll find a boulder and sand beach that can hold a big swell. Distinguishable because it's a nudist beach, there is good parking by all three beaches.

Water Quality: Extremely polluted – bad!

28. Verdicio

Faces northwest and has a sandy sea bed. The surroundings are very pretty. In good conditions it produces good lefthand waves with hollow sections. It's not very crowded with surfers. Take the road going towards Luanco from Aviles. The small beach town is very quiet.

Water Quality: Clean.

29. Playa de Xago

This beach also faces northwest and has a sand bottom. It's a good beach for the summer season, and, since it's very exposed, it works on very small swells. The best waves are on either side of the beach at low and high tide. It gets quite crowded since it's close to the nucleus of surfers in Aviles and Salinas. You'll reach it by going in the same direction as to Playa de Verdicio.

30. Salinas and Espartal

It faces northwest, like most of the best surfing beaches in Asturias. Personally, I think it's one of the best and I refer also to the local surfing atmosphere – the people are natural and they're good surfers.

Here I'll describe Salinas and Espartal since it's really one long beach. Starting on the right side, in San Juan or Espartal, there's a breakwater which forms a bank giving powerful rights with hollow sections; at low tide the favourable winds are from the NE while at high tide the break forms left peaks and you can have a wicked time! As you go along the beach, towards Salinas, there's an abundance of left and right peaks with good quality waves. Reaching Salinas you find a little town that's very well-kept. Whenever I go there, because of its structure and lay out, I get the sensation that I'm in Australia or California. In Salinas there are quite a few good quality peaks. The whole beach, because it's so long, picks up all types of wind and swell directions, so depending on the conditions, there is always something to choose from. I'll also add that you can surf here from 2 - 12ft. It holds a lot of swell. It's usually crowded since it's close to very populated areas but there's always a place to catch a wave. Easy parking by the beach.

Water Quality: Very polluted.

31. Playon de Bayas

As you make your way down the steep, winding dirt track to the beach, the entire stretch of Playon de Bayas can be viewed. It's a very good idea to stop, take a long look to find the best peak before heading down to the bottom. It's a consistent west-northwest facing beach, which is best from mid to high tide and from 2 - 8ft. Any bigger and the paddle out can be very hard. No crowds. Take the road to the airport, head to Santa Maria Del Mar and before you get there, you'll come to a village called Naveces. The beach is signposted from here, it's 4kms away.

Water Quality: Good.

WESTERN COAST
Surf Breaks 32 – 35

32. Playa de Otur

Playa de Otur is a quiet, sheltered beach break. It faces directly north and is good on all tides from 2 - 8ft. Works best in spring and autumn. The beach is signposted from the small village of Otur. A steep road leads down to an area for parking.

Water Quality: Good.

33. Playa de Frejulfe – Puerto de Vega

I have a deep affection for and good memories of this place. After a trip to Australia, I lived here for a year for work reasons. Puerto de Vega is a little fishing village set amongst wild surroundings. It's my favourite spot with powerful and hollow waves and no crowds. You can get to the beach through Navia and by Puerto de Vega.

Water Quality: Unfortunately affected by pollution from Navia. There are plans to make it into a nature reserve (perhaps specifically to protect it from contamination). We'll see what happens.

34. Navia

A long beach facing north, protected from SW and SE winds. On its left side the River Navia opens into the sea. In the middle of the beach a sand bar is formed that gives excellent lefts and rights which can hold a good swell. On the right side a point named 'El Moro' produces good rights on all tides. Parking beside the beach.

Water Quality: Highly contaminated.

35. Tapia de Casariego

The lovely fishing village of Tapia de Casariego has an excellent small beach with some good waves. It's here that some of the first surfing took place in Asturias and there's still a small but active surfing population. There are two spots: A beach break giving rights and lefts and a rock reef break on the western side of the bay. The reef breaks as a left and is best from 4 - 8ft at mid tide. The beach break is best at low tide with a small swell and high tide in a big swell. Both spots work best with a SW, S, or SE wind. A small dirt track leads to an area for parking just above the beach west of the town.

Water Quality: Clean.

36. Playa de Peñarronda

Faces north and gives good quality right and left peaks on all tides (best at mid). You can choose between here and Tapia because when the conditions are right for one, they're not for the other, and vice versa. Parking just above the beach.

Water Quality: Good.

Galicia

Galicia occupies a peculiar geographical situation and enjoys a humid yet sunny climate. It's a magic land where the mists creep down the valleys blown by the wind and inhabitants still tell tales of 'Santa Compaña' (the procession of ghosts) while the wind howls. A land of sweet green hills with a forested cloak gently merging with the ocean's incredible beauty.

The Galician coast has a tortuous outline and on its sandy beaches you can find a thousand and one different waves. Regardless of wind and swell direction, somewhere is working all the time. More than likely you will be alone with the ocean's roar, your footsteps perhaps alongside those of a fisherman who, with impassive gestures observes your manoeuvres without losing sight of his rod.

The sport's beginnings here were like in so many other places – the first glimpse of a big, beautiful Malibu was love at first sight, ecstasy from the first day. It was in Vigo in 1969 and La Coruña in 1970 where the first waves were ridden. In other countries, today's generation is curious about beginnings; the first surfers, the first surfboards etc... Here we are still in the 'prehistoric' phase.

I first fell in love with the sport at Pantin, 20 years ago, and despite the fact that a ProAm event (The Pantin Classic) is held here annually, nothing has really changed – the same waves break in the same places. I guess it's been only a second in the long history of the beach and twenty years in the multicoloured history of one man! I feel small when I contemplate the quiet cliff rocks that have presided over so many geological eras. Our history is short. In a land without haste, surfing has slept quietly for these 20 years.

I remember the first contest at Nemiña (100kms from La Coruña) that ended up as a beach party because the surf was small. We were always looking for new places to surf. You'd open a map and see hundreds of unknown beaches but nobody knew exactly where to go. With map in hand we discovered many spots. We could see Doniños from the shelter where we made our first boards at Ferrol. It was a white line in the distance. One afternoon we decided to try it. What we saw was the quintessential surf dream – an infinity of empty perfect peaks. I remember the crazy race we had down the hill. The water was crystal clear, and cold, but the sun shone. It was an unforgettable moment.

All of Galicia's coasts get waves in various conditions but generally speaking the breaks in the north are the most consistent and popular. In summer the area around Ferrol can be exceptional. Our main advantage is easy access to different beaches giving many waves which work in an array of conditions.

Carlos Bremón/Aqua Surf Shop

TRAVELLING AROUND

Area Code:	Coruña – 981
	Pontevedra – 986
Tourist Office:	Dársena de la Marina, s/n
	15001 La Coruña
	Tel: 981 221 822
Airports:	La Coruña
	Tel: 981 232 240
	Santiago – Tel: 981 597 400
	Vigo – Tel: 986 275 204
Railway Station:	La Coruña
	Tel: 981 230 309
American Express:	Viajes Amado
	c/ Compostela, 1
	La Coruña
	Tel: 981 225 732

Surf Breaks 37 – 55
Carlos Bremón/Aqua Surf Shop

37. Playa Reinante

Playa Reinante and the beaches west of Reinante face northwest, with a coast road affording good views of the sea. The waves here are good, with loads of unsurfed peaks, best caught from 2 - 6ft on all tides.

38. Playa de Barrerios/Foz

The wide sands that stretch from Playa de Barrerios across the river to Foz generally receive good quality beach break waves. Tides here play a major part in surfing conditions, with good peaks coming and going with the tidal flow. Low to mid tide is usually the best time to surf, but on big swells high tide is often better. Rips and swirling currents are strong here due to the river. Take extra care! Playa de Barrerios is on the eastern side of the River Foz. It's well sign-posted and there's easy parking by the Moby Dick restaurant.

39. Pantin

Pantin has some of the best beach break waves in Galicia making it a popular competition venue and also popular with local and visiting surfers. Facing northwest it picks up a lot of swell and will work throughout the tides. A channel on the right side of the beach, through the rocks, will take you into the best peaks. This part of the beach is the most popular and it does get crowded in summer and on weekends. Works from 1 - 10ft. Pantin is easy to find, though it's not marked on most maps. Parking is easy at the right hand side of the beach.
Water Quality: Excellent.

40. Valdoviño (Frouxeira)

A good spot to check when the other surrounding beaches are flat. The beach faces northwest and it's just the end part of a long, curving beach that extends for over 2kms. The waves at Valdoviño break over a sand and rock bottom, best surfed from low to mid tide up to 8ft.
Water Quality: Good.

41. Campelo

The waves here are excellent. Best at low tide they only work at high tide when there's a big swell. Offshores are from the NE. When it is big, a strong rip takes you into the impact zone. Being one of Galicia's best spots, and undoubtedly one of its most beautiful, this place can get crowded, especially in summer. Campelo is sign-posted from the main road. This leads to an unmarked crossroads. Turn left and within 500 mtrs there is another sign-post. This will direct you to Campelo where there is an area for parking.
Water Quality: Excellent.

42. Playa de San Jorge (Xorxe)

The southern end of Jorge's long, curving bay

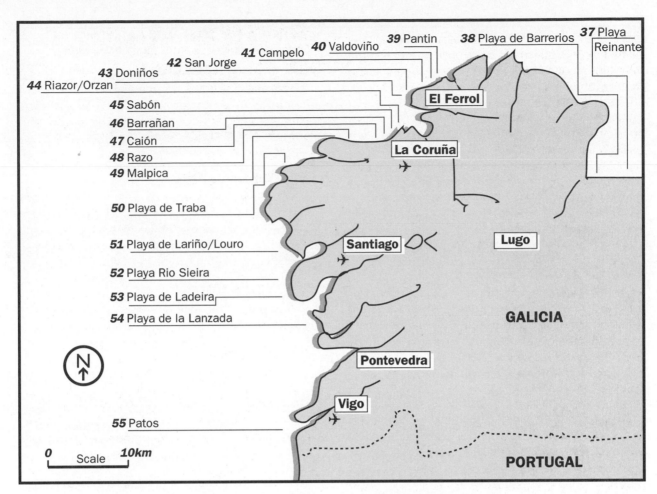

Map labels (north to south):

37 Playa Reinante
38 Playa de Barrerios
39 Pantin
40 Valdoviño
41 Campelo
42 San Jorge
43 Doniños
44 Riazor/Orzan
45 Sabón
46 Barrañan
47 Caión
48 Razo
49 Malpica
50 Playa de Traba
51 Playa de Lariño/Louro
52 Playa Rio Sieira
53 Playa de Ladeira
54 Playa de la Lanzada
55 Patos

El Ferrol
La Coruña
Santiago
Lugo
GALICIA
Pontevedra
Vigo
PORTUGAL

N

0   Scale   10km

faces northwest and is the place to head for when Doniños is blown out by S winds. From low to mid tide there can be an excellent, long, peeling lefthander breaking over a sand bottom, giving rides of up to 200mtrs. There's a useful channel near the rocks. The rest of the bay can also have some good beach break waves. These areas, especially the northern end, can be well worth checking out on big swells, when Doniños and the lefthander are closing out.

Water Quality: Good.

43. Doniños

Doniños beach provides good consistent tubey waves best surfed from low to mid tide. There are two access points – north and south, with the north end nearly always being the better spot. It's here that one might encounter a Galician crowd. Offshores are from the NE. There's parking at both ends of the beach.

Water Quality: Good.

44. La Coruña. (Riazor/Orzan)

There are a couple of mediocre breaks here; a lefthander in the middle of the beach which works best from 2 - 6ft at low tide, and a rock reef giving a righthander at mid tide. This is located to the left of the beach. Both Riazor and Orzan face north.

Water Quality: Can be badly polluted.

45. Sabón

The waves along this beach are highly regarded by Galician surfers. However, due to badly polluted waters we would only recommend surfing here if there's no good surf elsewhere. Sabón produces rideable waves when elsewhere is flat.

Water Quality: Gets very polluted.

46. Barrañan

A long north facing beach picking up most swells. Works on all tides up to 6ft. Watch out for rocks inconveniently placed along the beach.

Water Quality: Gets polluted from industries.

47. Caión (Cayon)

On lefthand side of Caión is a small beach which is relentlessly pounded by the Atlantic's N and NW swells. It's best from mid to high tide.

Water Quality: Good.

48. Playa de Razo

Faces north and gets some good, consistent beach break waves. It's surfable on all tides and one can always pick the best peak as there are no crowds here. It's exposed to N and NW winds which are common and often strong. Surfable up to 8ft.

Water Quality: Good.

49. Malpica

A beach break facing north, best at mid tide up to 6ft. Few crowds appear here, although in summer one may find several travelling surfers due to the good quality of the waves.

Water Quality: Good.

50. Playa de Traba

With a good clean NW swell and a S to E wind, one can find fun tubey surf here. There are a number of rough dirt tracks leading to the beach.
Water Quality: Good.

51. Playas de Louro/Lariño

Both beaches face SW and can have some fair rights and lefts breaking over a sand bottom. They work best on a W or SW swell and are only really surfable up to about 5ft. Louro is generally the more surfed of the two which can both be seen from the main road.
Water Quality: Good.

52. Playa Rio Sieira

A fairly consistent northwest facing break situated in some of Galicia's more remote and finest countryside. Crowds here are nonexistent and the quality of the water is as good as you'll find anywhere on Europe's Atlantic coast. Take the small sign-posted road just north of Xuno.
Water Quality: Excellent.

53. Playa de Ladeira

Faces southwest and is the place to head for when big NW swells are closing out the beaches on the north shore of this peninsula. Otherwise, this beach needs a W or SW swell. At its northern end a N wind is offshore and it's here that one can often find some good, small rights and lefts. The further down the beach you go, the bigger the waves get. Best at mid tide up to 6ft.
Water Quality: Good.

54. Playa de la Lanzada

This beautiful bay curves round from west to south and is well protected from N and NW winds. Unfortunately, this protection also blocks a large portion of the swell. Only a big NW swell, or a W or SW swell can make the waves worth a trip onto the peninsula. Best from mid to high tide from 2 - 5 ft. Very popular with windsurfers. Easy parking along the beach.
Water Quality: Excellent.

55. Patos

Patos beach, about 14kms south of Vigo, has some excellent rock reef breaks. On the lefthand side, a rocky point gives off some excellent rights and good lefts. In the centre of the beach another good righthander breaks over rock. Then, at the extreme right of the beach, a third good right breaks over another rocky ledge. The beach faces north and needs a big NW swell with S to W winds. The waves at the left hand side and in the middle are only safely surfed at high tide and the third break is best at mid tide. Another very popular windsurfing spot. Easy parking by the beach.
Water Quality: On the left hand side at the point of the rock, the water is usually somewhat polluted.

South West Andalucia

Surf Breaks 56 – 74
Marco Almaraz/Tarifa Wind System

56. La Cabañita

A hollow righthander breaking over a rock bottom. This wave is for experienced surfers only, due to the shallowness of the break. It can only be surfed at high tide and usually only breaks in winter. Located 4kms south of Cádiz.

57. Torre Gorda

A popular spot giving lefts and rights, 3kms south of La Cabañita.

58. Camposoto

Popular spot with San Fernando locals.

59. La Barrosa/Roche

A series of beaches giving reasonably consistent rights and lefts over a sand bottom. These beaches are very popular during the summer season.

60. Conil (Fuerte del Gallo)

A righthander of good quality breaks over a sand and rock bottom.

The village is called Conil, and the wave is called **Fuerte del Gallo**. Just off the N-340.

61. El Palmar

A popular surf beach with sand bottom rights and lefts that are best with a light E wind. For windsurfers, this is not one of the best places as it can be gusty but with a strong W wind it can be okay. Rips can be strong. Turn off towards the coast 1km from Vejer (60kms to Tarifa and 60kms to Cádiz).

62. Caños de Meca

Rock bottom lefts and rights, with the lefts better for both surfers and wave-sailors. Has good hollow sections and good walls for manoeuvres and when easterly winds are too strong for Tarifa, everybody heads here due to the lighter winds and better waves. If you're lucky enough to catch swell from the SW, then conditions can be similar to Hawaii. Gets very crowded in summer and be careful of rocks at low tide. Best winds for surfers are from the W and NW. Best sails for windsurfers 3.5m²-4m². It's 7kms from El Palmar, 50kms from Tarifa.

63. La Yerba Buena

A similar wave to Los Caños but it breaks right with more hollow waves, better for tubes. A wave for surfers set in nice surroundings. It's 7kms from Los Caños and 3kms from Barbate.

64. Bolonia

Four kms of beach which, like Caños, are popular when Tarifa is blowing strong easterly. Few dangers and good for medium to expert sailors.

65. Spot Secreto

Only good with strong E winds, which make fantastic waves. Ideal spot for expert sailors as the wind speed can reach up to 8 on the Beaufort scale – but it also pushes you out to sea. Never go here alone. This spot's speciality is the waves, careful of the rocks. Same road as to go to La Duna but continue along the road of Punta Paloma. Just before you reach a barrier, there's a road that goes off to the beach.

66. La Duna

A continuation of Los Porros and together these two beaches are the best spots to sail on an E wind. From June to September it's possible to sail every day and you can count on 30 days in a row with winds above force 5 Beaufort. A lake is formed in winter and spring that is ideal for beginners. 3m² – 4.5m² sails with an E wind, 4.5m² – 6m² with a W. Very crowded in summer.

67. Los Porros

Good with W winds and lots of fun if a strong E wind is blowing, creating good jumping waves. It's one of the places where the wind blows the strongest and these winds combined with the water depth help create big waves. It's not difficult to sail upwind on an easterly because of the current

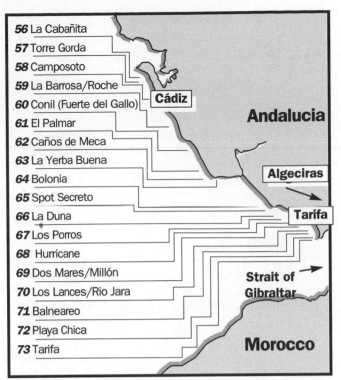

56	La Cabañita
57	Torre Gorda
58	Camposoto
59	La Barrosa/Roche
60	Conil (Fuerte del Gallo)
61	El Palmar
62	Caños de Meca
63	La Yerba Buena
64	Bolonia
65	Spot Secreto
66	La Duna
67	Los Porros
68	Hurricane
69	Dos Mares/Millón
70	Los Lances/Rio Jara
71	Balneareo
72	Playa Chica
73	Tarifa

Cádiz · Andalucia · Algeciras · Tarifa · Strait of Gibraltar · Morocco

heading in the direction of Tarifa. There's a break about 3 - 4kms east of here where great waves can be found. However, only go there in a group of experienced sailors and with a local, or you might end up in the Canaries! It's situated in front of 'Camping Torre de la Peña I,' and you can get there on a dirt road that goes to the beach.

68. Hurricane

Area from Millón to past the 'Camping Torre de la Peña I.' Same characteristics as Dos Mares - Millón but unfortunately some years the bottom can be rocky. However, it's convenient for those staying at the hotel or camping. Good waves and slalom for all levels, except when a strong E wind is blowing. Access through 'Camping Tarifa,' Hotel Hurricane and 'Camping Torre de la Peña I.'

69. Dos Mares, Millón

Site of the Regatta 'El Toro Andaluz.' This event in Easter has gained popularity over the last 10 years and has now been selected as Tarifa's second PBA contest site, making the Tarifa area the only place with two PBA events. One can sail here on all winds but the E wind blows lighter than in other spots making it a good one for beginners (don't go too far out from the beach). With W winds it's one of the best places for waves. Few dangers make it good for all levels. It's 4kms from Tarifa. Can get there on a road 1km from 'Camping Río Jara' or from Hotel Dos Mares, or from the entrance of Hotel Millón.

70. Los Lances, Río Jara

Almost 4kms of beach good for all levels of sailing. Good with E winds for speed sailing and, when there's a good swell to go with it, it's a fantastic place for wave-sailing. Good conditions for surfing are when there's a S swell. Bjorn Dunkerbeck beat the world speed record here on open sea in July 1991. It's 2kms from Tarifa. Take the lane going off at the end of the village or by the football stadium.

71. Balneareo

E winds are good for wave-sailing here. Be careful – when the wind comes from the land, it blows you into the strait, even when the sea is flat. W and S winds make this spot a favourite place for locals, especially in winter. Best for expert sailors, as there's danger of the offshore winds and some rocks at the foot of the beach. Good for surfers with a S or W swell with a light E wind. Access is through the village in the direction of Tarifa and the spot is on the right side of the island.

72. Playa Chica

Sailing is only possible here with an E wind and when it blows, it blows the strongest here. For those who like to get the heart pumping, sailing past the island is the thing to do. Strong currents (which generally go W – E), strong winds and one of the world's busiest stretches of water make it suitable for experienced sailors only. Can also have good sized waves in winter. Access is same as for Balneareo but to the left. Situated to the right of the port.

73. Tarifa

At the beginning of the 80's the first wave sailors began to arrive here from all over Europe looking for wind. The 14km straits funnel winds between Europe and Africa, especially those from the E, which blow very strong, normally between 5-8 on the Beaufort scale. This reliability has made it possible for ten windsurf shops and seven manufacturers of custom boards to set up here, making these the most exportable product in Tarifa. The combination of wind, waves and the night life in summer make holidays in Tarifa exhausting but great fun.

TRAVELLING AROUND

Area Code: Barcelona – 93
Gerona – 972
Tourist Office: Gran Vía de las Cortes, Catalanas, 658, 08010 Barcelona
Tel: 93 325 5829,
Rambla Llibertat, 1, 17004 Gerona
Tel: 972 202 679
Airport: Barcelona – Tel: 93 379 2454
Railway Station: Barcelona – Tel: 93 322 4142

Cataluña, Costa Brava

Cataluña (and specifically the Costa Brava) is an extremly popular windsurfing location. Agreeable temperatures both in the water and on land are common all year round (12°C minimum in the water) and the medium to strong winds are ideal to start learning funboarding. Some spots like **Surfbreak** have good waves. Others like at **Rosas** where the sea is calm, are great for practising speed sailing There are actually only two places that are good for surfing – **Pals** and **Castelldefels**. Many beaches along the Costa Brava are clean and well-cared-for in spring and summer. It's rare at this time of the year for a day to pass without winds reaching up to 10 knots and you will always find a group of windsurfers with whom to sail.

When you are tired of sailing, the restaurants are excellent and the night life thrives throughout the year. In winter and spring, the ski and snowboarding slopes are open, and are only 40 minutes away by car.

Access to the rest of Europe is easy along the A17 Mediterranean motorway and travelling from spot to spot is straight forward with newly built roads connecting them.

Jordi Fraguas/Surfbreak Test Centre

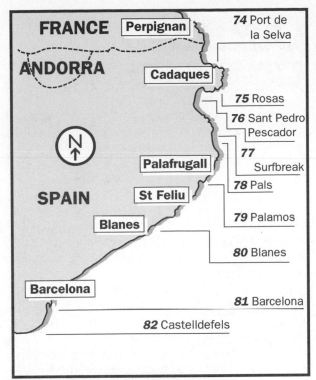

Surf Breaks 74 – 82
Jordi Fraguas/Surfbreak Test Centre

74. Port de la Selva

A small bay facing north by the border of La Jonquera. The winds blow strongly from the N, from force 4 - 10. There are big waves here that are ideal for wave-jumping but it's dangerous over the rocky bottom. Only for experts. Quiet atmosphere.

Water Quality: Beach and water okay.

75. Rosas

A bay facing southeast and that is excellent with all winds (magnificent regatta site). Ideal for all sailors. It's a sure bet that the winds from the southerly quadrant reach 10 knots minimum. Small waves with a N wind (offshore) are perfect for speed sailing. Good camping sites and night life.

Water Quality: Beach and water okay.

76. Sant Pedro Pescador

In the middle of "Bahía de Rosas" (Rosas Bay), at the mouth of the River Fluvia, the N winds come diagonally and allow one to jump small waves up to 1mtr. The thermal winds are excellent. A 5km beach is bordered by camping sites.

77. Surfbreak

In Torroella de Montgrí, in front of 'Camping Delfin Verde' in the middle of the bay of Pals, there are 9kms of fine sand beach. Due to its location, all winds come in, ranging from 15 - 90 knots, with waves from 1 - 3 mtrs that are ideal for wave-jumping and for surfing. The Tramontana wind blows throughout the winter and spring while there are thermals up to force 7 (Beaufort) in summer and autumn. Great night atmosphere and a windsurfing regatta scene happens every weekend.

Water Quality: Beach & water have EEC Blue Flag.

78. Pals

For lovers of big waves, this beach gets winds from the N (Gregal or Tramontana). It's right beside Surfbreak and is an excellent regatta site. Winds from the S reach force 3-6. One can also surf here.

Water Quality: Beach and water okay.

79. Palamos

A fishing population and a tourist spot. Ideal for sailing with winds from the S or thermals in the summer. The winds from the N are offshore. Excellent site for slalom regattas and course races. Winds reach from force 2 - 7 (Beaufort). Lots of night life being only 4kms from Playa de Aro.

80. Blanes

In the town furthest south in the Costa Brava, one sails next to La Pineda. Thermal and S winds reach force 2 - 5 (Beaufort), and at the mouth of the River Tordera there is a good wave-sailing break up to 1mtr. When in other places the wind is too much for you, come to Blanes to sail moderate conditions.

81. Barcelona

With the world's top sailors decending on Barcelona this summer (1992) for the Olympic sailing and windsurfing, a recent visit by Patrick Harty on behalf of the Clean Water Initiative has confirmed the worst fears of many of the sailing fraternity – he found results that indicate all will not be plain sailing this summer!

"Four out of six tests failed to comply with even the imperitive EC standards for faecal coliforms. The aesthetic quality of the water, the sheer number of panty-liners and hypodermic syringes on the beaches, along with the overwhelming smell, were all indicators of gross polution," said Patrick. For test results see page 179.

82. Castelldefels

Situated to the south of the Barcelona airport, windsurfers gather in front of the Club Naútico to sail with winds from the SW or E. A nice break is formed some 50 - 75 mtrs from the shore and it's perfect to wave-jump and to surf. Surfing is best close to the break water at Port Ginesta. Good vibes.

THE CANARY ISLANDS

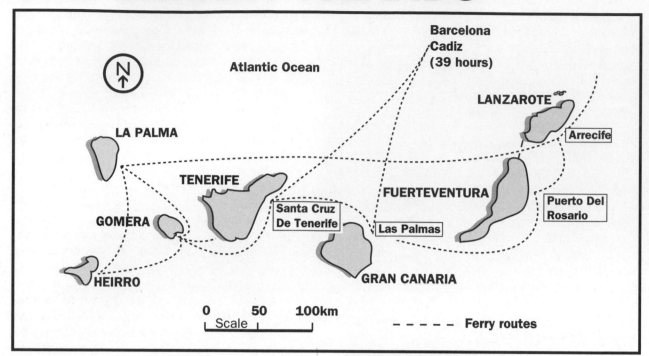

Language: Spanish
Currency: Peseta (Ptas)
Total Population: 1,135,000

THE LAND

The Canaries are a volcanic chain encompassing 7 main islands, lying at a latitude of 28°N and influenced most by the Atlantic Ocean. The Canary Islands have been called the 'fortunate islands' due to the mild, consistent climate. Temperatures range from 18°C to 24°C in winter and 24°C to 32°C in summer. Rainfall is low, especially on Lanzarote and Fuerteventura.

The local landscapes directly influence their respective climates. Mount Teide (3718mtrs) in Tenerife is snow capped in winter and often shrouded in mist. At the same time the south can be sunny (hence its popularity) and the north can be raining. This explains the desert-like landscape in the south and the much greener, luxuriant landscape in the north. Gran Canaria follows the same pattern, dry and arid in the south and wetter and greener in the north. Fuerteventura is desert-like from top to bottom with very little rain. Lanzarote is similar to Fuerteventura but receives some rain and consequently has a little vegetation.

Prevailing winds are from the NE to NW. These winds are occasionally interrupted by the dust-laden Sirocco, which blows over from Africa during winter in the Sahara. The Sirocco is not loved by tourists but is welcomed by surfers and windsurfers for the good surf conditions it brings to the Canary Islands west-facing breaks. The winds that blow over the Canaries keep the air feeling fresh even on the hottest of days. The sun's intensity can go unnoticed, especially in the water.

THE PEOPLE

The earliest inhabitants of the islands are believed to be the aboriginal Guanches but how they got there is open to debate. The most popular theory is that they were descended from the Berbers of North West Africa. History has left us little of the Guanches due to the ravages of colonialism. In the 13th and 14th century Portuguese, French, Genoese and Majorcan navigators visited the islands and at first were welcomed. Things began to change in 1402 and after about a hundred years of bloody warring, the Guanches were virtually wiped out. The Spanish had colonised the islands.

Over the years the Canaries established themselves as a major staging post between Europe and the Americas. Columbus sailed from Gran Canaria on his voyage of discovery to America in 1492. Cargo and passengers were plagued by pirates from many countries, including the English, the Dutch and the Moors. In 1797 Lord Nelson challenged the Spanish sovereignty but was defeated, lost an arm, and 226 of his men were killed.

Since then, tourists have been the only real invading force. English, German, Scandinavian, French and Spanish people flock to the islands on various package deals, especially in winter when the more northerly European countries get very cold. They come for the sun, sea and surf. Tourism is by far the biggest money earner across the islands now, with purpose built towns such as Playa del Inglés or Playa Las Americas offering package deals to hell. While elements of traditional society remain, many aspects of Canarian culture are facing pressures, not always compensated for by the benefits of the tourist trade.

THE SURF

The Hawaii of the Atlantic is the term most used by surfers when talking about the Canary Islands. In this chapter there's detailed information on 4 of the islands. Lanzarote and Fuerteventura are unquestionably better surf destinations than Tenerife and Gran Canaria but all the islands are very popular and they all receive good waves.

Memories of surf trips to the Canaries will conjure up images of gnarly, uneven, lava reefs, hollow waves and a power comparable to just about anywhere in the world. Hot, sunny days surfing in board shorts or a short wetsuit are also enticing aspects of Canarian surf. Winter is always the best season and consistent swells and good weather come at an affordable price. Many surfers and windsurfers hole up here for two or three months of the year before heading back home for spring surf. Water temperatures vary little throughout the year, remaining at a respectable 18°C in winter and 22°C in summer. A short suit will keep you comfortable most of the year although many people surf in a steamer on winter mornings.

Crowds will always be a talking point when discussing Canarian surf. On Gran Canaria and Tenerife the problems have led to a heavy 'locals only' attitude which, although partially understandable, should never have reached its present stage. Rip-offs and 'aggro' are an ugly, unnecessary side of surfing which is detrimental to the activity in every way. Possible explanations for this are the vast numbers of surf-hungry foreigners who probably have not shown enough respect to the locals for whom these breaks are home. A new attitude on both sides is the best hope of visiting these places as friends rather than enemies. Lanzarote is not as bad, although crowding is getting steadily worse, but less locals and more breaks ease the situation. Fuerteventura is the newest and least populated surf island in the Canaries. There definitely are still breaks that go unridden on all the islands.

WATER QUALITY

The Canary Islands are clean compared to most of Europe. Most towns discharge into the sea but outlet pipe locations vary and faecal coliform levels are low at most breaks. Avoid the tourist traps and main towns and you will have no problems. Unfortunately sea-borne flotsam, litter and remnants of oil spills are in evidence at various points around the coastline, which is disturbing but not yet severe. Oil spills are generally thought to come from tankers flushing and cleaning their tanks after leaving the refinery in Tenerife. New oil is seen all the time on the beaches. An environmental pressure group, **Associación para la Defensa del Surf (ADES)** – have supplied information on the breaks on Tenerife. Their formation was another spontaneous attempt to increase awareness of the problems of coastal development.

TRAVELLING AROUND

Although airfares and accommodation are cheap, food can be expensive. Camping is probably the cheapest way to stay there, though it's not encouraged by the authorities. Self-catering accommodation is freely available and is often most competitive as part of a package deal. Local foods include traditional Spanish standards; paella, tapas etc.

Spain's health agreements with other nations are applicable (see *Spain: Health and Living*). Naturally comprehensive health/travel insurance will save many headaches in the event of any serious injury in the surf or on the roads. Often it's possible to get insurance in a package deal.

FLIGHTS: There are international airports on Gran Canaria, Tenerife, Lanzarote and Fuerteventura. The cheapest way to get there is unquestionably via London and prices can be ludicrously low if you're prepared to travel at short notice (see London).

AUTO'S: Renting a car is just about obligatory but prices can vary considerably. Europeans may find that their national drivers license okay, otherwise an international licence is required.

FERRIES: The Canaries are serviced by a 'Transmed' car/passenger ferry that leaves the Spanish mainland from Cádiz and takes approximately 39 hours. One ferry leaves every two days in summer, one per week in winter. The boats are described as floating hotels with swimming pools, bars, sports facilities, cinema etc. The service runs Cádiz – Santa Cruz de Tenerife, Las Palmas de Gran Canaria and Arrecife (Lanzarote). They also operate inter-island vehicular and passenger ferries and jetfoils between all the main islands For more information contact:

UK	Tel: 071 499 6731
Cádiz	Tel: 284 350
Madrid	Tel: 456 0007
Gran Canaria	Tel: 260 070
Tenerife	Tel: 287 850

Telephones: From the Canaries out – first dial 07, follow with country and area code,and your number. To phone the Canaries dial your international access code where you are making the call from, then 34, then 28 (for Lanzarote, Gran Canaria and Fuerteventura), or 22 (for Tenerife, Heirro, Gomera and La Palma), follow this with your intended six digit number. Operator – 003

EMBASSIES & CONSULATES:
British Consulate
Alfredo, L.Jones 33
Las Palmas de Gran Canaria
Tel: 272508
American Consulate
Alfredo Primo de Rivera 5
Las Palmas de Gran Canaria
Tel: 271259

Lanzarote

Population: 50,000
Capital: Arrecife (30,000)
Area: 806 km²
Highest Point: 671 mtrs, Peñas de Chache

This astonishing union of fire and water is the easternmost in the Canarian archipelago and looks, to all intents and purposes, like the surface of the moon.

A canal called El Rio (The River) separates Lanzarote, on the north bank, from the island of La Graciosa (The Graceful One). To the south the 10km wide strait of Bocaina separates it from Fuerteventura. The islands of La Graciosa, Montaña Clara and the farthest one, Alegranza, all fall under its jurisdiction. A large part of the island is covered with a layer of ash and lava called **malpais**, which, together with the countless volcanic cones, represent the predomminant features of its landscape.

Lanzarote lives on fishing and horticultural produce, but by far the biggest industry is tourism and related service industries.

The first Guanche inhabitants called it 'Tite-Roy-Gatra.' To Europeans it was first known as Capraria or Caprasia (Goat Island) though its present name was bestowed on it in 1320 by Genoese navigator Lanzarotto Malocello. The original capital, San Miguel de Teguise, was burned by Algerian pirates in 1586. Ten years later, English corsairs sacked it when it had hardly risen from the ashes. In 1618 Barbary pirates fell on the island and again San Miguel de Teguise was fuel for flames. Many of its inhabitants were murdered, a fortunate few took refuge in Cueva de los Verdes.

In 1730 eruptions occurred in the Timanfaya massif. 30 craters poured a 10mtr layer of lava over ten villages and 200sq km of the most fertile land. The eruptions continued until 1736. A long period of volcanic activity followed till 1824 when three more cones appeared within as many months. Erosion has hardly had time to work on the landscape and only a few lichens survive on barely cold lava.

THE SURF

Lanzarote has been surfed regularly for at least a decade by surfers and windsurfers from many countries, and has now become one of the hottest spots in Europe to find powerful, consistent surf.

The best waves on the island are generally to be found in the north with both coasts hosting classic reefs offering good surf in a variety of conditions. Swells from the N to W produce waves on the west coast and islands. N swells strike the east coast from Playa de la Canteria in the north to Arrieta further south. S swells, most common in summer can produce good waves around the south and east coasts, although it's the winter N and W swells that have built Lanzarote's reputation amongst the surfing community world wide. Virtually without exception, the best waves are shallow lava reef breaks. Playa Famara can produce excellent conditions but these pale against the power of the reefs. The La Santa area is the most impressive and consistent with all N and W swells surfable somewhere, given correct winds.

When the west coast is onshore or badly cross-shore, the east coast breaks can go off and the reefs north of Playa de La Garita can be just as challenging as the west coast breaks. At Costa Teguise, a resort complex has been developed which provides many facilities for windsurfers/wave-jumpers and windless days are surprisingly few. Whilst we have detailed most breaks where access is possible by road, there's no doubt that more

TRAVELLING AROUND

Most travelling surfers will arrive at the national and international Aeropuerto de Lanzarote at Arrecife, 6kms south of Arrecife. Public transport is virtually non-existent. There are several rental companies at each arrival point and others (usually cheaper) in the towns - with prices generally negotiable. Roof racks are usually available but a pair of soft racks would be a valuable back up. If you're travelling spontaneously you will find tourist apartments, especially at off peak times. We encountered no difficulty when camping at La Santa, San Juan, etc., other than that presented by hard ground and fear of rip-offs.

Rental Cars: Best company we found was Autos Cabrera Medina; they have offices at the airport, Playa Blanca (500mtrs from the ferry terminal) and in Costa Teguise.

Bus Services: Calle Garcia Escamez, 71. Tel: 81 15 46. This can be found on the main road to San Bartolomé to the NW of town. The service is infrequent and destinations are limited, but are rapidly improving.

Ferry Services: The Alisur line: 6 daily services between Corralejo (Fuerteventura) and Playa Blanca, 45 mins and a single fare costs approximately 1500 ptas – or vehicle and two passengers, 5,500 ptas. Ferry Betancuria is a more modern but less frequent and more expensive competitor servicing the same route. Trans Med routes to Tenerife and Gran Canaria are serviced at least twice weekly, usually overnight.

Tourist Office:
Parque Municipal, Arrecife.

National Police:
Tel: 81 23 50/54.

Hospital: Hospital Juan de Quesada, Arrecife. Tel: 81 05 10.

Clinica: Gonzalez Medina, Garcia Escamez, Arrecife.
Tel: 81 13 24.

surfable reefs exist, but these would be reached either by boat, 4wd vehicle – or by the keen walker. Lanzarote can hold big waves! Surf of up to 15ft has been occasionally ridden. Big boards are common here – as are broken boards.

The majority of foreign surfers are English, with a complement of Kiwis, Australians, Americans, Scandinavians and Germans. There's a strong local surfing population which includes a high proportion of body boarders who keep largely to themselves. Whilst the spirit of 'localism' is strong here, it hasn't led to the behaviour seen on other Canary Islands. The choice remains with the individual whether or not to foster good relations in the water and on the land, but may we state what should be obvious to 'aware' people, that only by adopting a relaxed attitude to wave selection can surfing remain an enjoyable sport. Especially when at foreign breaks, you should be prepared to sacrifice a percentage of waves in order to show respect to a hierarchy which already exists and which will continue to do so after you leave.

Surf Breaks 1 – 20

Vaughan Smith/Midnight Hour Surf Charter

1. Playa del Janubio (Salt Flats)

The southern-most of the known surf locations on the west coast. A kilometre of black sand beach faces southwest in front of the Janubio salt flats. Waves break on the beach and on reefs at the northern end of the bay. Park at either end of the beach.

2. El Golfo

The outside reefs at the town of El Golfo can produce some tubey righthand waves. They face northwest and are surfed less frequently than the other breaks on the island, but can prove excellent without the crowd problems. The reefs are visible from the town.

La Santa & Famara Area

The stretch of coastline running from the village of La Santa to the northern tip of Playa Famara, must rate as one of the best wave locations in

Europe. It picks up all N and W swells and offers a variety of breaks facing in numerous directions. There is a good beach break for beginners, a number of easily accessible world class reefs combined with the strong smell of undiscovered surf.

One can find accommodation at the bungalows of Famara, possibly in La Santa village and also at the La Santa Sports complex next to La Isleta, the peninsula that holds **Morro Negro** and **Boca del Abajo**. Many people camp adjacent to Morro Negro in a levelled off site overlooking the break. Also at **San Juan**. Security, however, is a problem – be warned.

A rough dirt road connects La Santa with Famara. It is difficult to give directions as the road is almost indistinguishable from the ground around, and there are several dead end and deceptive turn-offs. It pays not to be in a hurry.

3. Village Left

A short sucky lefthand reef breaking close to the shore in front of the village of La Santa. Optimum swell is from the W to NW with accompanying S to E winds. Being a town break, it does get crowded quickly. From the village of La Santa, walk to the harbour.

4. La Santa Left

Located just north of La Santa and directly across the bay from Morro Negro, La Santa Left is rapidly gaining fame as one of the best lefts in Europe. A thick lipped tube breaks over exposed rock at low tide, but as the water covers it, the reef turns on the goods – fast, sucky and consistent. It collects the maximum amount of swell and is often the only break working on the island when the wind is in the northern quarter and the other west coast spots are onshore. A righthander which is always shorter is often rideable. The break is visible from the main road.

5. Morro Negro (La Santa Right)

One of Europe's finest waves, a serious righthand reef breaking on the south end of 'La Isleta.' The reef can hold big swells and has been ridden up to 15ft. It generally has three sections which work independently, though on a good day all can connect up giving long, powerful rides.

Not as renowned for its tubes as other breaks on the island, nonetheless it's one of the biggest draw cards in the Canarian archipelago, at its best when the swell is N to NW at mid tide (though it breaks on all tides depending on the swell direction). The best winds are from E – S. Getting in and out can be a difficult exercise, some of the locals jump off the end of the point straight out the back, whilst others are content to paddle around the break from the inside section. Morro Negro breaks on the southern side of La Isleta.

6. Boca Del Abajo

A lefthand reef on the northern tip of La Isleta which sucks off the sea bottom and breaks into a calm, deeper bay. Offshore is from the S to E. The wave is excellent to 10ft plus, and even when the swell is big, the paddle out remains relatively easy. The left works like a point giving long, fast and hollow waves on all tides. Follow the road around La Isleta and you will definitely see it if it's working.

7. Chicken Left (Caleta del Caballo)

A lefthand reef located on the left hand side of the bay breaking in shallow water on a N or NW swell and S to SW winds. Best at high tide. The last dirt road heading east on the road from La Santa village to La Santa Sports Complex, leads to the small village of Caleta del Caballo.

8. Ghost Town (Caleta Del Caballo)

A spectacular peak breaks in the bay to the right of the town of Caballo when other breaks are 2mtrs+. Has a reputation as one of the Canaries foremost big wave breaks. Best at low tide, offshores from the SW.

9. Outside Reef (Caleta del Caballo)

A bombora breaks 500mtrs out to sea when the swell is max N, from 4 – 5mtrs and up. We've no confirmed accounts of anyone surfing it – very little in the way of real information on it exists. It could be the big wave of the Canaries, it could be a myth.

10. San Juan

A killer left and a shorter, less consistent right. Can be surfed through the tide though it's best at low, with a N or NW swell. Offshores are S to SW – a valuable backstop when La Santa can be cross shore. San Juan is a powerful wave which can have swell when other breaks are too small to surf. 1km after the village of La Caleta de Famara, an unmarked dirt road leads to the coast just before the waves. Paddle out to the break to the west of the peak in the channel.

11. La Caleta de Famara

A lefthand reef in front of the town visible from several points, produces more dredgy lefthanders best surfed between 1 and 3mtrs in a S to SE wind. Paddle out from the breakwater. Best at high tide.

12. Playa de Famara

A crescent-shaped bay facing from north-northwest. Three distinct waves. Firstly, the **beach break** gets wicked, without hassles of shallow reefs and intense crowd scenes. Generally the north end has bigger swell but to get there you have to drive up the side of the mountain range (which shelters it from the NE winds) before descending again to the coast. This beach is one of Lanzarote's best and most popular windsurfing spots especially in Sirocco conditions.

Also located at the north end of the bay is a reef which breaks a couple hundred metres to the south west of rocks called **Las Bajas** – quite a long paddle out to sea but obviously worth it if conditions are right. The break is visible from the road north of the beach and it's best at low tide. It's a dangerous wave that should only be attempted by experienced surfers.

A **shipwreck** is clearly visible from the shore at the south end of the bay. Sand bars form off either side depending on recent storms, and from mid to high tide can produce good waves. Obvious caution should be exercised when dealing with wrecks.

13. Graciosa Island

Graciosa covers an area of 42km² and is separated from Lanzarote by a 1km stretch of water called the 'Strait of El Rio.' The island is populated by about 800 people who rely on fishing and increasingly, tourism, for their livelihood. Graciosa is an ideal place to get away from the world and catch some empty waves. The coastline has many deserted white sandy beaches and around these beaches unridden reefs await the adventurous. The

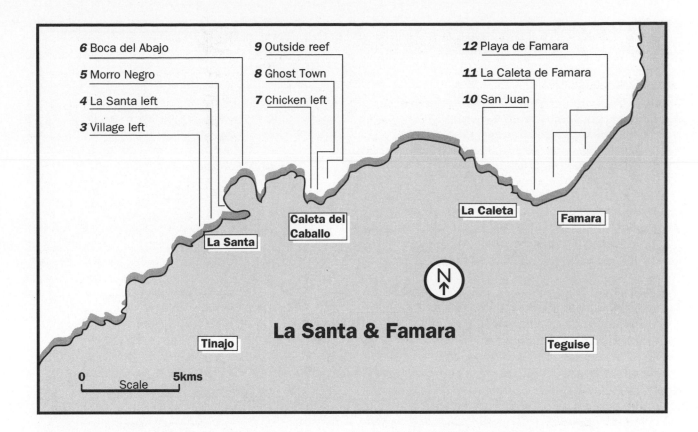

Map labels:

6 Boca del Abajo
5 Morro Negro
4 La Santa left
3 Village left
9 Outside reef
8 Ghost Town
7 Chicken left
12 Playa de Famara
11 La Caleta de Famara
10 San Juan

La Santa
Caleta del Caballo
La Caleta
Famara

Tinajo
La Santa & Famara
Teguise

N

0 Scale 5kms

main town is Caleta del Sabo where the ferry arrives from Orzola. There are places to stay, bars, restaurants, a supermarket, a post office, taxis and a disco (good on weekends). The island doesn't like a lot of wind due to its flatness. The ferry leaves in the morning from Orzola in the northern end of Lanzarote. The price is 1200 ptas. Before deciding whether a visit to Graciosa is worthwhile, a trip to Mirador del Rio (Viewpoint of the River) in the northern mountains of Lanzarote is a good idea. From here there is an excellent view of the island.

14. Playa de la Cantería

1,500ft below the cliffs of Mirador del Rio, at the extreme north of the island there is a good lefthand reef break, which is perhaps the most exposed to a N swell. It gets maximum possible protection from winds from the S or W. The location is breathtaking – the cliffs loom straight out of the ocean, dwarfing everything else. Works best at high tide. Take the dirt road from the village of Orzola.

15. Jameos del Agua

The northernmost in a string of lefthand reefs and points. They work in a northerly swell with a wind from SW to NW. S swells do break here in summer with accompanying N trade winds. The two peaks can either connect or close out depending on the conditions. The outside reef is a favourite amongst wave-jumpers and one will sometimes find good sailors practising here. Works on all tides. Located north of the car park at Jameos del Agua.

16. Punta Usaje (Los Caletones)

A shallow lefthand point break half a kilometer south of Jameos del Agua breaking close to the shore. It works only on a big N swell. NW winds are offshore and it's best from mid to high tide. A dirt track leads to the break from the car park at Jameos del Agua.

17. Los Picachos, Espinos (Punta de Mujeres)

Yet another shallow lefthand reef break just south of the village, which works in N and S swells. It faces east southeast and works best in a W or NW wind at high tide. Located off the highway south of the village. Park where possible.

18. Arrieta

There are a few reefs facing E–SE at the town of Arrieta, all are invariably very sucky, very shallow and very dangerous.

19. Playa de la Garita

At the south edge of the town of Arrieta there's a small sand beach with a rocky left point. Lefts and rights provide a beginners break which can get very good. Easterly winds are offshore, best at low tide. Waves are under threat due to the construction of a pier and beach front/promenade area.

20. Costa Teguise

Major sailing resort on Lanzarote geared mainly towards flat water sailing – not too much swell gets in here. Full facilities include shops, bars restaurants, etc, and though designed for sailors, package deals including accommodation often attract many other different types of people here (including girls!)

Fuerteventura

Population: 30,000
Capital: Puerto del Rosario (15,000)
Area: 2020 km²
Highest Point: 807 mtrs, Pico de Zarza

Fuerteventura is the second largest island in the Canary group located only 90km from the coast of Africa. It is commonly known as 'Isla de Soledad' (island of solitude) and has more km's of sand beaches than any of the other Canarian islands. Consequently there are several large scale tourist developments on the island, restricted mainly to the east coast which receives less swell. The capital hosts the main port and the international airport at Los Estanions.

Fuerteventura's existence is a result of intense volcanic activity approximately 12 million years ago. Nowadays the island is almost devoid of trees except for occasional planted palms, small desert plants and cacti.

The lack of high mountains accounts for the extremely low rainfall and also makes Fuerteventura a great windsurfing location – winds pass over the island with little interference. Volcanic peaks and strange shattered cones dot the landscape in the centre of the island, funnelling breezes – whilst in the south and east, desert like sands and long beaches create a shifting landscape.

Fuerteventura had already been mapped when early in the 15th century Jean de Bethencourt began his conquest from Lanzarote. The two ruling tribes of 'Maxorato' and 'Jandia' were subdued and the two kings, Guize and Ayoze, baptised. The Christian name for the island became Forte Adventure. Pirates made regular, plundering visits here throughout its history, as they also did on Lanzarote.

The island folk have existed since then on horticulture and fishing. The fishing grounds are bountiful and common fish are shark, swordfish, tunny, durada, corra, sea bass, sea dace, eels, octopus and crabs.

Obvious problems present themselves to the farmers here; the Sirocco blows hard and soil and water are scarce, and water is a precious resource as it is on Lanzarote, desalinated water is drinkable but bottled water is recommended.

Corralejo in the north has always been an important port and is now home to a small but flourishing tourist industry. Other main tourist resorts are at Flag Beach and Sotavento.

THE SURF

Fuerteventura is a large island. Many beaches remain almost deserted and the island rates as one of the best places in Europe to surf heavy, un-crowded waves. The north and west coasts and Lobos Island are the main surf areas, with the eastern and southern shores offering better windsurfing and swimming conditions. Access to the north coast is easy, a track runs for 20kms alongside volcanic reefs which pick up all N swell.

TRAVELLING AROUND

Accommodation on the island is similar to Lanzarote...tourist villas can be rented either in a package with air fares or they can be negotiated on the spot. The package deal is once again often the cheapest. Various options present themselves in Corralejo if you arrive with nothing booked. Signs advertise places to rent, travel agents have information and various of the surf shops might be able to point you in the right direction. Camping is again similar to Lanzarote. Though not encouraged, it is probably safer. Soft ground is impossible to find...that leaves the beach, the car or a good air mattress.

There are several good restaurants, supermarkets, patisseries and cafés in Corralejo so it's an easy place to look after yourself, though once again not extremely cheap. The fish restaurant overlooking the harbour is a winner.

Airports: Los Estancos International Airport is located 6km south of Puerto del Rosario.

Rental Cars: Most surfers will arrive at either Puerto de Corralejo or Puerto del Rosario. The best deals in rental cars appear to be around Corralejo though getting there from further south can be tricky.

Driving/Roads: The road which runs the length of the island and some of the peripheral routes are good with next to no traffic, but when the surface deteriorates as on most of the rest of the roads, then the definition of 'road' is explored. With a 4wd vehicle, travel is relatively easy though road signs and facilities are few and far between. This is a large island with few petrol stations, although a 24 hour filling station south of Antigua on the GC610 has recently opened.

Buses: The bus station in Puerto del Rosario is on Calle Alfonso XII, 25.
Tel: 85 09 51.
The service is hardly used by tourists due to its infrequency.

Ferry Routes: There are two main ports - Puerto del Rosario and Corralejo: Both hydrofoils and ferries connect Fuerteventura with other Canarian islands and the mainland (as per Lanzarote).

Tourist Office: Ministerio de Trabajo, Avenida General Franco, Puerto del Rosario (8.30-3.00).

Hospital and Medical services: The hospital is on the southern edge of town, on the main road to the airport.
Hospital, Carretera General al Aeropuerto. Tel: 85 03 12
Ambulance, Puerto del Rosario. Tel: 85 03 12

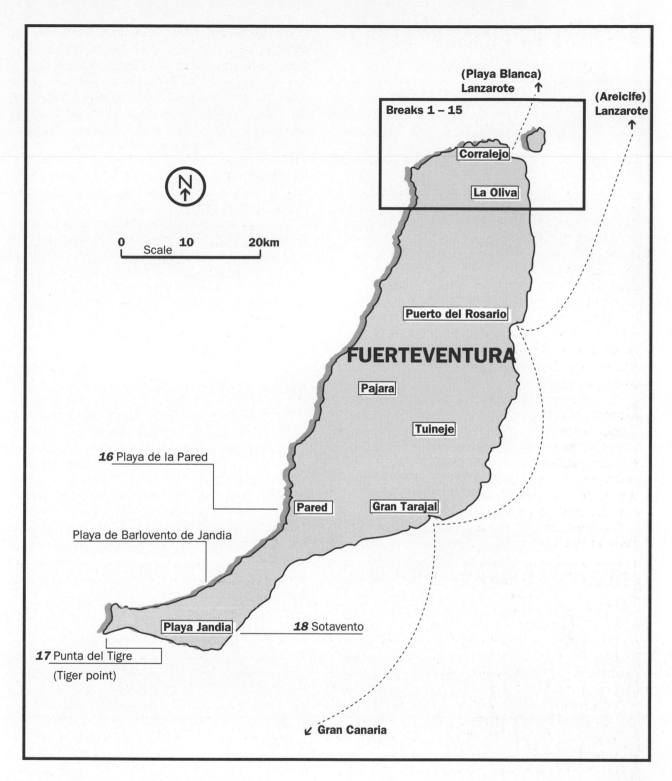

(Playa Blanca)
Lanzarote ↑

(Areicife)
Lanzarote ↑

Breaks 1 – 15

Corralejo

La Oliva

Puerto del Rosario

FUERTEVENTURA

Pajara

Tuineje

16 Playa de la Pared

Pared

Gran Tarajal

Playa de Barlovento de Jandia

Playa Jandia

18 Sotavento

17 Punta del Tigre
(Tiger point)

↙ Gran Canaria

The west coast receives masses of swell but access is extremely restricted. Between Corralejo and Sotavento miles and miles of reefs with occasional sandy beaches form a coastline that has little protection from Atlantic swells. Because of its desolate nature and wild seas, only a few fishing villages punctuate its length. Roads to the coast are few and even 4wd vehicles experience difficulties.

The Jandia Peninsula receives heaps of swell and there is still tremendous undiscovered potential in the south of the island. The sandy beaches which line its eastern shores are beautiful, if a little empty, but the water is turquoise blue and crowds are not commonplace around most of the surf spots – the best waves break miles from most tourist activity. Playa de Sotavento is the most popular centre and can be a good place to base yourself.

All the coasts are regularly windsurfed and Fuerteventura is a great place for both sailing and spectating because as the wind moves around the compass, sailors can follow the coast to find the wind direction they desire.

Various organisations cater to those members of the windsurfing fraternity without travelling equipment and more information can be obtained from Nouveau Monde in France or in the UK.

Surf Breaks 1 – 17

1. Glass Beach, Tres Islas, Flag Beach

Saharan sands blown across from Africa by the Sirocco winds have deposited themselves along the east coast of Fuerteventura. There are many kilometres of idyllic beaches, some visible and accessible from the main road, others are hidden away and can only be reached by 4wd or by foot. The extensive sand dunes that run south of Corralejo for almost 6kms have become a nature reserve and the coast has become a popular windsurfing centre. Normally the seas are calm here so wave riding is only possible on a big N or S swell. For the rest of the time it's a busy sailing location with many facilities.

2. Rocky Point

Faces north and is one of Fuerteventura's most popular wave spots. Rights break in a decent sized N or NW swell best from mid to high tide. When the breaks further north start closing out then Rocky Point starts to suffer from crowding, from both surfers and wave-jumpers. Located to the south of Corralejo's beaches, it's easily seen from town.

3. Los Lobos

The righthander breaking along the south east coast of Lobos is one of Europe's best waves. Los Lobos is a small volcanic island (6.5km²) named after the seals (lobos marinas) who used to feed in the fish rich waters that surround it. With a N or NW swell and S or E winds, this wave can provide 400 metre rides with fast walling sections and clean tubes. On a big swell (10ft+) the wave can clearly be seen from Fuerteventura as it powers its way around the island. The boat to the island is caught from Corralejo, by the town pier. It leaves at about 10am or when the boat is full and returns at 4pm. Cost is 1200ptas (1992). From the ferry it's a walk west. Take liquid as it can get hot and dusty.

4. El Muelle (Harbour Wall)

Behind the harbour wall in Corralejo breaks a deservedly popular lefthander. Many of the locals learnt to surf at this break due to its proximity to Corralejo. A N swell with a S or SW wind will provide long rides in surf from 2 - 12ft. All tides are surfable though low tide is preferred. Parking is possible near the harbour wall.

5. Shooting Gallery

A lefthand reef break facing northeast. Low tide at Shooting Gallery is hollow, shallow and fast. The higher the tide gets, the easier it becomes to ride. A popular wave jumping and boogie boarding spot which can get crowded. On a good swell a righthander can also be surfed. Shooting Gallery is the first break along the northern track. Take a right turn by a small power station.

6. Henarossa

Another hollow lefthand reef break located about 1km further along from Shooting Gallery. The waves can be good here and it doesn't get as crowded as many of the other breaks. It requires a N or NW swell and a SE or S wind. About 1km after Shooting Gallery is a slight run off to the right. The wave will not be visible unless the swell is huge.

7. Suicides

A good but seldom surfed righthand reef breaking in shallow water. Suicides implies correctly that mistakes can be painful! This break is a high tide spot best with a S to SE wind. There is no indicator as to the location of the break. It is about 1km west of Henarossa.

8. Mechihonas

Faces north and picks up more swell than most of Fuerteventura's breaks. The waves here are peaky rights and lefts that break in relatively deep water (for Fuerteventura) and they can be surfed on any tide. This is a popular spot but because the peaks shift the crowds tend to get spread out around the point. The waves are easily seen from the road. There are two places where cars have smoothed out areas for parking.

9. Majanicho

About halfway along the car battering northern track lies a ramshackle fishing village. The bay, around which the village has been built, can provide some good righthand reef/point waves. They can remain surfable up to 10ft but even if it isn't big, watch out! It can be a dangerous place to wipe out. Park in village.

10. The Bubble

One of the sweetest and most consistent waves on Fuerteventura's north shore breaks on the reef at the eastern fringe of the bay. A righthander of exceptional quality and consistency, it tubes mercilessly on a typically sharp and shallow volcanic reef.

The break faces north and is surfable on all tides although mid to high tide is safer and more popular. The break can get crowded but it's the kind of wave where quality can make up for quantity. Paddle out off the rocks to the west of the wave. Located about 1km west of Majanicho. Small circular shelters have been set up a bit beyond a wrecked VW Kombi van.

11. Yarro, Backdoor Bubbles

Just across the bay from the righthander is another wave that can provide excellent surfing conditions. Not as tubey as the right, it's more of a wall leaving room for manoeuvres. Faces north and picks up a lot of swell, giving fun rides even when it's small. It can get crowded. Access is the same as The Bubble.

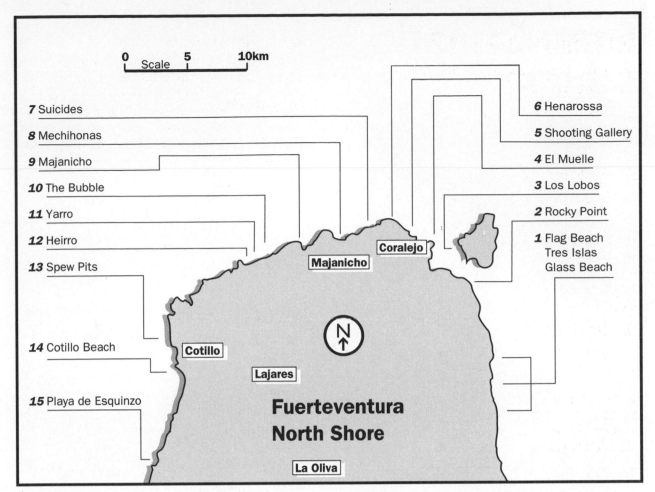

7 Suicides
8 Mechihonas
9 Majanicho
10 The Bubble
11 Yarro
12 Heirro
13 Spew Pits
14 Cotillo Beach
15 Playa de Esquinzo

6 Henarossa
5 Shooting Gallery
4 El Muelle
3 Los Lobos
2 Rocky Point
1 Flag Beach
Tres Islas
Glass Beach

Coralejo
Majanicho
Cotillo
Lajares

**Fuerteventura
North Shore**

La Oliva

12. Heirro

In the same bay west of Yarro. More good quality righthand waves but the crowds often don't travel this far along the track. Optimum conditions here are a N or NW swell of any size (it can hold a swell) and a wind from down south.

13. Spew Pits

A west facing lefthand reef break that has its name for a reason! It works with a SW, W or NW swell and needs an east wind. The breaks around here are well worth checking if the north shore is flat. If the Sirocco is on, then winds will often blow easterly for long periods of time, and that's offshore! Just north of the harbour in Cotillo.

14. Cotillo (South Beach)

At the southern end of this dusty, Mexican style outback village is a long sandy beach. The sea bed has a distinctive ledge which causes the waves to jack up in virtually the same place whatever the tide state or swell size. It's a popular wave-jumping spot and the northern end of the beach receives some protection from N winds. The beach is easy to find.

15. Playa de Esquinzo

A west beach which is hard to find and consequently always crowd free. It receives a lot of swell and works on all tides though high tide can be best. Esquinzo is signposted off the main road north of La Oliva. From there the road leads through the desert following an unmarked road with many unsignposted turn-offs. It's hard to find but if you don't end up at this beach, then you could well end up by another unmarked surf spot. Good luck! The Gorge lies about 7kms (5m) south of Cotillo along a rough dirt track, 15 minutes south of Cotillo.

16. Playa de Pared

A northwest facing black sand beach break that picks up loads of swell. As yet the area is little explored but potential is immense. This beach will break on any tide from 1 — 10ft. Rips are strong along this part of the coast so take extra care.

17. Punta del Tigre (Tiger Point)

Swells come out of deep water and break with force and speed over a shallow lava reef. Rarely surfed due to it's remoteness but can be well worth a check if there's a S swell with N to NE winds. The break is located at the southwestern end of the Island.

18. Sotavento

One of the world's most famous windsurfing/ beaches with winds above force 5, 23 - 25 days a month! Beware of strong offshore winds unless you're planning a trip to South America. On big tides (new and full moon) a lagoon is created near the hotel that's perfect for speed sailing, except for the crowds that such a good spot attracts. Many sailors launch at Las Dunas to avoid having to carry equipment far.

Gran Canaria

Population: 550,000
Capital: Las Palmas de Gran Canaria
Area: 1532 km²
Highest Point: 1932mtrs, Pico de las Nieves

Las Palmas de Gran Canaria is the biggest city among the islands and is the administrative, commercial and cultural centre for the Eastern Canaries. Gran Canaria is often referred to as a continent in miniature due to its contrasting landscapes. The island is shaped like a cone with Pico de las Nieves as the central point. The north is lush, with moisture coming from the prevailing north winds, and it's here that the local people live and work. The peak will often be covered in snow, and the south is hotter, sunnier and drier.

Like elsewhere in the Canaries, Gran Canaria had a history of Guanche settlement ended by a bloody colonisation process. In 1478 Juan Rejón landed with an army of men and preachers on La Isleta. He was ordered to convert the island to Christianity which he achieved, within 5 years, by wiping out the native population. Christopher Columbus sailed from Las Palmas on his epic voyage of discovery to unknown continents in the west in 1492.

THE SURF

Gran Canaria's roughly circular shape offers a choice of coasts with surf under varying conditions. The north coast picks up the most swell and is easily the best and most popular area on the island. All the surf shops on Gran Canaria are in Las Palmas where the majority of surfers stay. Gran Canaria, like Tenerife, is not as favourable for travelling surfers as Lanzarote or Fuerteventura due to heavier crowds and 'localism' problems. The best waves on the island are harder to enjoy due to these factors and although other areas do get waves, they're not of a quality or consistency comparable to the north coast. Still, good waves can definitely be had on Gran Canaria if you do end up here. There are some uncrowded surf spots not marked on the map which are easy enough to find. These are the places that a travelling surfer must seek out if he or she is to get the best out of Gran Canaria's surf.

Surf Breaks 1-24

Miguel Ortega/Orca Surf Shop

1. Bocabarranco

A consistent spot with a powerful righthander that breaks over a sand bottom. Breaks throughout the year with surfable waves up to 6ft. Works best at high tide. Follow the North Road until you reach Galdar then turn off towards the coast. It's 25km from Las Palmas.
Water Quality: Contaminated with sewage water.

2. El Agujero

A short and hollow peak breaking over a rock bottom. Popular with locals from Galdar and it's best at high tide. 300mtrs from Bocabarranco.
Water Quality: Average.

3. La Guancha

A righthander breaking into open sea, short tubey and dangerous since it's surrounded by cliffs. Works at high tide. Access is the same as Bocabarranco and El Agujero.
Water Quality: Good.

4. Vagabundo

This beach is situated at the end of San Felipe and has various sand bottom peaks. It works all year round, but especially in the summer months. Turn right off the North Road towards San Felipe.
Water Quality: Good.

5. El Circo

There are two breaks here; the first is a right and left peak with a very quick and hollow take-off that breaks at high tide. A lefthander that's not as hollow but is longer works at low tide. Same access as to Vagabundos. The breaks are situated in the town of San Felipe itself, behind the restaurant 'Los

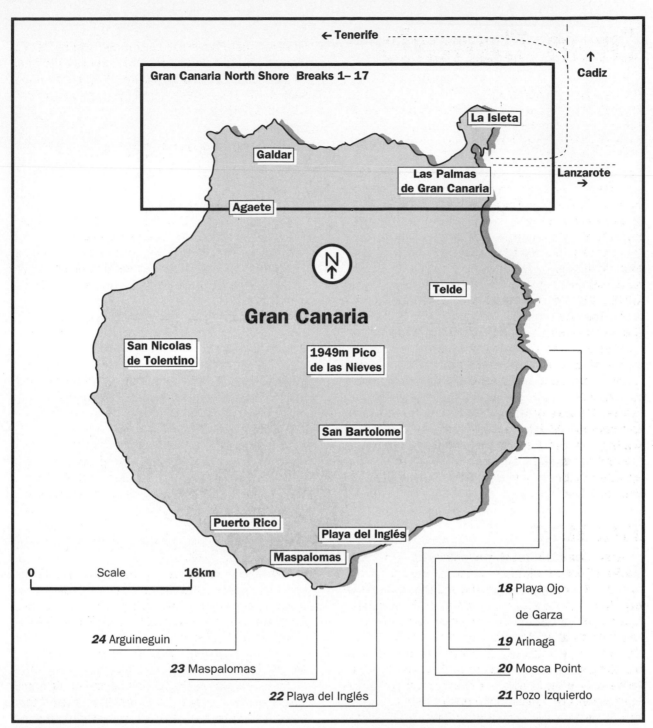

Gran Canaria North Shore Breaks 1– 17

← Tenerife

↑ Cadiz

La Isleta

Galdar

Las Palmas
de Gran Canaria

Lanzarote →

Agaete

N

Gran Canaria

Telde

San Nicolas
de Tolentino

1949m Pico
de las Nieves

San Bartolome

Puerto Rico

Playa del Inglés

Maspalomas

| 0 | Scale | 16km |

18 Playa Ojo
de Garza

24 Arguineguin

19 Arinaga

23 Maspalomas

20 Mosca Point

22 Playa del Inglés

21 Pozo Izquierdo

Pescaditos.'

Water Quality: Contaminated from restaurant garbage. Be warned of the presence of sharks.

6. El Paso

A great break situated some 300mtrs out to sea. It's the only wave on the island that can be surfed when the swell reaches 12ft. The peak breaks both right and left, with the right being a much longer ride. Take the North Road until 'El Parador.'

Water Quality: Good.

7. El Roque

200mtrs out to sea, a good lefthander breaks in front of a big rock. It has a fast take-off, followed by a slower section and is best from mid to high tide. Works in the summer months. Drive 17kms from Las Palmas on the North Road until you reach 'El Altillo.'

Water Quality: Good.

8. Las Piscinas

A good long tubing righthander that breaks over a rock bottom. It works at mid tide. Access is the same as El Roque.

Water Quality: Good.

9. Boquines

A wide bay with rocky reef breaks at both ends. On the eastern end is a righthander, giving long rides and lots of room for manoeuvres. Best at mid tide. The wave on the western side of the bay may be shorter but can be fun due to the radical take-off. The break is in San Andrés.

Water Quality: Good.

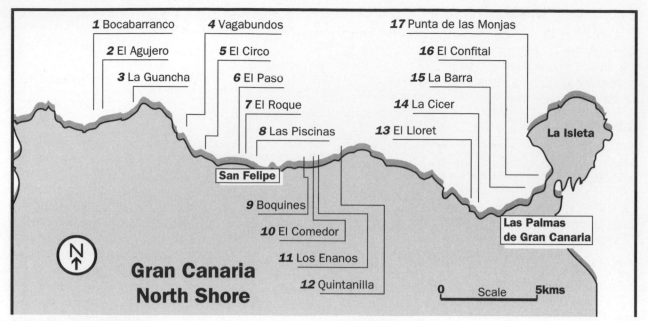

The map shows:

1 Bocabarranco
2 El Agujero
3 La Guancha
4 Vagabundos
5 El Circo
6 El Paso
7 El Roque
8 Las Piscinas
9 Boquines
10 El Comedor
11 Los Enanos
12 Quintanilla
13 El Lloret
14 La Cicer
15 La Barra
16 El Confital
17 Punta de las Monjas

San Felipe

La Isleta

Las Palmas de Gran Canaria

N

Gran Canaria North Shore

0 Scale 5kms

10. El Comedor

A powerful lefthander begins breaking over a rock bottom and finishes on sand. Best at low tide. The break is in San Andrés.

Water Quality: Good.

11. Los Enanos

A beach break which starts getting good at around 3ft. Rights and lefts over various sandbars. Take the North Road until the entrance of the village of San Andrés.

Water Quality: Good.

12. Quintanilla

This lefthander breaks over a rock and sand bottom and can have perfect long rides when on. Take the North Road until you reach the dance hall 'Quintanilla.'

Water Quality: Good.

13. El Lloret (La Lloreta)

Left and right peaks break over a rock bottom. When there's a big swell, the two waves can connect up and close-out, making the place very dangerous. El Lloret does get crowded but the atmosphere here is reasonably friendly. Winds from SW and S blow offshore, and a SE can be okay too. Access is at the exit of the North Road.

Water Quality: Average.

14. La Cicer

La Cicer is one of Europe's most popular boogie boarders' break. There are three named areas, each offering their own characteristics.

Los Muellitos lies at the west end of the beach, next to the breakwater and has a rock bottom with fast and tubey waves.

El Bufo is the area in the middle of the beach where good sand bottom waves make a good venue for competitions. The waves here aren't long but good peaks provide tubes and good walls for

manoeuvres.

El Piti Point has a sand and rock bottom and is a very popular area of La Cicer. Longer waves here than at El Bufo but they break with less power. Located on the west side of Playa Las Canteras.

Water Quality: Average.

15. La Barra, Playa Las Canteras

Excellent set-up with a fine golden sand beach, a turquoise lagoon and a lava reef handily positioned 500mtrs from shore. Not a big wave venue, but with up to a 2mtr swell, the waves are good and especially popular with boogie boarders. Sunrise and sunset are particularly nice times to surf La Barra. Park where possible.

Water Quality: Good.

16. Confital

Faces west and picks up good amounts of swell. Confital is famous for two things, great waves and heavy 'localism'. The main attraction is a righthand reef break considered to be one of the best waves in the Canaries. A sucky take-off followed by some clean barrels best caught at full tide.

However, all of this is only relevant if you choose to surf here. Most people don't. Foreigners are not really welcomed! Park at the end of the street called Calle Lujan Perez on the left. Do not leave a vehicle here unattended.

Water Quality: Good.

17. Las Monjas

Picks up as much swell as just about anywhere in Gran Canaria and is known for its powerful surf. There's a good left and right with the left being the hollower wave.

Like Confital, shanty towns back the break, and 'localism' is rife. The waves break over a lava bottom and are best at full tide with a S to E wind. Access is the same as Confital.

Water Quality: Good.

18. Playa Ojo de Garza

Beach break facing east-northeast. Only works on big N swells. Not a great place. Waves break by the airport so you can get a swell check if you fly in. Take the main S road and it's next to the airport.

Water Quality: Good.

19. Arinaga

Lefthander breaking over a lava bottom. A very fast wave which is both hollow and short. It works with from the east-northeast and the fact that it's often offshore makes it the most esteemed wave on the east coast of the island. Best at low tide. Take the main South Road until you come to Km 26.

Water Quality: Good.

20. Mosca Point

A right and left peak with the latter being a good spot giving a fast take-off followed by long rides. Best at a low tide. Take the old South Road until Vecindario and look for the way down by the Cemetery of Vecindario.

Water Quality: Good.

21. Pozo Izquierdo

A beach famous for its unbeatable conditions for funboarding. Has a righthander which needs a SW wind but this only comes in the winter as the rest of the year, east-northeast winds predominate. It's located at the end of the village of El Doctoral.

Water Quality: Good.

22. Playa del Inglés

Another freeze block city built purposefully for the tourist industry. Sand dunes cover 8kms and these dunes provide perfect sunbathing areas. Swells are rare. Conditions needed are a big S swell with a W to NW wind. Although clean swells are rare, onshore swell waves are common and these can be fun for wave-jumpers.

Water Quality: Good.

23. Maspalomas

There are two peaks on either side of the lighthouse. The one on the east is a great right with a long ride which breaks over a sand bottom, best at dawn and dusk. On the west side the break is formed by different peaks breaking over a rock bottom. The two breaks work on all tides and are best in winter. There is parking by the beach.

Water Quality: Good.

24. Arguineguin

One of the few green areas left in the southwest of Gran Canaria is in danger due to decisions by political leaders. It's a fun, long righthander that was very popular amongst the 'Surfer Freaks' during the 70's. A low tide break. Sunsets are beautiful here. Take the main road south until the village of Arguineguin.

Water Quality: Average.

Tenerife

Population: 607,000
Capital: Santa Cruz de Tenerife (185,000)
Area: 2053 km²
Highest Point: 3718 mtrs, Pico de Teide

Tenerife is the largest of the Canary Islands and the capital, Santa Cruz de Tenerife is the centre for the Western Canaries.

A mountain chain running roughly east/west divides the island in sharp contrast. Pico del Teide (Mt Teide) is famous as the highest mountain in Spanish territory, and is snow capped in winter.

Tenerife was the strong hold for the Guanche resistance to Spanish colonisation. Some of the islands welcomed the new colonisers but on Tenerife they resisted bitterly and with great ferocity. It was in 1496, nearly 100 years after the Spanish first arrived, that they were finally overcome. Santa Cruz was where Nelson lost his arm in 1797 at his only defeat in battle.

Information for this chapter has been provided by **La Asociación para la Defensa del Surf (ADES)**. The developments forced on this island by the encroaching tourist trade threatens many of the best surf breaks. Artificial beach formation and jetty developments are the biggest problems with several locations already irreparably altered.

THE SURF

There are two main areas to find waves here – firstly on the southwest coast from Playa de las Américas to los Gigantes approximately 25kms to the north, and secondly along the north coast up to Playa de los Troches. Main roads service these areas and they're also the scene of intense urbanisation. Playa de las Américas is one of the ugliest examples of the mutating tourist fungus, and although the northern coast of Tenerife is uniquely beautiful it's also the most heavily populated region in the group.

The atmosphere in the car parks and the water at most of these breaks can often be described as 'gnarly.' We suggest attempts to communicate in Spanish as the best way travellers can aleviate this problem. Don't be drawn into arguments, be polite! Be friendly and you can meet good people everywhere.

Tenerife has not been covered as extensively as the other islands because we felt the negative aspects of surfing here can outweigh the positive aspects, especially when compared to the other Canarian locations. The problems of 'localism' encountered by many of the surfers of the 80's, can destroy the whole essence of a surf trip. However, should you end up here, bring a board, keep a low profile, hunt around for the many unlisted surf breaks and you'll get waves.

Surf Breaks 1 – 13

ADES

1. El Confital

Most tubey left on Tenerife. Not good for beginners, S-SE-SW swell, N to NE wind, mid to high tide, lava bottom, up to 2mtrs, best in spring and summer.

2. Las Galletas

Breaks both right and left with the left being the better ride. The wave's length has been shortened considerably due to the construction of a pier. S-SE-SW swell, NE to N wind. Best at low tide up to 2mtrs, lava bottom, best in spring and summer.

3. La Fitenia (The Desert)

One of the best waves in south Tenerife will disappear due to construction! Left and right with the right being a better ride, S-SE-SW swell, NW to N winds, any tide, lava bottom, waves up to 3mtrs.

4. La Derecha del Cartel (Billboards)

Threatened wave! Excellent right with NW-W swell and E to SE winds. Best at mid tide in autumn, winter and spring, rocky bottom, breaks up to 3mtrs, located in front of the Hotel Conquistador.

5. La Izquierda (Spanish Lefts)

Threatened wave! Undoubtedly the best wave of Tenerife, long tubey left with a NW-W swell and an E to SE wind, all tides up to 3mtrs, lava bottom, autumn, winter spring. Many foreigners come to surf this wave – you can see it in front of the main drag at Las Américas.

6. Punta Blanca (K-16)

Threatened wave! Left, short and intense due to steepness and power of wave. NW swell, E wind, mid to low tide up to 3mtrs, rocky bottom. A popular break with foreigners. Other waves in the vicinity are also threatened.

7. La Izquierda & Derecha de la Caleta

A right and left both threatened by construction! N-NW swell, S winds, all tides up to 3mtrs, rock bottom with waves all year round. Both waves are somewhat hazardous.

8. Playa del Socrorro

Sand and rock bottom, N swell, S to W winds, all tides up to 3mtrs. Popular break with waves all year round.

9. El Charco

Threatened by construction of swimming pools! A big long left for experienced surfers. NW swell, E to SW winds, high tide up to 4mtrs. Rock bottom waves best in autumn and winter.

10. Fuera de la Bajeta

Threatened wave! A very good long righthander, N-NW swell, E to NE winds, all tides up to 4mtrs, best in winter.

11. Los Dos Hermanos

Powerful right and lefts, big, tubey and popular with more experienced surfers. N-NE-NW swell, S winds, high tide up to 4mtrs, rock bottom, best in winter.

12. La Derecha de Almáciga

Righthander, good for beginners, works on all tides and any swell, S to SW winds, sand bottom waves up to 2mtrs all year round.

13. Igueste de San Andrés

Good long tubey left with long walls. NE-N-SE swell, N to NE winds, all tides though best at high, breaks over smooth rocks and sand, best in winter up to 2.5mtrs.

TRAVELLING AROUND

AEROPUERTO: Los Rodeos (inter island – in the north). Tel: 257940. Reina Sofia (international – in the south). Tel: 380267
BUSES: Buses in Tenerife are reliable and are a cheap way of getting around the island. The main bus station is at the beginning of the motorway in Avenda Tres de Mayo. Tel: 218122.
FERRY: Aucona, Marina, 59, Santa Cruz de Tenerife. Tel: 287850.
TOURIST OFFICE: Palacio Insular, Santa Cruz de Tenerife. Tel: 242227.

HOSPITALS AND MEDICAL SERVICES:
Centros Medicos Salus have a multilingual service at Las Américas (24hr). Tel: 791253 and at Puerto de la Cruz. Tel: 380267.
GENERAL HOSPITAL Santa Cruz de Tenerife. Tel: 641011.

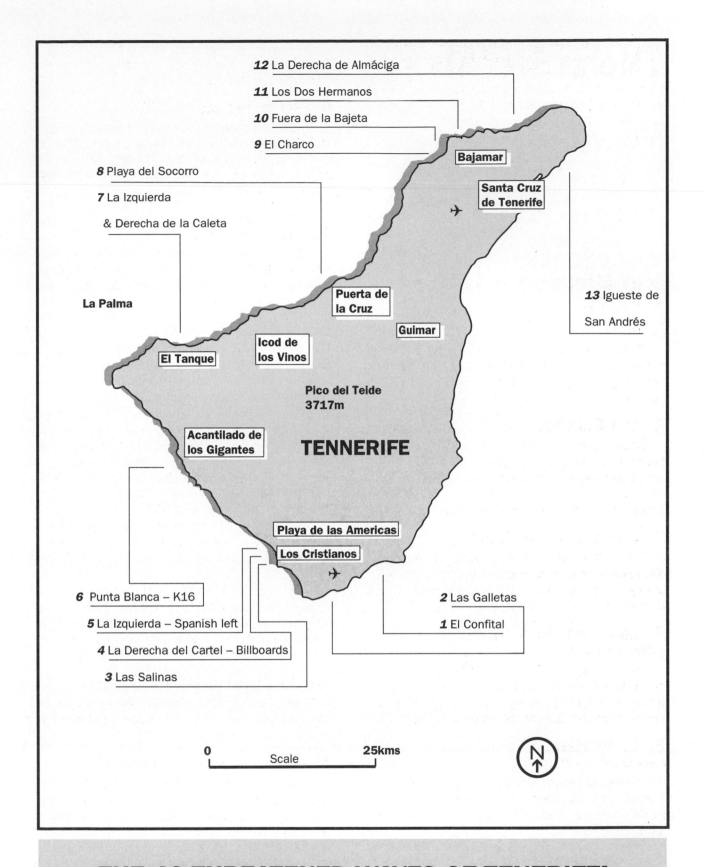

12 La Derecha de Almáciga

11 Los Dos Hermanos

10 Fuera de la Bajeta

9 El Charco

Bajamar

8 Playa del Socorro

Santa Cruz
de Tenerife

7 La Izquierda

& Derecha de la Caleta

La Palma

Puerta de
la Cruz

13 Igueste de

San Andrés

Icod de
los Vinos

Guimar

El Tanque

Pico del Teide
3717m

Acantilado de
los Gigantes

TENNERIFE

Playa de las Americas

Los Cristianos

6 Punta Blanca – K16

2 Las Galletas

5 La Izquierda – Spanish left

1 El Confital

4 La Derecha del Cartel – Billboards

3 Las Salinas

0   Scale   25kms

N

THE 46 THREATENED WAVES OF TENERIFE!

Tenerife Tour; Candelaria; Pal-Mar; La Izqueirda del Cristian-mar; Las Salinas; El Guincho; El Conquistador; Derecha del Cartel 'Billboards'; El Bunquer; La Ballena; Izquierda de Tenerife 'Spanish Left'; Punta Blanca 'K-16'; La del Medio; La del Chalet; La Concha; La Izquierda del Pueblo; La Izquierda de la Caleta; Punta Brava; Juan Galán; El Charcón; La Derecha del Castillo; El Muelle; La Derecha del Lago; Baja del Diablo; Baja del Bizcochado; Pico de Fuera; El Charco; Fuera la Baja Nueva; Baja Nueva; El Desague; La Derecha de Candelaria; El Roquete; Fuera del Roquete; El Lastradero; La Baja Chica; La Cueva de Mejia; La Bajeta; Por Allá de la Bajeta; Fuera de la Bajeta.

PORTUGAL

Capital: Lisbon
Population: 10,470,000
Area: 92,389km²
Time: GMT (summer time GMT+1)
Religion: Roman Catholic
Language: Portuguese
Currency: Escudo (Esc)

THE PEOPLE

Portugal retains the various influences of successive conquests by such far flung peoples as the Moors, Visigoths, Romans, French, Spanish and the English, all of whom left some genetic, architectural and social impression.

Portugal remained one of the least penetrable of European states to the Romans. Since then the country's fortunes have been inextricably linked to the ebb and flow of the Atlantic. Prince Henry, The Navigator, focused the Church's attention and finances seaward. He founded a school of navigation on the promontory at Sagres (then considered to be the world end!) within sight of some tubey surf. Madeira and the Azores were consequently discovered in 1419 and 1427 respectively and by Henry's death in 1460, the Cape Verde Islands and the west coast of Africa to Sierra Leone had been explored. In 1487 Bartolomeu Dias navigated the southern tip of Africa and named it Cabo da Boa Esperança in the hope of good things to come. Within 10 years, Vasco de Gama had opened up trade routes with India and the small cargo of pepper he brought back on his first expedition was enough to pay its expenses 60 times over. Portugal promptly became the richest monarchy in Europe.

In 1494 Spain and Portugal divided the world between them along an imaginary line 370 leagues west of The Cape Verde Islands. Portuguese wealth and power reached its zenith during the next 30 years but a combination of social and political factors brought a rapid end to the dynasty of the House of Avis.

Since then, its political life has been tumultuous. On April 25th, 1974, a bloodless coup ended half a century of near-fascist rule and gave independence to all Portuguese former colonies. The period since 1975 has been one of consolidation and the main concern in recent years has been Portugal's move towards full membership of the EC in 1992.

THE LAND

Portugal, along with Ireland, occupies Europe's most westerly seaboard and the Atlantic Ocean exerts a primal influence over a country of stunning variety. While the northern interior is mountainous, lush and green, the south experiences a Mediterranean/ African climate which rarely gets cold.

Unfortunately the water remains cool all year round so a full wetsuit is necessary for autumn, winter and spring. A spring suit is all that's required for summer. Booties are also a good idea year round – the water can be cold enough to numb the feet and sharp reefs and urchins abound – be warned!

The coastline is vast and wonderful with many fine stretches of beach break and some world class reefs, points and jetties. Most swell comes from North Atlantic lows, though W and S swells are also common.

WEATHER INFO: Newspaper: *Diario de Noticias* B & W Satellite picture and map, both excellent. **TV:** Channel 1, 8.15pm, includes maps, satellite pics, and often swell size on the Azores. Watch out for *Roger Ramjet* re-runs after the weather.

WATER QUALITY

Portugal, like most other European nations has many waste disposal problems but the Portuguese surfing community is not yet environmentally active. Coastal destruction is a topic people still have to be educated about before they will take action. Some beaches are very polluted, mostly with human sewage. In the Lisbon area, all of the so-called Estoril Line (from Cascais to Lisbon) has serious sewage problems, with Carcavelos being the most affected area.

Carcavelos is one of the main surf spots around Lisbon, and many cases of eye and skin irritations have been reported and, the way it's going, things are getting worse. Oporto, at Matosinhos Beach (another main spot), has the biggest problem, with human sewage mixing with the blood coming from a slaughterhouse! All the beaches are commercially concessioned during summer, and this happens to be the only season when they are clean. Once the holidays have finished, the dirt starts to invade the sand again and nobody seems to care too much.

Summer surf schools, besides teaching the sport, are trying to induce a conservationist ethic among children, and during the days of classes, many clean-beach groups go around with plastic bags, collecting trash and setting a good example to other beach users. But this is the only initiative that is surf-born. There is much more to do, but we're not yet united enough to protest or to take any action on a national level. Through the magazine, we're trying to help in the best possible way, but it is never enough. The next step will be a donation by *Surf Portugal* to the Surfrider Foundation, and closer contact with the organization in order to get some help with this matter.

João Valente/*Surf Portugal*

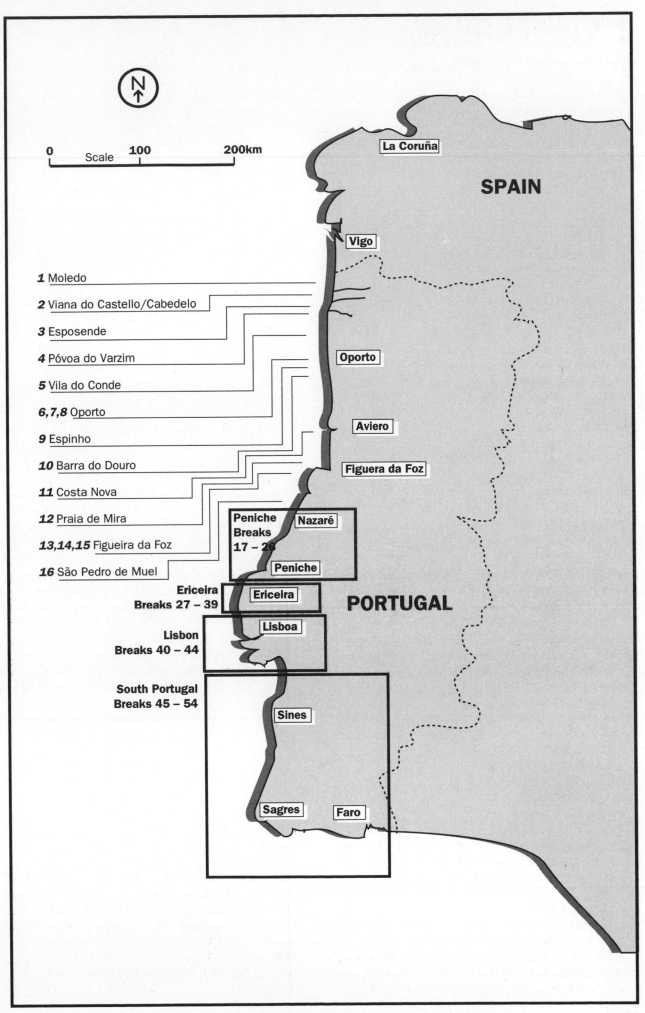

N

0 Scale 100 200km

1 Moledo
2 Viana do Castello/Cabedelo
3 Esposende
4 Póvoa do Varzim
5 Vila do Conde
6,7,8 Oporto
9 Espinho
10 Barra do Douro
11 Costa Nova
12 Praia de Mira
13,14,15 Figueira da Foz
16 São Pedro de Muel

La Coruña

SPAIN

Vigo

Oporto

Aviero

Figuera da Foz

Peniche Breaks 17 – 26

Nazaré

Peniche

Ericeira Breaks 27 – 39

Ericeira

PORTUGAL

Lisbon Breaks 40 – 44

Lisboa

South Portugal Breaks 45 – 54

Sines

Sagres

Faro

THE SURF

Portuguese surfing is at a very decisive point of its history, trying to pull itself together after years of total chaos.

After the early years of indiscriminate growth, the sport only began to feel the need to organise itself in the mid 80s. Surfing became more than just a sport practised by a group of fanatical enthusiasts; it was becoming good business too. By that time, almost every major international surf company was already installed here, with commercial representations and franchises, and a small local industry grew up alongside. In 1988 the Portuguese Surfing Federation (FPS) was founded, but it never took off as it should have. Despite some good initiatives in its first year of activity, (the Portugal/ NSSA cultural exchange and an attempt at a national ranking) the FPS was too dependent on government benefits and those were never enough.

Now the FPS has new members and has prepared a different approach. A private source has sponsored a national circuit, and it sounds like this time they've got it together. If by the end of 1992 the planned six contests have been held, we'll know our first national champion.

The new FPS is run by members of the Viana Surf Club, from the north of Portugal. This is one of the strongest surf associations in Portugal, and they've been working well in the last years. Plus, surfers' parents and local officials are giving it a big push. However, they have a lot of work ahead of them to restore the Federation's credibility in the eyes of a broad surfing community, which probably numbers around 30,000 by now.

João Valente/*Surf Portugal*

THE LOCALS

Portuguese surfers have a special feeling (like most others) about their homeland. They really enjoy it and surf around as much as possible. That's probably one of the reasons why they don't travel as much as other surfers. They know the surf-trip potential they have on their own doorsteps.

Due to this awareness, Portuguese locals can sometimes seem a little difficult, but after the first verbal contact, and if the sport's laws are respected, they can be really friendly. The Portuguese level of performance is high on a European scale, due to the climatic conditions that allow one to surf 12 months a year. In Portugal, surfing has never been seen by its aficionados as a fashion, but rather as a true sport. Although there are some signs of the typical 'surfer look' (the long blond hair) Portuguese surfers aren't very much into the 'all-surfer look,' preferring to build their image in an individual way.

THE COMPETITIVE ARENA

There have been some good surfers in our short history, one being a guy from Carcavelos named Paulo Inocentes, the best of the 70s generation.

But it was during the 80s that the 'new generation' began to appear. Today, names such as Dapin, Jorge Leote, João Antunes, Bruno Charneca, Rodrigo Herédia and Nuno Mata are well known to any concerned European surfer. There are some hot young upstarts that nobody outside Portugal has ever heard about, who will rapidly follow the European routes opened up by the aforementioned. Names to look out for include; Marcos Anastácio, Felipe Gatinho and Hugo Zagalo. There's a big wave crew of guys that almost never compete, but who don't miss any of *those* days. Anyone who has spent some good times at Ericeira, must have known guys like Miguel Fortes and Miguel Ruivo, Faneca, Zé Menezes, João Pedro and the soon to be famous Tó Gama, a guy that besides being a great big-wave surfer, is also one of the best 'forcados' in Portugal. ('Forcado' is a typical Portuguese bullfight in which the bullfighter grabs the bull with bare hands.)

THE MARKET

Despite the big increase it has been enjoying since the beginning of the 80s, the market estimate of 30,000 constitutes a small share of a population of 10 million and their average ages are still young (15 to 18) which means that the biggest part of the consumer mass is not financially independent. This problem will sort itself out with time. We are only now seeing a generation of older surfers appear to help the younger ones into the water. The older generation can take control of the sport's basic organisational structures more easily.

There are companies trying to give Portuguese surfing an individual face, developing new brands etc – but they face stiff competition from the big overseas labels. However, they have their piece of the market, and one can find all kinds of products, from surf wear to wetsuits and accessories, made in Portugal, to high standards.

The most advanced is the surfboard industry and companies such as Polen and Semente rank among the best in Europe, both in terms of quality of materials and in shaping performance. Polen is one of Europe's biggest factories and Semente one of the most hardcore.

Media coverage has been improving in the last years. Today there are two magazines, one 100% dedicated to surf (*Surf Portugal*) another that puts it among other nautical sports (*Surf Magazine*). Also, there's an all bodyboard publication (*Body Board Portugal*), and a newspaper that covers the surf and bodyboard scene on a regular basis (*Notícias do Mar*). There are about five regular radio programmes and at least two TV series are being prepared on radical sports subjects, with surfing predominant in both. Besides that, there is a surf hot-line on the phone, called 'Disc Surf' for information about wave conditions from Lisbon to Peniche, and a new line covering the north is being prepared.

WAVE-SAILING/FUNBOARDING

Although Portugal has the sun and the waves on its side, the natural conditions for this sport would be much better if the wind was more consistent. There's no single spot where the wind constantly blows strongly enough to satisfy the hardcore funboarder.

It can reach 45 knots (force 9 on the Beaufort scale) but the average classic conditions would be force 6. As a good practitioner puts it, "Portugal would be a dreamland, but we have to wait about 8 months before the summer arrives with its northwest winds." Sadly, and despite the good efforts of the people involved with the sport, windsurfing in general is not well established in our country. After the tremendous impact of the first years, the number of practitioners has been decreasing year after year. It seems that people looked at it more as a trendy thing than as a serious sport, and there haven't been any new faces appearing for the last three years.

On the other hand, funboarding has been slowly increasing. The highlight of the competition scene is the annual Guincho Wave Classic, an international event, and one that brings this sport closer to the wider public through strong media coverage.

In the national domain, there was only one contest held in 1990, it was in the Peniche area and attracted 50 contestants from all over the country.

The Champ Luís 'Luisinho' Cruz Gomes is widely considered to be the best Portuguese funboarder. Other good athletes worthy of mentioning are Luis Caliço, Pedro Soares and Miguel Dória. The actual number of practitioners is between 2,000 – 2,500 with some 500 hardcore enthusiasts.

The national association, the APF (Portuguese Funboard Association) is a very amateur organisation and its performance hasn't been as good as one could wish. There are no professional organisations in Portugal.

BODYBOARDING

Like in many parts of the world, bodyboarding is developing fast in Portugal. The sport is controlled by the Portuguese Surfing Federation (FPS) and there's an estimated number of about 10,000 seasonal and regular enthusiasts.

Since its first appearance, about five or six years ago, bodyboarding has been experiencing non-stop growth. The reasons seem obvious: It's cheaper than a surfboard, it's easier to learn, less dangerous in parents' eyes and, of course, it's lots of fun.

From the very beginning, competition has been present in the sport. Isolated contests and circuit attempts promoted by local businesses have helped a lot. The market is advanced, with virtually all the major worldwide companies being represented locally and sponsorship is lavish.

Although 1991 was a relatively confused year, there were lots of contests and some of them offered good prizes, such as air tickets to Hawaii. In the first years, there was an annual circuit, promoted by Morey Boogie, but not any more.

Other kinds of promotional events happen, such as the visits of Keith Sazaki and Mike Stewart (the latter bringing a big crowd to Praia Grande for what turned out to be the greatest event for Portuguese bodyboarding last year.)

The number of adepts has been growing year after year. The biggest group is in the 12 – 15 years old range, but there are many younger and a few older.

The performance level is as high as anywhere in Europe and names like Paulo Costa, Rodrigo Bessone, Gonçalo Faria, Nuno Silva and Dora Gomes are recognised to be some of Europe's best performers. A specialist magazine called *Body Board Portugal* covers every aspect of Portuguese and international bodyboarding.

João Valente/*Surf Portugal*

STRANGERS IN A STRANGE LAND

I first travelled to Portugal in 1978 with no intention of surfing. I was ignorant of the quality and quantity of surf available in this strange and beautiful country.

It took me roughly two days to change my game plan, having seen perfect barrels at Carcavelos. Surfboards and wetsuits were unavailable at this time so I was forced to head up to France where I bought a second-hand board and wetsuit.

Upon return I spent two months surfing perfect waves at Carcavelos. It was fall of 1978, and those who surfed in Portugal at that time numbered no more than 200 people. They will remember it was a classic year and there have been many more since.

It was a magic time, as I guess it must have been anywhere in surfing's early days. The general public were always amazed by the madmen who would paddle out into 10ft waves. It was a crowd pleaser and people would stand for hours watching the few surfers in the water at any spot on any given day.

Like the rest of the world, wherever surfing starts it explodes with an almost cancerous growth pattern. Portugal is no exception and in the 13 years that I have been here the surfing population has grown into the thousands.

Board builders have grown to meet the demand and where we worked with national foam resin and glass in the early days, we have progressed to meet the needs of a more informed and demanding public.

New materials from the U.S. and Australia are imported by many manufacturers and, with the input from travelling shapers, professional surfers and the waves – local surfers and surfboards have evolved with the rest of the world.

Most travelling surfers will be found on a 50km stretch of coast from Ericeira to Peniche for reasons that become obvious when you get there.

Some PORTUGUESE language

SURF SPEAK

back wash ....ressaca
bad waves ....puta mar
bay ....baia
beach ....praia
big......................................grande
bottom ....cavada or fundo
bottom turn......................cavada
checking waves ....
......................chaca los ondas
coast ....costa
cut back ....cut back
deep..................................profundo
ding ....buraco
drop ....dropar
east ....este
fibreglass ....fibra da vidro
fins ....quilha
flat ....poco mar
good waves ....bom ondas
high tide ....maré cheia/alto mare
high pressure ....
..............alta pressão or cyclone
hollow..................................oco
in front........................em frente
late ....tarde
left....................................esquerda
leg rope ....shope or leg rope
low pressure .....baixa pressâo or
....................................anti cyclone
low tide....maré vazia/baixo mare
map ....mapa or carta
near....................................cerca
north ....norte
offshore ....offshore
onshore ....onshore
outside ....outside
peak ....pico
point....................................point
re entry................................batida
reef ....rife or reef
resin....................................resina
right....................................direita
rip..corrente
rivermouth ....boca do rio/foz
rocks ....rochas
rocky bottom ......fundo de rochas
sand....................................areia
sandbank ....saco de aria
set ....set
shallow ....baixo or poco profundo
slow ....lento
small..................................pequeno
south....................................sul
surfboard............prancha de surf
swell..................ondulaçoa/vaga
the weather....................o tempo

prediction..................prognostico
wall ....muro
walled up..................amurallada
water ....agua
waves ....ondas
wax ....cera
weather map.......mapa do tempo
west ....oeste
wetsuit................goma or
......................fato de borracha
wind..................................vento

USEFUL WORDS

all ....todo
before ....antes de
because ....porque
behind................................atrás
boat ....barco/navio
cold......................................frio
condom..................preservativo
everybody....todos/todo o mundo
fast......................................rapido
fire ....fogo
God....................................Deus
good................bom/boa
here....................................aqui
high....................................alto
hot......................quenta/picante
little ....pequeno
lost......................................perdido
many ....muitos
no ....não
old ....velho/antigo
please ....por favor!
rain......................................chuya
slow ....lento/vagaroso
snow..................................never
soon.............. logo/brevemente
thank you ....obrigado
thunder............................trovão
under..................debaixo de
up ....alto
very ....muito
well ....bem
when?............................quando?
why?..................................por quê?
with ....de, do, da
without ....sem
yes ....sim

USEFUL PHRASES

Good morning..........bom manha
Good day ....bom dia
Good afternoon ....bom tarde
Good night ....bomnoite
I'm sorry/pardon ....desculpe
Do you know...? ....sabe?

I don't know?................não sei?
Could you?......................pode?
How do I get to...?....para ir a...?
How much is it? ....quanto custa?
It is expensive ....é caro
What is your name? ....
......................como se chama?
My name is..............chamome...
Can we camp here? ....
..............pode-se acampar aqui?
I'd like a room...queria um quarto
Can I look? ....posso ver?
What is that?.........O que é isso?

PUBLIC SIGNS & NOTICES

open....................................aberto
closed....................fechado
entrance....................entrada
exit ....saida
free......................................livre
occupied ....ocupado
ladies ....senhora
gentlemen........................senhor
lavatory ....privado
forbidden ....proiber
no parking................estacionam
......................ento proibido
no smoking..........proibido fumar

SHOPS & PLACES

bank ....banco
bakery................................paderia
chemist........................farmácia
fish shop ....peixeiro
grocer ....mercearia
library ....biblioteca
market................................mercado
newsagent..................papelaria
post office....................corrieo
shop .... loja
travel agent ....agencia de viagem

RESTAURANT

bill ....conta
bottle..................................garrafa
breakfast ....cafe de manha/
......................pequeno almoço
cup .... xícara/chávena
dinner................................jantar
drink .... bebida
fork ....garfo
glass ....vidro
knife....................................faca
lunch............comida/almaço
plate ....chapa
sandwich....................sandvíche

spoon ....colher
table ....mesa

DRINK

beer...........................cerveza
coffee -black......................bika
   -white ....gallao
ice ....gelo
juice ....saco
tea ....cha
water ....agua
wine............................vinho

FOOD

apple ....maça
avocado ....abacate
banana ....banana
beans ....feijao
beef....................carne/rosbife
biscuit ....biscoito
bread ....pao
butter.......................monteiga
cabbage ....couve
carrot ....cenoura
cauliflower ....couveflor
cheese..........................queijo
chicken ....galinha/frango
cream..............................nata
cucumber......................pepino
egg ....ovo
fish ....peixe
garlic ....alho
grapes ....uva
ham...........................presunto
lamb ....cordeiro
lemon ....limao
lentils.........................lentilha
marmelade/jam................geléia
milk...............................leito
mushrooms ....fungo
mussels ....mexilhao
mustard ....mostarda
oil..................................óleo
olives ....azeitona
onion ....cebola
orange ....laranja
peach..........................pêssego
pear ....pêra
pepper(veg) ....pimenta
pepper(table) ....salpicar
pork...................carne de porco
potato .... batata
salad ....salada
salt................................sal
sauce ....molho
sausage ....salsicha
shrimps......................camarao?
spinach ....espinafre
strawberries ....morango
sugar ....açúcar
toast ....torrada

vegetables....................vegetal
vinegar ....vinagre
yoghurt ....iogurte

COUNTRIES

Scotland ....Escócia
Ireland ....Irlanda
Wales...................Pais de Gales
England.......................Inglaterra
Channel Islands...................
.............Ilhas Anglo-Normandas
France...........................Franca
Spain ....Espanha
Canary Islands .....Ilhas Canárias
Portugal ....Portugal
Azores...............Ilhas dos Açores
Italy ....Itália
Germany ....Alemanha
Switzerland ....Suiça
Australia.......................Australia
New Zealand........Nova Zelãndia
United States......Estados Unidos

NUMBERS

one ....um/uma
two ....dois
three ....três
four ....quatro
five..............................cinco
six ....seis
seven ....sete
eight.............................oito
nine ....nove
ten..............................dez
eleven ....onze
twelve ....doze
thirteen ....treze
fourteen ....catorze
fifteen ....quinze
sixteen ....dezesseis
seventeen...................dezessete
eighteen ....dezoite
nineteen ....dezanove
twenty ....vinte
twenty one................vente e um
thirty ....trinta
fourty............................quarenta
fifty.............................cinquenta
sixty ....sessenta
seventy ....setenta
eighty ....oitenta
ninety..........................noventa
one hundred ....trinta
two hundred................duzentos
five hundred..............quinhentos
one thousand......................mil
one million.................um milhão

DAYS OF THE WEEK

Monday ....segunda feira
Tuesday ....terça feira

Wednesday ....quarta feira
Thursday ....quinta feira
Friday ....sexta feira
Saturday ....sabado
Sunday......................domingo

MONTHS

January.........................Janeiro
February ....Fevereiro
March ....Março
April.............................Abril
May ....Maio
June ....Junho
July..............................Julho
August ....Agosto
September...............Septembro
October ....Outobro
November ....Novembro
December ....Dezembro

SPACES OF TIME

minute ....minuto
hour ....hora
day................................dia
week.............................semana
month............................mês
year...............................ano
decade..........................década

MECHANIC WORDS AND PHRASES

oil..................................óleo
petrol..........................gasóleo
puncture ....furo
Something is wrong with..............
Há qualquer cosaque nao funciona
the engine....................no motor
the clutch...........na embraiagem
the gearbox ....
.................a caixa de velocidades
the breaks ....nos travôes
the steering...............na direcçâo
the suspension ....a suspensâo
My car...has broken down ....
...................O meu carro...avariou
...has run out of gas...................
.....................ficou sem gasolina
...is...kms from here ....
.......................é a...km daqui
Can you...?.....................Pode...?
................tow the car to a garage
rebocar o carro para uma garagem
...repair the car .....arranjar o carro
When will it be ready? ....
.........Quando é que está pronto?
How much will it cost?................
.....................Quanto vai custar?
I don't have sufficient cash..........
....Nâo tenho dinheiro que chegue
Will you accept credit cards?
..........Aceitam cartas de crédito?

Numbers have greatly increased in the past few years due to magazine exposure and a series of E.P.S.A. and A.S.P contests held in Portugal. But that's all just part of the evolution of surfing.

Travelling anywhere in the world, one must treat people as one would wish to be treated. People here are very friendly and helpful in general.

Treat people and their property (rented house or room) with respect so you and other surfers will find yourselves welcome in the future. As far as surfing goes, all surfers pay out on crowds at their local break, especially if visitors lack respect and good manners. No one likes a wave hog or a bad attitude. Remember you're travelling and are here to surf and have a good time, not to create enemies!

Nick Uricchio/Semente Surfboards

North Portugal

Surfing is strong here but numbers in the water are generally much fewer than further south. The coast is especially good for wave-jumping/funboarding with predominant winds coming from the NW. The whole area holds potential for further wave discovery. Entry points into Portugal at Valença or V.N. de Carveira (car ferry).

TRAVELLING AROUND

Portuguese National Tourist Office:
New Bond Street House,
1-5 New Bond St,
London W1Y OND
Tel: 071 493 3873

PLANES: Most of the cheapest flights to Portugal from within Europe are charter flights. They have fixed and unchangeable outward and return dates and a maximum stay of one month. Scheduled flights offer more flexibility or longer stays. Most common routes are London to Faro, Lisbon or Oporto.

T.A.P. (Air Portugal) service these routes and have connecting deals with BA and other airlines. Flights from Australia and America would come via another main European travel centre.

Airlines:
T.A.P. (Air Portugal),
19 Regent St,
London, SW1
Tel: 071 889 1031

Discount Flights: See newspapers or Student Travel Association: 86 Old Brompton Rd, London SW7 Tel: 071 937 9921.

Airports: There are three main international airports in Portugal.
Lisbon   Tel: 889181
Porto   Tel: 9482141
Faro   Tel: 23538

● For other information on services within Portugal see *Lisbon: Travelling*.

TRAINS: Similar to other European countries, though unless you have a Eurail pass it would normally be cheaper to get in and out by air. Trains and buses within Portugal are government-run and pretty good.

DRIVING:
Car: The traditional route is via the French coast road south of Bordeaux entering Spain at Irín and choosing a destination from there. Roads in Portugal are radical and the accident rate is among the highest in Europe. This becomes evident quickly. Especially bad is the Cascais coast road and the main highways to both Porto and Faro from Lisbon. Rental cars can cost from £60.00 – £100.00 per week, often best to sort it out when you buy your air ticket.

Maps: T.A.P publish a very good tourist map with good coastal detail. Some land and survey maps can be bought in London, otherwise the address in the Lisbon area section is the best bet in Portugal.

Breakdown services:
Lisbon   Tel: 736121
Porto   Tel: 316732

Coaches: Supabus and Eurolines operate twice weekly services from London to Lisbon and Algarve via Coimbra. Fares are from about £65.00 one way to £110.00 return. All from Victoria coach station. Tel:730 3453.

Return bookings can be made at "Intercentro" (Avda Casal Ribeiro, 18) in Lisbon.

TELEPHONING:
International dialling
Dialling in code: 351
Dialling out code: 00
Operator: 144
Directory enquiries: 166
International Operator: 097
European Operator: 098
Emergency services: 115

Opening times:
BANKS (Bancos): Banks are open from Monday to Friday, 8.30am – 3pm. Larger banks open on Saturday mornings.

POST OFFICES (Correios): Post offices are open from Monday to Friday, 9am – 6pm. Larger branches are open on Saturday mornings.

SHOPS (Lojas): Virtually all the shops in Portugal, like those in France and Spain, close for siesta, usually from 12.30 – 3pm. They generally open at 9am and close at 7pm. On Saturdays they remain open until lunchtime. Closed on Sundays.

PUBLIC HOLIDAYS:
1, January
25, April   (74 revolution)
1, May
early June   Corpus Christi
10, June
15, August
5, October
1, November
1,8,25, December

SURF BREAKS 1 – 16

1. Moledo

A half-ruined fort guards the rivermouth from a long spit. A good beach break offers good conditions for surfing and wave-sailing.

2. Viana do Castello/Cabedelo

Beach breaks hold surf from 2 - 10ft, both sides of the rivermouth. Focal point for northern funboarders. Lively town with great restaurants. A ferry takes you to Cabedelo.

3. Esposende

Another stretch of west facing beach broken by a moderate sized river.

4. Póvoa do Varzim

Lefthand waves off the reef and bars on the beach. The rocks are sharp making mid to high tide a safer bet. Both need a good sized swell to work.

5. Vila do Conde/Azurara

Beach breaks south of Varzim. Frequently good sailboarding conditions.

6,7,8. Oporto: Leça, Matosinhos, Barra do Douro

Beach breaks, a reef break and a rivermouth make this city the home of good but very polluted surf–the River Douro empties sewage and industrial waste into the Atlantic at an alarming rate.

9. Espinho

The busy seaside town of Espinho is home to several good jetty breaks, giving good rights and lefts from 3 - 10ft. The heavy backwash at high tide can affect the wave quality on smaller swells. Busy in summer, otherwise pretty laid back.

10. Barra

Now only works on big swells. Breaks both ways. Beach development killed this one…

11. Costa Nova

The sandbanks created by the jetties in Costa Nova, south of the River Vouga, produce some of the best waves along this stretch of coast. Long tubey rights and lefts regularly grind off the breakwaters and along the beach. When it's big the paddle out can be long and arduous, so finding a rip to go out in can be well worth while. Surfable on all tides.

12. Praia de Mira

Typical beach town and consistent beach break waves set amongst extensive dunes. Surfable on all tides and generally uncrowded.

13, 14, 15. Figueira da Foz

BUARCOS (13), Tamagueira: Very long right reef and sand break in front of the Hotel Tamagueira. Best conditions are a clean NW/W/S swell, NE winds and low to mid tide. The beach holds good sized swells and has no crowd problems outside high season.

CABEDELO (14): On the south side of the Rio Mondego, a tarmacked pier runs out to sea for about ½km. Long, classic righthanders break on the sandbanks with thick lips and grinding barrels best at mid to high tide. A useful rip runs alongside the pier. **Cabedelinho:** can be good when Cabedelo is huge – it's on the other side of the pier.

GALA/COVA (15): Five jetties in Gala/Cova produce more excellent rights and lefts. The banks change continuously but there's usually a spot to be found.

Water Quality: Large sections of coastline south of Leirosa, almost as far as São Pedro de Muel have been reported by beach walkers as being heavily polluted. Stretches of ocean apparently foam red and stink badly as a consequence of emissions from two paper plants at Leirosa. What a Nightmare.

16. São Pedro de Muel

Rarely surfed reef and beach breaks west of Marinha Grande. A seasonal Youth Hostel open from May 1 – Sept 30 sits right on the sea.

Peniche

Peniche is one of Portugal's busiest fishing ports and was an island until the 12th century – now joined to the mainland by a narrow isthmus. Its other cause for repute is the 16th century Fortaleza, it was once one of Portugal's most notorious jails, expanded in the 1950's and 1960's to accommodate growing numbers of political prisoners and today is an impressive monument against fascism.

The town has been a magnet for surfers and sailors for over a decade. A variety of breaks all working in different conditions lie within a 20 mile radius. N swells which hardly register around Ericiera can be breaking on the beaches north of Baleal, and when swell comes from the SW, **Supertubes** throws out barrels which often snap boards.

The beach at Nazaré shows good potential as a big wave break and, when its good, one can sense many other secret spots pumping and empty. In all, it's one of the most versatile surf venues in Europe.

The surrounding towns are small and the vibe is generally pretty relaxed. Things can get a bit hassley in the water at the main breaks when they're small, and foreigners might need a bit of patience with drop-ins – we strongly advise you exercise it! From Peniche northwards, the crowds thin substantially and the coast could best be described as 'semi-explored.' Jetties, rivermouths and the odd well-placed rock, break the miles of almost empty beaches which stretch to Spain.

Peniche Area:
Surf Breaks 17 – 26

17. Nazaré

The Surf Report calls it: "Portugal's big wave spot...6 - 22ft...sand bottom." Certainly a stretch of beach which holds large waves. A long finger of deep ocean points to Nazaré and consequently swells hit the beach from extremely deep water.

Very radical conditions and probably "Portugal's most underrated wave," according to João Valente.

18. Foz do Arelho

The beach runs from here to Peniche and begins to reach northwards. Good rivermouth and beach break.

19. Ferral/Lagide

You can see the beach from Baleal and in a small N swell when everywhere else is crap and the wind SW, Ferral can be head high and pumping. A track runs from town along the lenght of the beaches – finding it can be tricky but worth while. Various banks break on all tides in various offshores.

20. Baleal Reef

High quality lefthander breaks over an urchin infested rock ledge. Faces north and remains surfable on all tides, though dangerously shallow at low. Loads of campervans in the car park.

21. Praia do Baleal

Protected scallop-shaped beach north of Peniche best in large swells and SW to SE winds. Mid to high tide often best. A good learners and boogie board break.

22. Molho Leste

Protected righthanders break on the beach just south of the harbour at Peniche. Similar conditions to Supertubes.

23. Supertubos/Supertubes

The name speaks for itself. This is one of those breaks, (like Escondido in Mexico) that's described as "a close-out you can sometimes make." The nearby fish factory lends flavour to the experience and although the lefts are wicked, crowds and sometimes filthy water can mar the experience. Supertubos is a S swell break, offshores NE to NW. One of the most publicised waves in Europe and also a spectacular wave-sailing location.

24. Consolação

Point break south of Peniche works in similar conditions to Supertubes.

25. Praia da Areia Brancã (White Sands)

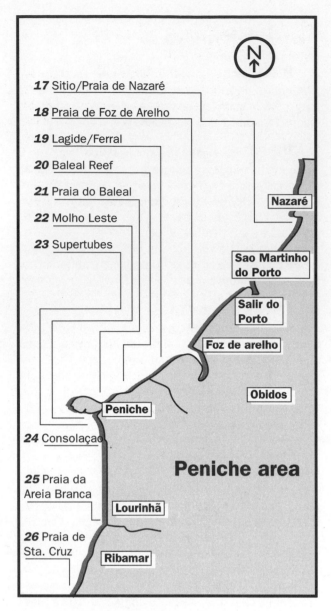

17 Sitio/Praia de Nazaré
18 Praia de Foz de Arelho
19 Lagide/Ferral
20 Baleal Reef
21 Praia do Baleal
22 Molho Leste
23 Supertubes
24 Consolaçao
25 Praia da Areia Branca
26 Praia de Sta. Cruz

Nazaré
Sao Martinho do Porto
Salir do Porto
Foz de arelho
Obidos
Peniche
Peniche area
Lourinhã
Ribamar

Unusual beach break with a river draining into it, forming good bars at low tide.

26. Santa Cruz

Particularly good beach. Works in similar conditions to the Ericeira breaks at various tides. Also a popular wave-sailing venue, especially in summer.

TRAVELLING AROUND

Tourist Office/Turismo:
Rua Alexander Herculano
2520 Peniche
Tel: 062 79571 Fax: 062 74049
They can advise on most basic tourist requirements, including rental cars, accommodation, maps etc... 'Quartos' or 'Dormidas' are cheap rooms for rent, otherwise there's a camping ground towards Baleal. Ask in bars for private accommodation. There's a good youth hostel above the beach at Areia Branca south of Peniche, Tel:061 42127.
Surf Report "Disc Surf"
24hr Portuguese language surfline covering Peniche – Costa Caparica. Tel: 01 486 8335

Ericeira

Ericeira was and is the Mecca of Portuguese surfing. In the early days, trips to Ericeira were pretty rare, and it was always a real adventure to surf up there. Ericeira itself was still a small fishing village where the bulk of visitors people were Portuguese on summer vacations. Rooms and food were dirt cheap, and surrounding towns were beautiful, white-washed houses, farm lands, just a general country look to it all. Beaches were rugged and car parks nonexistent. Crowds were never a problem.

Ericeira has grown up fast. Apartment buildings, restaurants and hotels have been built to keep up with the growing tourist population and a steady stream of Portuguese people in search of a get away spot relatively close to Lisbon. Many things were not taken into consideration, and the area has suffered. Beaches that handle a large crowd in the summer months have no clean up program. Even trash cans are scarce on most beaches. Sewage outlets which were originally set up to deal with a small town do not meet the demand of Ericeira as it is today. Pollution may be a major factor in Ericeira's future.

I still have great hopes for the future of this area and perhaps in time the pollution and littering will be controlled. I think anyone who has tasted the power and grown attached to this rugged bit of coastline would hope and work for the same.

THE SURF

The spots in and around Ericeira cover about 20kms by road and around 11kms by water. I have done a rough map of what I consider our major surf spots, and laid them out explaining tides, swell directions and bottom conditions. I'm an avid skin diver so the bottom conditions have been studied pretty well. Offshore winds for all these breaks come from the easterly quadrant.

Nick Uricchio/Semente Surfboards

Surf Breaks 27 – 39

Nick Uricchio/Semente Surfboards

27. São Lourenço

The first spot on the map is our version of Sunset. A deep water platform, a long paddle out from the beach, can hold giant surf if the swell direction is correct. Keep an eye out for sneaker sets from the west when its big. Wave characteristics include elevator drops and very fast hollow sections (because of the abruptness of the reef). N – NW swell is best but São Lourenço has seen some good days with extreme S swell. Will hold a little south wind without blowing out. 4 - 15ft.

28. Coxos

Said to be the best righthander in Europe. Swells come from deep water out the back and unload on an even reef platform. Best on N-NW swells on mid to low tide, but can be surfed right through high tide (exits get sketchy!!) Can also be extremely hollow and fast on S swells. It's a small bay if compared to other point breaks, so when it's big currents can be heavy as the water tries to find a way back out. Lots of paddling and clean-ups. Unforgiving, powerful and humbling on big days. Depending on swell direction and size it changes the type of wave you're surfing, always fun, 2 - 15ft.

29. Crazy Left

A tubey lefthander breaking over a rock reef bottom on the south side of Coxos bay. On S - SW days, hollow, fast and very powerful waves break from mid to high tide. On low tide Crazy Left closes out. Considered to be one of the best spots in the area. 3 - 10ft.

30. Pontinhã

Paddle or walk north from Ribeira. A high tide peak breaks right on N-NW swells, usually closes when direction becomes too westerly. Flat, sea-urchin infested reef bottom. Has some classic days. 3 - 8ft.

31. Ribeira D'Ilhas

A versatile bay with various peaks. Will work on most swells but best on W-NW. When good, one of the longest waves in the area and it works on all tides depending on the size and direction of the swell. One of the most consistently surfed spots during summer months. Rock sand bottom with long reefs running from deep ocean. 2 - 12ft.

32. The Reef

The first break on the Ericeira side of the hill, just a hair to the north of Backdoor right. Solid reef bottom, very shallow. It's 20ft deep right next to the peak and 3ft where you are dropping and gets shallower on the inside. When it's on it's pure magic! but no one surfs it a lot without paying the fiddler. Best one hour either side of mid tide (can be stretched depending on wave size). N-NW swells. 3 - 6ft.

33. Backdoor

Sits on the other side of this same bay. Usually a summer time break. Works best on N-NW swells. A rock sand bottom with strips of reef running towards land. Holds some very hollow sections. Sketchy on low tide. 3 - 8ft.

34. Pedra Branca (White Rock)

A deadly lefthand reef located in front of the camping ground north of Ericeira. Works best on S and SW swells and can handle large surf if direction is perfect. The bottom is another rock platform with big holes, and swell comes out of deep water, so it peaks with speed and power. Best from mid to high tide, (suicide at low), it's got a pipelinish look to it on good days. 3 - 10ft.

35. Praia Do Norte (North Beach)

From the northern side of the piling to the chapel on the end of the beach. Rock sand bottom, with long reef fingers throughout and an especially big platform at the northern point. Will work with all swell directions, but best known for the long rights from the N. S swells occasionally put out some good peaks, best 1 hour after low tide right through high. The point is very dry on low tide. 3 - 12ft.

36. Praia do Peixe (Fish Beach)

On the southern side of the Ericeira piling at the fisherman's port of entrance, you'll find a sandy

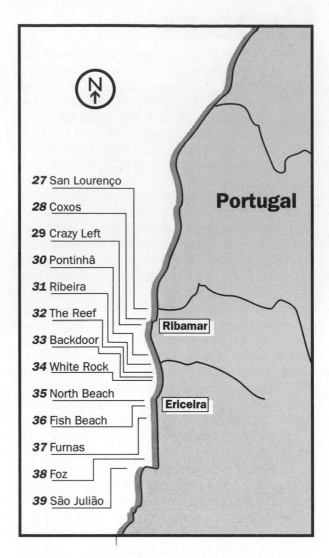

27 San Lourenço
28 Coxos
29 Crazy Left
30 Pontinhâ
31 Ribeira
32 The Reef
33 Backdoor
34 White Rock
35 North Beach
36 Fish Beach
37 Furnas
38 Foz
39 São Julião

Ribamar

Ericeira

Portugal

bottom lefthander that's usually pretty gutless. Best from low to mid tide. Needs a solid swell; best with SW, sometimes works on a big N. Can get very polluted in summer months because of a raw sewage outlet, thus definitely not the kind of place you travel to find.

37. Furnas

Right in front of the Ericeira Tourismo Hotel. Only works in a big N or NW swell, best coming off low tide right up through high. Lots of power, not too much tube. A last chance when everything else in Ericeira is impossibly big and you don't feel like driving. Rock bottom with patchy sand. 6 - 12ft.

38. Foz De Lizandro

A classic lefthand rivermouth wave forms when the fickle sand formation settles correctly. Best on a S or W swell from low to mid tide, with a strong backwash on high tide. Can hold some size and deal out some power. 3 - 10ft.

39. São Julião

A beach break that works on most swell directions and tides depending on sand flow. Sand bottom with scattered rocks in deeper water. This is a small (2 - 6ft) day spot that maxes out easily.

Lisbon

Lisbon lies on seven low hills at the mouth of the river Tagus. Her origin is shrouded in legend though the name originates from the Phoenician 'Allis Ubbo' or 'delightful port.' The city was successfully occupied by Greeks, Carthiginians, Romans, Visigoths and Moors, finally conquered in 1147 by Portugal's first king with the aid of English crusaders. It became the capital and the seat of the monarchy in 1255.

The old town was razed in a massive earthquake in 1755 and much of the modern city is a result of 18th century rebuilding. For both Lisbon and Portugal, the earthquake seemed to close an era. Nonetheless, the capital reflects the architectural and cultural influences of a prosperous and diverse history and still remains Portugal's centre for communications and transport across Europe and the world.

Both the castle of São Jorge (which stands on the site of the original Phoenican settlement on the hill above the city), and the various royal palaces in Sintra, are breathtaking for the glimpse into history they provide. They must be seen to be believed.

THE SURF

It was undoubtedly along the Estoril/Carcavelos coast that wave sports had their birth. The whole area pumps with various breaks offering killer conditions for Lisbon's surfers and wave-sailors and a good percentage of the surf industry can be found here, close to international travel routes, markets and good surf beaches.

N and W swells break consistently on the beaches at Guincho, Praia Grande and Costa Caparica. In big W or average S swells, the 'Estoril line' beaches and points become the scene of frantic surf activity for Lisbon's bustling surf community.

Various problems are emerging, however, along this area of coast as a result of increasing population pressures. Unfortunately the water at the inner harbour beaches is almost alive with filth. Many Portuguese parents prevent their children swimming here and though many people surf here, it would have to be pretty good to tempt me in.

Both Guincho and the Costa Caparica offer cleaner alternatives to the main city beaches – vote with your feet.

TRAVELLING AROUND

As with all European capitals, Lisbon offers a huge array of things to do, places to stay etc.. Most surfers will find the areas south or north more desirable places to stay, but as most roads lead to Lisbon, you'll end up there for sure.

TOURIST OFFICES: These are mines of information where English is widely spoken. You'll find them at Lisbon airport, Rocha and Sta Apolonia Railway Stations and;
● Arcadas do Parque (Estoril) Tel: 2680113
● Avenida Dom Carlos 1, (Cascais)

EMBASSIES AND CONSULATES:

UK: Rua S. Domingos a Lapa 37.
        Tel 661191

US: Avda. das Forcas Armadas
        Tel 726600

AUS: Avda. da Liberdade 244-4
        Tel 523350

There'is also an English language information line on Tel: (1) 369450

AIRLINE OFFICES: Most are along Av de Liberdado B.A. No 36-2, Air France 224A, Air Maroc 225. Airport Info: 721101, 802060

BANKS: Many Portuguese and foreign banks open standard hours 8.30 - 11.45 & 3 - 7pm. An 8am-8pm currency exchange at Santa Apolonia Railway Station

EMERGENCIES: Tel: 115

HOSPITAL: British Hospital at Rua Saravade de Carvalho #49, Tel: 602020.
Emergency Tel: 603785.

MAPS: Topographic maps of the whole country from: Servicios Cartographicos de Exercito, Avda Dr Alfredo Bensaudé, Olivais Norte, 9 - 11am & 1-4.30pm.

TOURISM POLICE: (24hrs) Rua Capelo 13, Chiado. Tel:366141

TRAIN & BUS INFO: From the Rossio information office Tel:876025. Trains to Madrid leave from Santa Apolonia station.

TRAVEL AGENTS: They are everywhere; try, Tagus Juvenil, Praca de Londres, 9B Tel: 884957, otherwise ask at the tourismo.

SURF REPORT 'DISC SURF'
24hr Portuguese language surfline from Costa Caparica – Peniche Tel: 01 486 8335

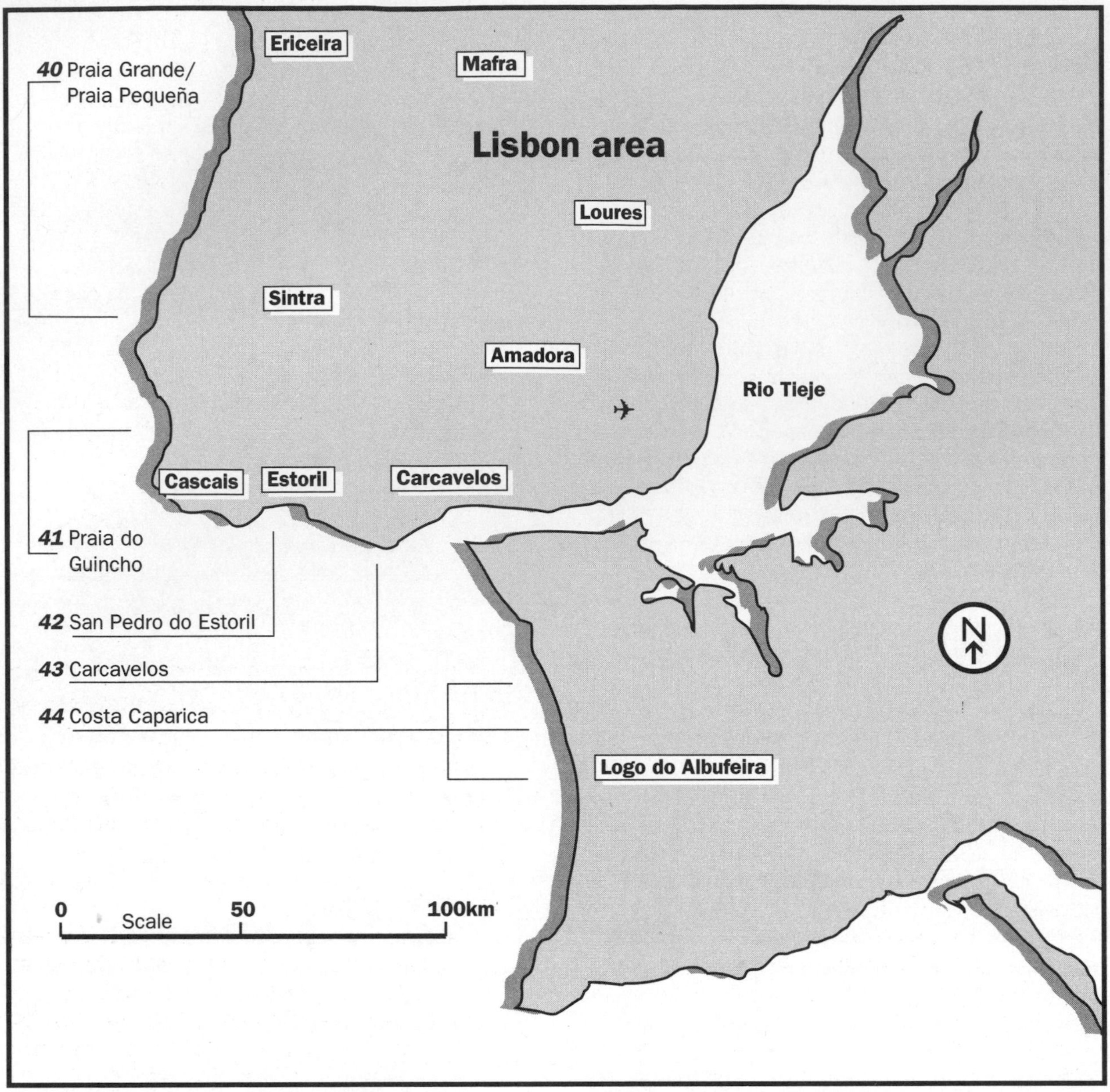
Ericeira
Mafra
40 Praia Grande/
Praia Pequeña
Lisbon area
Loures
Sintra
Amadora
Rio Tieje
Cascais
Estoril
Carcavelos
41 Praia do
Guincho
42 San Pedro do Estoril
43 Carcavelos
44 Costa Caparica
Logo do Albufeira
N
0
Scale
50
100km

Surf Breaks 40 – 53

Eduardo & Alvaro/Polen Surf Designs

40. Praia Grande/Praia Pequena

The most consistent location in the Lisbon area, which can provide powerful, beach break waves on all tides. An infamous shore break is very popular with bodyboard enthusiasts. Summer often sees small, crowded surf, but from September, swell up to 4mtrs and colder water produce a more acceptable balance of conditions. Praia Pequena is the northern continuation of the same beach with similar characteristics but less crowds. A dirt road leads to a small parking lot. Offshores for both beaches are in the easterly quadrant.

Water Quality: The beach can get dirty but the water isn't too bad.

41. Praia do Guincho

A popular west facing beach. Photos of huge surf published in *Surfer Magazine* in September 1967 first made the waiting world aware of Portugal's surf potential. Guincho is Portugal's most popular wave-sailing location, and the venue for the Guincho Wave Classic, an annual stop on the Peter Stuyvestant Tour. Strong summer NW winds provide classic sailing conditions. Strong winter swells do the same for surf conditions.

42. São Pedro do Estoril

Righthand point break near town of Estoril. Best at low tide. Works in similar conditions to Carcavelos.

Water Quality: A pioneering location, now very polluted.

43. Carcavelos

One of the first Portuguese surf breaks to be ridden, Carcavelos is a powerful and tubular beach break. In a strong NW swell lefts predominate. S swells get in easier and waves tend to break right. Low tide often closes out and high tide can get fat – mid tides usually the best bet. Being a central city break, crowding gets bad with the best peaks being dominated by locals.

Water Quality: As already mentioned, water quality here is highly suspicious and this is a major cause of local concern, yet we seem powerless to effect change. This depressing state of affairs is already the breeding ground of some strong sentiment.

44. Costa Caparica

South of the River Teijo, this crescent-shaped stretch of coast collects a lot of swell. Costa Caparica is also the name given to its most northerly town but the coast works in different conditions along its entire length. Praia Nova is the most popular bodyboarding location – by tradition more than for any other reason. There's easy parking for the first 8kms with numerous beach restaurants. Other spots down this stretch of coast to Cabo Espichel can be reached with a bit of effort, including Praia do Meco and other more secluded destinations.

South Portugal

Southern Portugal remains one of Europe's surfing enigmas. Various good peaks have been discovered and many are rumoured. The Atlantic coast is without doubt more consistent but the South Coast between Sagres and Faro definitley gets surf. The climate is one of Europe's most favourable and if you avoid the tourist traps, the water is remarkably clean. Faro is the cheepest palce to fly to in Portugal and car rentals easy to arrange. Late winter is often the best time to head here. Regardless of the waves a good time can always be found on the beaches.

Surf Breaks 45 – 53

45. Comporta

One beach stretches from Comporta all the way to Sines. The further south one travels, the more exposed the coast becomes. Access is restricted by a shortage of beach roads but the best banks can often be found around **Santa André**.

46. Sines/São Torpes

An uncrowded south to west facing beach stretching from Sines to Porto Covo. The best season is autumn and winter and crowds are generally not a problem. The area works on all tides in S to W swells with offshores from the N to E.

47. Vila Nova de Milfontes

Various reefs with a small beach located just south of the river Mira. 'O Canal' – (The Channel) is the best known spot – a long righthander located north of the village which holds swell from 3 - 15ft! Other breaks also provide good conditions in big winter surf.

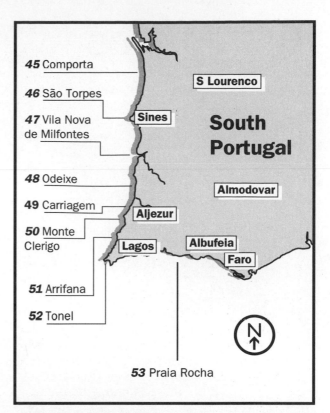

48, 49, 50. Odeixe, Carriagem and Monte Clerigo

Three beach breaks which pick up all N and W swells and share similar conditions that work well in summer time. Unpolluted and uncrowded, Offshores come from the E.

51. Arrifana

The road descends steeply to a protected southwest facing bay. Constant sand bars that form over rocks in the middle of the beach hold powerful waves in S or big NW swells. When the surf gets above 2mtrs, a righthand reef on the edge of the bay goes off, long and fast with a hazardous reputation. Offshores are from the NE. A totally chill place to catch some waves in the off season.

52. Tonel/Sagres

Sagres used to be considered 'Lands End' by early Portuguese navigators. Tubular waves break over rocks in the centre of a compact beach. The water is exceptionally clean but its proximity to the Algarve can lead to crowding during peak summer months. Winter is usually the best time to surf and whilst the water remains cool, air temperatures this far south stay pleasant even in February. Access is somewhat confusing – a small path leads to the beach from the road to Cabo S. Vicente.

53. Algarve (South Coast)

Surf happens in the Algarve but S swell is less frequent than W and N. Various spots catch swell most often in late winter including Praia Rocha and the sand bars protecting Faro (visible from the plane when landing from the south). There are a couple of superb, *very* secret spots on the south coast but you'll have to use initiative to find them.

The Azores

A massive sub-sea volcanic chain extends north to south along the Atlantic from Iceland almost to Antarctica. The Azores archipelago represents the highest peaks of the Mid Atlantic Ridge. Nine main islands and many smaller protrusions make up the group which lie some 700 miles west of Lisbon in mid Atlantic. Like Madeira, Portugal's other Atlantic island colony, much of the land masses subside steeply into the sea, especially on S. Jorge.

The Azores are climatically influenced by the 'Azores/Mid Atlantic High,' a consistent zone of high pressure centred in this region contributing to the prevailing N and W winds. Air temperatures, like on the Canaries are moderated by the Atlantic and vary between 55°C in winter and 75°C in summer.

The water is cold in winter, warm in summer and filled with wierd marine life including some of the the planet's largest species of shark and squid, with great whites being the most common. On S. Miguel, there's even a restaurant specialising in shark meat, appropriately named 'White Shark.' Yeah, right! There's not much to say about this – avoid cutting your feet on the reefs!

THE SURF

The Azores are a sparsely populated group of islands which receive abundant swell. The first semblance of surfing reportedly appeared at the turn of the century in the form of bodyboarding. Home-made surfboards were first ridden in 1962 or 1963, but little contact was made with foreign surfers until the mid 70's when a group of US Air Force personnel based on Terceira got wise to the potential surrounding them. The word has spread, but not very far yet. As all roads lead to Lisbon, Portuguese surfers are the most common visitors, though growing numbers of adventurous Australians, Americans and other European nationals can be found on this dramatic and verdant island group. The locals are not exactly friendly to visitors, especially on the north of San Miguel, but with respect and modesty, problems be few.

Swells come from the N, NW, W and S, though it is once again from big North Atlantic lows that the largest waves originate and it gets **big**! Like on the Canaries, the best peaks break over lava reefs.

Surf Breaks: 54 – 72

ILHA DO FAIAL
54. Praia do Norte.

A left point break in Baie da Ribeira das Cadras. Holds surf up to 3mtrs plus in W to N swells. Faces north.

55. Praia do Almoxarife

Situated north of the main town, Horta, a sand and pebble beach breaks in big N or SE swells. Lefts also break off the small jetty (Cais).

ILHA DO PICO

North swells undoubtedly hit the northwest section of the coast, especially around Mourato and Baia do Cachorro. The quality of surf has yet to be fully explored. Lots of spots pick up south swell, especially around S. Mateur and Lajes de Pico.

ILHA DE SAN JORGE

The steepest of all the group. The land tilts madly into the sea. Several points on the north coast are accessible and visible from the main coast road.

56. Faja dos Cubres

Two breaks, the first reputedly Portugal's longest left. Another fast righthander breaks off the northern face of the point. Also visible from here are other breaks formed by huge landslides.

57. Punta da Caldeira

Long lefthand point, rarely surfed. Further north, good potential exists around Faja do Ouridor and Faja da Ponta Furada.

ILHA GRACIOSA

The smallest of the main group, Graciosa receives no protection from N and W swells. Two breaks near the town of Praia:

58. Lagou

Breaks left and right over volcanic reefs.

59. Porto da Praia (South)

Another left and right peak. North from Sta. Cruz de Graciosa. Pta. da Barca and Porto Alfonso show good potential.

ILHA TERCIERA (From The NW)
60. Pta do Queimado

Shows good potential for good lefts.

61. Baie des Quarto Ribeiras (Four Rivers)

At the village of the same nam, another left and right reef.

62. Vila Nova

A north facing right point that breaks best at high tide.

63. Praia Vitoria

Around this town various spots can be surfed including Sta Catarina, a fast right with a smaller, usually hollower left, located north of the pier at Vila Praia da Vitoria.

64. Porto Martins

Small village south of Vitoria holds three breaks.

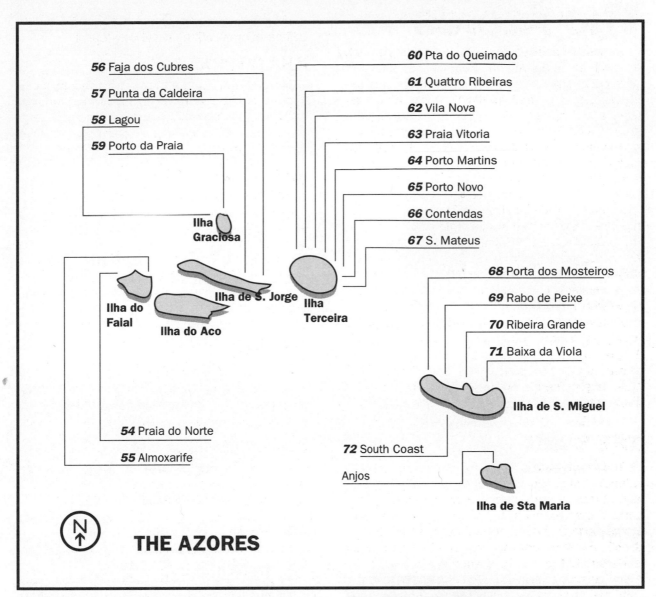

56 Faja dos Cubres
57 Punta da Caldeira
58 Lagou
59 Porto da Praia

60 Pta do Queimado
61 Quattro Ribeiras
62 Vila Nova
63 Praia Vitoria
64 Porto Martins
65 Porto Novo
66 Contendas
67 S. Mateus

68 Porta dos Mosteiros
69 Rabo de Peixe
70 Ribeira Grande
71 Baixa da Viola

Ilha Graciosa

Ilha do Faial
Ilha do Aco
Ilha de S. Jorge
Ilha Terceira

Ilha de S. Miguel

54 Praia do Norte
55 Almoxarife

72 South Coast
Anjos

Ilha de Sta Maria

THE AZORES

Porto Martins (a righthand point in the village) Ponta do Negro and Pescador (two left points close to town).

65. Porto Novo
Right reef in front of the town.

66. Contendas
A lefthand point breaks in big N swells.

67. São Mateus da Calherta
South facing righthand point which picks up all S swells.

ILHA SAN MIGUEL
A bizarre and lush volcanic island more populated than the others. Three volcanic cones have large crater lakes, two have settlements built around them. The north coast offers the groups most versatile surfing location of the islands, but 'localism' is strong here.

68. Ponta dos Mosteiros
Various right and left reefs located on the extreme northwest tip of island. Must get massive!

69. Rabo de Peixe
A small promontory breaks right and left in front of village of the same name. Big potential.

70. Ribeira Grande
Beach breaks in front of the biggest town on the north coast, 5kms east of Rabo de Peixe.

71. Baixa da Viola
Good potential exists around much of the north coast – not too steep with a lot of indentations to break swell. 2kms north of Maia, four rivers funnel into the ocean. Strictly a walking mission.

72. South Coast
Various south coast spots hold S swell including Ribeira Quente and Ponta Delgado. Check it out!

ILHA DE SANTA MARIA
Ilha de santa maria is a small island. The western coast is extremely steep with little access to it. Anjos is the best northwest facing break and is yet another righthand reef. One of the main beaches is named after the town of Praia and it faces south.

ITALY

Capital: Rome
Population: 57,400,000
Area: 301,268 km²
Time: GMT +1 (+2 in Summer)
Religion: Catholic
Language: Italian
Currency: Lira

LIGURIA

Luca Garibaldi

Surf Breaks 1 – 7

1. Ventimiglia

Sandbank, south swells, only break in Liguria that works on a N or E wind (common in Spring and autumn).

2. Andorra (between Albenga and Imperia)

Sandbank between two rock jetties. Closes out when big.

3. Varazze

The best break in the north of Italy. Beautiful characteristic Italian town, good restaurants etc. Long tubey lefts break over artificial reefs. Ten people is a crowd.

4. Bogliasco (between Genova and Savona)

Surfing in north Italy started here and today there's a small surfing community. It's a pretty place that's protected from most winds. Just east of Genova. (Marco Fracas, was perhaps Italy's first surfer and this break was probably surfed for the first time in 1975).

5. Chiávari

Two breaks: One near the harbour wall handles huge swells. The other near the rivermouth...very dirty unfortunately but works in smaller swells.

6. Lévanto

Varied break which you can surf in various conditions. This town is nothing special but is a convenient location. Strong rips. Sandbanks and rock bottom.

7. Lérici

Beach on rock bottom. Nice town. Last break in Liguria, just south of La Spezia.

TUSCANY

More noted for its inland beauty and historical pedigree than for its huge surf. From Lerici south, all the beaches are very similar but one can find some particularly interesting artificial reefs.

Surf Breaks 8 – 9

8. Viareggio

The most popular location – two or three shops (including Natural Surf).

9. Livorno

A big town, many surfers, seven or eight breaks mostly sand and rock bottoms. Friendly place with a party atmosphere.

ROMA

All the coast from Orbetello to Rome gets S swell. The Roman coast is consistent and some of Italy's best surfers come from here. Competitions and clubs are common. Check it out!

Surf Breaks 10 – 14

10. Santa Marinella – Banzai

Just north of the city, heavy tubes break over rocks.

11, 12. Ostia & Circeo

The closest breaks to town are Ostia and Circeo. As in the movie *Wind in Your Hands* – filmed in Ostia! – check out the waves!

13. Napoli

South Italy is cheap and fun! Wes Lane lived here as a kid for two years and apparently surfed loads. Due to a NATO base, many US Navy personnel are based here.

South of Napoli is new territory, you'll have to go see for yourself but it gets lots of swell, especially in autumn, winter and spring.

14. The Boot And The Heel Go Off!

...So they say.

SICILY

15. The Pearl of the Med

Good all around the island especially the west and northwest tip, near Licata, also the small islands, Liparicca etc. One of the most beautiful and historic places on the planet holds other reasons to travel here, but if you bring your board you could well get surf.

SARDINIA

The best place to surf and sail in the Med! The Mistral winds from the NW and Sirocco from the SE both bring swell. Locals report surf on average 23 days per month during autumn, winter and spring – up to 12ft!

The landscape is incredibly varied, as are the surf breaks. Sardinian hospitality is legendary!

Much of the island still needs discovering.

Carlo Marazzi

16, 17. Isla la Rosa and Badesi

Two spots popular with Romans and Genoese that are considered amongst the best breaks in the Mediterranean. Compared to the Atlantic for power and consistency. Touristy area – and not especially cheap.

18. Porto Ferre

Another excellent spot. Long, extremely consistent and works in the Mistral. The bottom is rocky at take-off and ends up over sand. Often over 2mtrs and often protected or offshore as a result of mountain valleys funnelling breezes. 15km from Alghero. Accommodation is easy – best is Agro Tourismo (Farm Cottages) at £4 - £6 per night.

19. Alghero to Bosa

There's a road 100mtrs above the sea from which you can see the works – many breaks are visible, some surfed, most not. The coast south of Bosa offers the best surfing in Sardinia, with waves often over 6ft. The best spots are:

20. Putzu Idu.

Around this peninsula northwest of Oristano, the best surf can be found on SW and NW swells. At least four famous spots. The south facing **Capo Manu** and **Mini Cap**o are best and work in all breezes due to natural protection. The sea bottom is granite and the waves long powerful righthanders. Two other famous spots are **Su Pallosu** & **Sa Rocca Tunda/La Laguna**. They work with NW winds giving powerful waves over a sharp rocky bottom. The locals are friendly, they're called Bobo Lutzo and Georgio Stagno.

21. Portieddu (Little Harbour) & Buggerru

Two villages where you can find powerful surf. Only possible to surf on an abating swell, exposed

and unsurfable otherwise. These breaks are often uncrowded.

22. Chia

Faces southeast, 50km from Caglari. One of the most beautiful spots on the island, surrounded by dunes – also the best spot on the south coast. Consistent swells, surfable from 180° at two main spots, both sandbanks. **Il Pontille** (the jetty) – Winds from SE, take-off over rocks covered by sand. Long but can be less powerful than Pipe. **Pipeline** – The name is an indication when the wind is east (offshore) in SE swell, up to 8ft extremely fast, steep waves break on almost dry sand. The most fun spot on the south coast but prices for accommodation can be high.

23. Caglari/Poetto

Like Malibu – main break in a main town. Everyone learns to surf here in waves up to 6ft which break on consistent sand banks. Best months are Sept/Oct and March/April. **Torre Della Stella**; good spot in W winds.

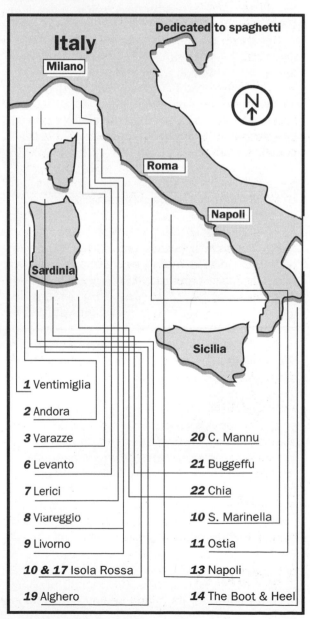

Map: Italy — Milano, Roma, Napoli, Sardinia, Sicilia. Dedicated to spaghetti.

1 Ventimiglia
2 Andora
3 Varazze
6 Levanto
7 Lerici
8 Viareggio
9 Livorno
10 & 17 Isola Rossa
19 Alghero

20 C. Mannu
21 Buggeffu
22 Chia
10 S. Marinella
11 Ostia
13 Napoli
14 The Boot & Heel

Surf & Co
"Gigi" Camba
Via Paoli, 71 Caglari

Sardinian Surf Association (SSA)
c/ Maurizio Spinas, Calgari
Tel: 070 654607

water quality

Marine Pollution

A recent survey has shown that the three main environmental concerns of the public in the UK are all about the marine environment: Chemicals put into rivers and seas, sewage contamination of beaches and bathing water, and oil spills at sea.

The problems encountered result from the entirely legal discharge of effluent through outdated and inadequate outfalls which have been in place since Victorian times, and from a continued dependence on dilution, and the decomposition of pollutants by sun light and sea salts.

Pollution occurs with the introduction into the sea of any substance which is harmful to wildlife, threatens human health or reduces marine activities and amenities. An enormous range of such substances enters our seas – deliberately, accidentally, or through sheer negligence – often creating pollution problems far from their source.

Beaches littered with rubbish, raw sewage at the water's edge, panty liners, sanitary towels, toilet tissue, condoms and other sanitary products not to mention oil on the rocks and lumps of tar on your surfboard – these are the most visible signs. But there are other, more insidious pollutants like poisonous chemicals, pesticides and radioactivity. Such pollutants may be invisible but their effects are not, and they can be equally as damaging, or more so than the obvious ones. The sea has no fences. The effects of polution are never solely isolated – it spreads throughout the ecosystem, combining with other pollutants to create compounded problems.

Types Of Marine Pollution

Waste can be classified under three main types: domestic, industrial and agricultural. **Domestic waste** includes sewage, silt, oil, lead, tar and de-icing chemicals which are used on the roads. **Industrial waste** includes, for example, radioactive waste, toxic chemicals, thermal discharges, refuse and oil from ships, as well as degradable organic waste from the paper, pulp and food processing industries. **Agricultural waste** such as fertilisers and organic matter are all potentially dangerous.

For years the sea has been used as a cheap and easy waste disposal system on a vast scale. Nine million tonnes of sewage sludge (the by-product of sewage treatment works), 42 million tonnes of dredged spoil – the silt removed from harbours and estuaries to keep them clear for shipping – and over two million tonnes of industrial waste, are dumped off UK shores each year. The wastes also contain high levels of chemical contamination with the result that the North Sea, for example, receives over 10 tonnes of mercury, 12 tonnes of cadmium, 1,250 tonnes of lead and 200 tonnes of copper each year.

Sources Of Pollution

The source of a pollutant may be easy to identify – an outfall pipe or dump ship deliberately discharging waste into the sea. However, sewage outfall pipes are very rarely marked for the public to see, which can be disastrous. Waste also enters the sea via rivers, from ships, through land run-off, and from the atmosphere. Some of the sources are easy to locate, others are less easy to define, and hence to control. An estimated five million tonnes of oil enter the sea each year, but only 4% comes from major tanker accidents. The majority is released during routine shipping and oil refining operations. In many cases individual pollution incidents are neither obvious nor devastating to the local area. However, their cumulative effect means that all the trade routes and ocean currents abound with tar balls, many of which will eventually end up on beaches.

The sources of pesticides and other agricultural chemicals which find their way into streams, rivers and eventually the sea are difficult to locate accurately. These chemicals, particularly the organo-chlorines like aldrin and dieldrin, are extremely stable and persistent. They accumulate in the sea and have been found in virtually all marine mammals – and in humans.

The Effects Of Pollution

In some cases the effects of pollution are easy to identify and link to specific causes:

Plastics

Plastics discarded overboard entangle wildlife causing death by drowning or strangulation. It has been estimated that 2 million seabirds and 100,000 marine mammals are killed each year due to marine debris, either by ingesting it or becoming entangled in it. The death of a marine animal may not be as easy to attribute to marine litter if the animal has eaten the refuse and died either because of some poisonous chemical in the waste, or starvation due to a permanently full stomach. On the shoreline, where much refuse ends up, it remains a hazard for wildlife and the beach user.

Oil

The consequences of oil pollution are not only the obvious oiled seabird or oil-spotted sands – there are also toxic effects. Water-soluble chemicals in oil are poisonous to animals and plants. The dumping of solid wastes also causes direct physical damage to marine life, smothering animals and plants, but as with many pollution problems there are combined effects. For example, dredged spoil is highly contaminated with chemicals. Dumping wastes offshore not only does physical damage to the environment but the chemicals are released and may poison wildlife, or affect their growth and reproduction.

Toxic Chemicals

Thousands of chemicals like mercury (used in the paper and pulp industry), lead from petrol, titanium dioxide (a whitener in the paint industry), polychlorinated biphenols (found in electrical components), pesticides like organichlorines (e.g. DDT) are released into the sea and have been found in all marine life. They have been linked to fish diseases, the disappearance of species and breeding failure.

In very low concentrations the chemicals may have minimal effect but the danger increases as they become concentrated up the food chain. A single shrimp may have a tolerable amount of a chemical in its body but when a fish eats lots of shrimps it absorbs all the chemicals from each shrimp and the result can be lethal. For example, around Minamata Bay in Japan, 46 people died and 2,000 people suffered from crippling mental and physical deformities. The tragedy was the result of eating shellfish from the bay which had accumulated methyl mercury released to the waters from a local factory.

Radioactive Waste

A radioactive atom disintegrates by emitting particles – radioactive decay. This is the process which causes the problem. The half-life is the time taken for half the radioactivity to be emitted. Radioactive decay can be slow: Strontium 90 and Caesium 137 have half-lives of about 30 years; plutonium 239 has a half-life of about 25,000 years – these are discharged from nuclear plants. The particles emitted may be alpha, beta or gamma, each having different biological and physical effects. Nuclear plants discharge radioactive waste into the air, rivers and sea.

Radioactive pollution occurs in the normal working of nuclear plants. But widespread radioactive pollution can occur after accidents, the most severe being the explosion at the Chernobyl nuclear power station in Russia. Other nuclear plants have also suffered accidents.

High doses of radioactivity quickly kill animals. Lower doses cause cancers, tumours and leukemia that can kill in the long term; very low doses cause mutations and genetic abnormalities. Radioactive materials accumulate in marine life and can travel up the food chain. Or they can reach humans in contaminated sea spray and in sediments moving shorewards.

Sewage

Sewage is a particular problem that has direct effects on beaches and bathers, surfers, windsurfers, divers and sailors. Over 300 million gallons of sewage are disposed of in our coastal waters each day! Of 590 significant sea outfalls in the UK (i.e. serving populations of 10,000+) 37% have no treatment, 50% have preliminary treatment (i.e. usually screening of larger solids), 11% have primary treatment and only 2% have secondary treatment. It's frequently discharged close to the shore and the raw sewage, often toilet paper, fat balls and other nuisance solids, is washed back on to the beach with the incoming tide or moved about offshore by the currents.

This is not only very unsightly but also harmful to health. The sewage contains bacteria and viruses that can cause a number of infections of the ear, nose and throat, gastro-enteritis (diarrhoea) and skin infections all of which are common place. There's also the added risk of more serious infections such as Viral Meningitis and Hepatitis B.

An example is a report recently published in the *British Medical Journal* which concluded that paddlers were 25% more at risk from minor infections than those who stayed on the beach, swimmers 31% and people participating in active water sports 80%.

An upset stomach or a bad throat suffered on holiday might have been caused by swimming, surfing, diving or sailing in polluted water or by eating shellfish that had accumulated the bacteria filtered from the sea water.

The discharge of sewage also affects marine life. The decomposition of the sewage requires oxygen, and the reduction in oxygen that occurs as the sewage is broken down can lead to a decline in the number and variety of plants and animals.

Sewage also releases a large amount of nutrients into the water which can result in algal blooms. There are two kinds of algae: Animal (zooplankton) and plant (phytoplankton) and these plankton thrive on the high nutrient levels in the water, causing a bloom at the expense of less tolerant species. As the algal colonies die, they break up and create foam which can be evil-smelling and is frequently washed up on to the shore. An additional problem caused by this increase in organic load results from the recent discovery that large amounts of organic matter can overcome the bactericidal effects of sea temperature and light thus resulting in an increased risk of infection.

Pollution Control

There are several international and national agreements which aim to control pollution. The problem with many of these agreements is achieving their successful implementation. For example, the International Agreement on the Prevention of Marine Pollution from Land (the Paris Commission, 1974) lists a series of chemicals that must only be discharged in 'trace amounts.' It is the interpretation of this definition that has caused problems in its implementation.

The International Convention for the Prevention

of Pollution from Ships (MARPOL 73/78) and its five annexes were originally drawn up in 1973. But they were only to come into force when enough countries, representing 50% of the world's shipping tonnage, signed each part of the agreement. Until then it could be effectively ignored even by those that had signed. The Convention and Annexes 1 and 2 were agreed and became law in 1978. It was not until the end of 1987, ten years later, that the United States signed Annexe 5, concerning dumping of refuse from ships. This took the tonnage over the 50% mark, making the Annexe law 12 months later in December 1988.

As of January 1989 it became illegal to dispose of any plastic from ships at sea. Added to this, other forms of garbage, biodegradable food waste etc, can only be discharged at sea under strictly controlled conditions. The refuse now has to be deposited at special reception facilities which should have been set up at ports and harbours.

It is hoped this will improve the colossal problem of marine litter. Unfortunately the law only applies to the countries who have signed the Annexe (approximately 75% of the world fleet). How the regulations are to be enforced remains to be seen. Annexes 3 and 4 of the convention are not yet ratified by sufficient countries.

The European Community has introduced legislation to control pollution, but there have been problems with the implementation of these regulations also. The Directive on Discharges into the Aquatic Environment, which attempted to stop dumping, was never introduced because of a UK veto: However, the UK Government is now much more committed to cleaning up the seas and has said it will stop dumping sludge by 1995.

The EC Bathing Water Directive was introduced in 1976 when, after three years and much persuasion, Britain designated its 'bathing beaches'. It designated only 27. France designated 1,498, Italy 3,308, and even Luxembourg, with no coastline, came up with more bathing sites than Britain – 34.

Resorts such as Brighton and Blackpool (without a doubt one of the largest bathing resorts in Europe) did not feature within the 27, indicating a lack of commitment to the spirit of the Directive. It was not until 1987, after much criticism, that the Government yielded to pressure and the number was increased to 391. By 1990 this has risen to 446. The problem is that of defining and agreeing on terms, and such dogma has plagued the EC Bathing Water Directive throughout its existence. Even now, there is no standard European interpretation of the Directive and thus the results from each EC country are not comparable.

The EC bathing water directive (76/160/EC) has two main objectives:

● To improve or maintain the quality of bathing water for reasons of amenity.

● To protect public health.

The EC standard was apparently based on that of the United States Environmental Protection Agency, although it is considerably less stringent.

Comparisons of International Standards

Standards set by the EC and other countries are shown below;

County/Authority	Sampling Frequency	Faecal Coliform Std
EC STATES	Fortnightly (summer only)	Guide – 100/100ml Mandatory 2000/100ml
TORONTO	Daily	Geometric mean <100/100ml
U.S.E.P.A	5/Month	Geometric mean <200/100ml <10% to exceed 400/100ml

The coliforms are bacteria which are used as indicators of faecal pollution and their presence in bathing water also signifies the presence of harmful disease-causing pathogens.

The National Rivers Authority, Britain's government funded watchdog, presently bases its water quality assessment on a weekly sampling regime conducted through the summer months. The only microbiological parameters taken in to consideration are those of total and faecal coliforms. However, these organisms rapidly die off in sea water, whereas the potentially harmful pathogens can persist for weeks and thus should be monitored. Other flaws in the EC directive include a lack of data from which to assess the compliance of various beaches. This problem can be overcome by monitoring water quality through the winter months, more frequently in the summer and at more than one location on each beach.

In the past, pollution control has very much been about the implementation of regulations to solve problems when they have been proved to be damaging the environment.

If we are to solve the problems of our seas, however, we must adopt a precautionary approach.

This acknowledges that we don't know the effects of all substances that are discharged and should therefore err on the side of caution and not discharge these materials, **even if there is no scientific evidence that they actually cause damage.**

Widely accepted throughout Europe, this concept is only just beginning to be given consideration in the UK. The sea is not infinitely self-cleaning and we cannot continue to use it as a huge dustbin.

Bob Earll/The Marine Conservation Society

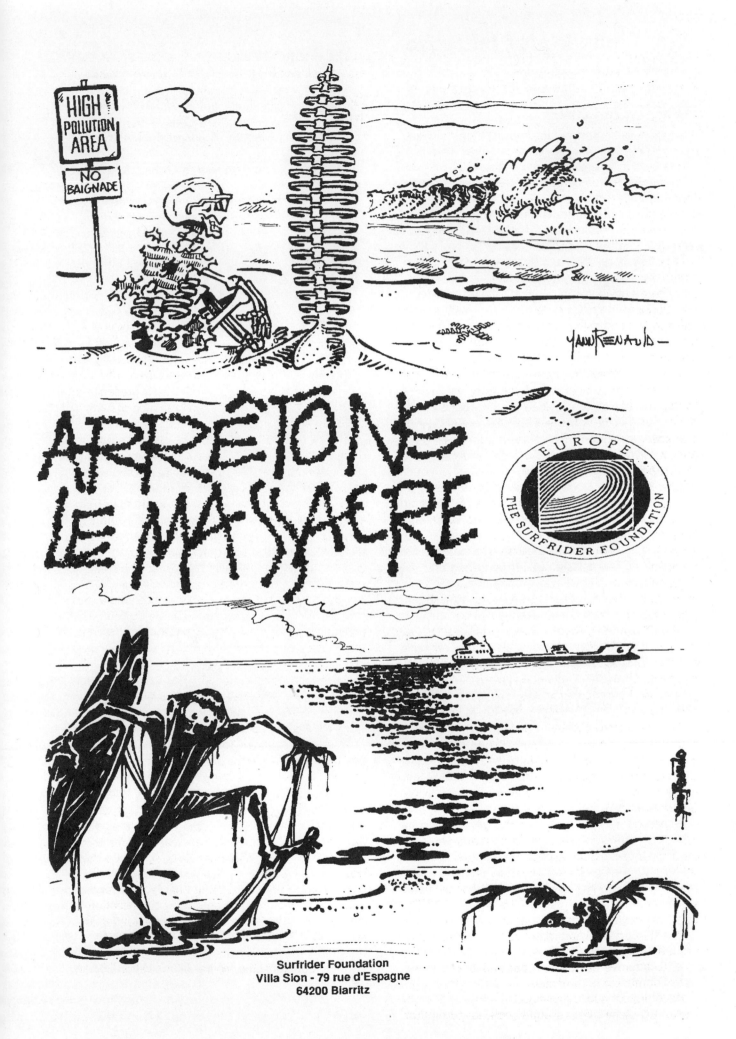

Surfrider Foundation
Villa Sion - 79 rue d'Espagne
64200 Biarritz

The Clean Water Initiative (CWI)

What is the CWI?

While we stand around scratching our heads wondering what we can do, our oceans are being systematically raped by organisations, policies and individuals that constantly escape the attention that their activities deserve.

The biggest problem currently faced by the public and marine conservationists is the lack of hard evidence to back up pleas for restraint by those responsible for the revolting discharges of every kind, regularly found around Europe's beaches.

The Clean Water Initiative has been founded as an educational aid organisation providing scholarship-type grants to students working on problem finding and solving within European recreational coastal environments.

The first project has been the funding of Patrick Harty (BSc Hons) in a testing scheme covering many of Europe's key bathing locations. Initial samples will be analysed for the faecal coliform bacteria using equipment supplied by the University of Surrey.

The study is being overseen by an independent group of reputable scientists and conservationists including the Robens Institute, The Plymouth Marine Laboratory and The Surfrider Foundation (Europe and USA).

Indisputable evidence derived from advanced scientific investigation, experimentation and development would supply environmental groups with the ammunition they need to fight the fat cats who consistently ignore rapidly deepening problems.

The CWI was formed on order to provide just this sort of information for groups like Surfrider Foundation, A.D.E.S., Surfers Against Sewage and Friends of the Earth.

What has CWI done so far?

In its first year the CWI has forged links between a number of educational and research establishments as well as environmental groups, and is now trying to get industry involved in debates and projects.

Research has been conducted throughout Europe and the findings submitted for publication in science journals, newspapers and magazines.

The CWI is responsible for the only pan-European survey of faecal pollution based on techniques that allow inter-comparisons of data from the various EC member states.

Detailed studies of particular beaches have also been conducted. Findings provided evidence to support the request for a revision of the EEC bathing water directive having demonstrated patterns of faecal dispersion that result in surfers and many bathers regularly being exposed to levels of pollution far in excess of those reported by the authorities.

Appendix

'Thermo-tolerant faecal coliforms' are exclusive to human sewage. A specific bacteria (E-coliform) is tested for, using equipment and methods which comply with EC guidelines. Levels are as follows:

Imperative level: 2,000 bacteria per 100ml sample.

Recommended guideline: 100 bacteria per 100ml sample.

Clean Water: 0 bacteria per 100 ml sample.

	CWI Faecal coliform per 100ml		NRA Faecal coliform per 100ml	
CORNWALL	High	Low	High	Low
Portreath	188	10	630	0
Porthtowan	190	<10	>10000	0
Trevaunance	3140	146	4900	30
Perran Village	304	66	>10000	2
Holywell	498	100	1400	4
Crantock	1980	60	1400	8
Fistral	1100	10	380	0
Towan	3200	160	4200	0
Watergate	700	40	44000	0
Mawgan Porth	2300	420	3700	0
Polzeath	358	96	2400	2
WALES				
Langland Bay	1740	1310	800	<10

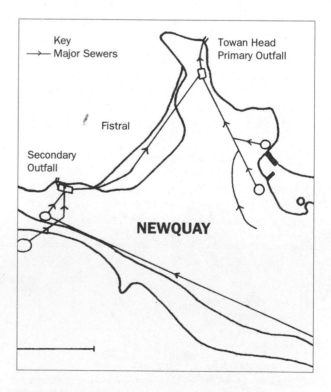

Plan diagram of Newquay Sewer System.

Results of a Preliminary Investigation into Human Sewage Pollution on the Coast of SW France

During the peak August public holiday period, Patrick Harty BSc., representing The Clean Water Initiative, conducted a preliminary sample-testing programme at a number of popular French Atlantic surfing and bathing locations.

Visual and analytical inspections were made at the locations listed. Samples were taken in a variety of conditions in an attempt to provide a more accurate picture of potential problem areas for water sports enthusiasts who use those areas.

Initial analyses indicate high faecal coliform levels at several popular locations. On the basis of these accumulated results, we believe that further studies would be beneficial in order to provide a more accurate picture of current water quality at these and other French and European recreational aquatic locations.

FRANCE	CWI Faecal coliform per 100ml	
	High	Low
Hossegor	200	70
Souston	470	-
Chambre D'Amour	>2000	-
Biarritz	1149	10
Côte des Basques	0	-
Bidart	>2000	-
Guétary	>2000	100
Lafitinia	150	-
Les Cavaliers	150	-

It's A Foul Wind That Blows

With the world's top sailors due to descend on Barcelona this summer for the Olympics, a recent programme by the Clean Water Initiative has confirmed the worst fears of many of the sailing fraternity.

Four out of six tests failed to comply with even the imperative EC standards for faecal coliforms. "The aesthetic quality of the water, the sheer number of panty liners and hypodermic syringes on the beaches along with the overwhelming smell were all indicators of gross pollution."

Patrick Harty BSc./CWI

SPAIN & CANARIES	CWI Faecal coliform per 100ml	
	High	Low
Barceloneta Pipe	3120	940
Barceloneta Mid	>4000	2290
Barceloneta End	1900	-

Ten beaches along the coast of Lanzarote in the Canary Islands were also tested for faecal coliform levels and were found to be free of faecal pollution.

Who wants to swim in Sewage

The NRA stated in their report entitled 'Bathing Water Quality in England and Wales, 1990';

"The widening pressure for increased recreational use of coastal and inland waters have been recognised by the NRA. It is important that water users understand that there is a degree of risk in any water contact sport. Wherever possible the risks need to be quantified and the users educated accordingly so that they can excercise individual choice on when and where to swim. Those requiring minimal risk will choose to swim in well managed disinfected swimming pools."

People of all ages have the God given right to swim in unpolluted seas without the fear of contracting ear, nose and throat infections, diarrhoea, vomiting, other gasto-intestinal problems, skin infections, hepatitis, menangitis or septicaemia.

Danger or no danger, who wants to swim and play in sewage?

What Comes Next?

In the immediate future the CWI will expand its bacteriological survey of European surf beaches. Faecal streptococci and viral surveys will be carried out as well as dispersion studies. Faecal streptococci can be used as an alternative indicator species and it may prove that they are more suitable than coliforms as they are more persistent in the marine environment and hence may more closely reflect the persistence of many pathogenic organisms such as viruses.

New research projects are in development such as the investigation of a non-culture genetically based procedure which hopefully enable the detection of DNA sequences specific to certain viruses thus providing a simple technique for the monitoring of viruses in the marine environment.

In addition to the scientific research, the CWI will continue to educate the public, investigate potential solutions and help substantiate relations between the scientific community, industry and conservational organisations.

In order to maintain its momentum and continue to develop, the CWI needs active support and financial assistance.

What's The Solution?

The only solution to sewage pollution is sewage treatment. Rather than pump millions of gallons of raw or semi-treated sewage into rivers and seas the water companies must be encouraged or pressurised into treating the sewage to render it harmless and to recycle the by products for other uses.

At present the vast majority of sewage discharged into estuaries or at sea, either under goes no treatment or receives only preliminary treatment.

In the case of **No Treatment** (37% of coastal and 11% of estuarine outfalls), it means that what ever you flush down your toilet ends up in the sea, in the rivers and on the beaches.

Preliminary Treatment (received by 50% of coastal and 24% of estuarine outfalls), is also known as screening, which basically means that the raw sewage is passed through a screen before being discharged. This is supposed to remove sewage debris. What a joke!

There are however, 3 main forms of sewage treatment that could and should be used on ALL outfalls:

1. PRIMARY TREATMENT. This is where raw sewage is held in sedimentation tanks to allow gross solids to settle to form sludge which is then removed.

2. SECONDARY TREATMENT. This is the process of oxidation and a form of biological digestion. Its purpose is to treat the liquid effluent from primary treatment in order to reduce the bio-chemical oxygen demand (BOD) and remove suspended solids.

● The sludge from the above can then be used on farm land as fertiliser, used as land fill, incinerated (SAS not to keen on that one) or – wait for it – dumped into the sea! (Dumping in the sea actually has to cease by 1998 under EEC law).

3. TERTIARY TREATMENT. This improves the effluent quality after secondary treatment and can take various forms, including rapid sand filtration; micro-screening; reed bed treatment; nutrient removal. And/or in addition, terminal disinfection can be applied to reduce levels of bacteria and viruses. Some of these techniques include chlorination, ozonation, peroxyacetic acid, liming or UV light.

SAS DEMANDS FULL IMPLEMENTATION OF THE HOUSE OF COMMONS ENVIRONMENTAL SELECT COMMITTEE REPORT WHICH RECOMMENDS THAT ALL SEWAGE OUTFALLS SHOULD RECEIVE PRIMARY AND SECONDARY TREATMENT, AND ULTIMATELY TERMINAL DISINFECTION.

Chris Hines/SAS

That The Sea Might Remain Beautiful

To surf is to discover and to feel the energy of the ocean. More than anyone else, the surfer is close to the sea and aware of its increasingly polluted state. Therefore it is logical that we get together to stop the degradation of the oceans and beaches. In 1984 The Surfrider Foundation came into being in California.

They started life as a small association but very quickly became well known in the fight against the barbaric management of Californian coastal zones containing a number of surf spots. It was a fight led through the courts as is often the case in the United States. But the Foundation, through its work in research and education has also contributed to a wider public awareness of the problems of the environment. in creating a European chapter in 1990, we decided to lead the same fight with the hope that surfers from the whole world would discover the importance of the role they have to play in safeguarding our oceans. The situation in France and Europe is different from the US both in mentality and action. Surfrider Foundation Europe has decided to organise itself step by step like an agency or information crossroads whose actions would support the structures or the associations already working in the same direction.

Because of the high press profile of surfing, Surfrider has the potential both to educate the population and also to support deeper research into the specific problems of the marine environment.

To create an organisation dealing with French and wider European issues is by no means an easy task. The first time the Foundation acted locally was on the Côte Basque to make the local authorities aware of our grievances by a huge demonstration on the River Adour. We also support a number of associations in their work to denounce serious pollution of water in other places.

The Foundation is in collaboration with the Clean Water Initiative and Surfers Against Sewage, two British based organisations facing problems that would blow your mind.

Like every association we are starting with donations of time by the people involved, and we are still building the strength to act efficiently and effectively.

I especially want to thank all who have helped so far. Since the *Planet Surf Initiative* at Meñakoz, our first organised event, we have tried to share our work with you.

The sea and its waves are vital for our pleasure as surfers, but also for the happiness and growth of humankind. It is up to all surfers and others who love the ocean, to ensure that the oceans remain beautiful...

Tom Curren/Surfrider Foundation Europe

Can you Help?

If you have information on:

1. Water quality in your area or a break that you have visited

2. New breaks you have discovered which aren't included in this volume

3. Comments or corrections about surf breaks that this guide has described

4. To purchase The Stormrider Guide, please send £14.95 plus £2 p&p by cheque or postal order.

Please tear this form along the dotted line and return it to Low Pressure

Your name ....

Your Address..

....

Your telephone no ....

Comments on Water Quality/Surf Breaks

....

....

....

....

....

....

Fold here

Low Pressure
186 Kensington Park Rd,
London W11 1EF

Affix stamp Here

A.D.E.S

(Asociacion Para la Defensa del Surf)

Tenerife is a mountainous island covering an area of 2,000 km² in which 700,000 people live, most from tourism. The main touristic areas of the island like Playa de las Américas, Puerto de la Cruz and Bajamar began developing in the 1960's close to the best surf points. The construction of jetties and artificial beaches brought on the disappearance of many of these before they could be surfed by most of us. In March 1990 we lost the Canaries' two best waves that worked on a southerly swell; 'La Izquierda de la Casa' and 'La Fitenia' (The Dessert). This fact was the reason that a group of surfers united to create ADES, although a group had already existed for more than five years who had been opposing the destruction of 'Spanish Left', the most internationally well known wave of Tenerife.

Our association is young, and currently we have 800 members who pay 1,200 ptas (£7.00) a year. Our activities include:

● Interviews with politicians and authorities, whereby we try to convince them of the economic potential of surfing revenues on an island that depends almost completely on tourism. We also talk about the waves as the natural arenas where ever growing numbers of youngsters can practise a healthy and spectacular sport.

● Demonstrations.

● Surf promotion through contests held around the island. The major event is at Christmas every year and this year (1992) we had special guests like Tom Curren and Bjorn and Britt Dunkerbeck. We have also created the Tenerife Surf Circuit which has five events in different parts of the island. We feel that these championships help to the type of attitude necessary amongst surfers to continue the struggle.

● Vigilance and denunciation of possible illegal construction that may damage the waves.

● Cooperation with other associations like 'The Clean Water Initiative' and 'The Surfrider Foundation'.

● Raising public awareness in general about the waves which nature has given.

And The Future?

We will encourage the growth of an ecological consciousness to save not only the waves but also the whole island. We have in mind trying to bring an important event of the A.S.P. to the island which will help to promote surfing throughout the population and this will demonstrate that this could be a good way to bring Tenerife to the attention of the outside world. We would also obviously like ADES to expand to the other Canary Islands as well as to Spain and the rest of Europe, providing there are enough people who are worried about the state of the sea and have energy to work for it.

Our coast constantly suffers horrifying attacks. The 'Jefatura Provincial de Costas' (The Provincial Chief of the Coast), the Civil Government, the Town Hall and the City Council remain impassive, almost as if these problems did not exist.

An urban development program, lacking in good taste and etiquette, with no initiatives prepared to prevent or control unpurified dumping of waste from the town, confirms this lack of interest that the official organisations seem to have in these matters.

And now with one stroke they are prepared to destroy the waves of our coast. They are trying to bury them with breakwaters in order to create vulgar beaches without life. It is not fair! That's why ADES was born in March 1990, as a consequence of these and future attacks against our coast.

We believe the whole coast should be declared a 'Natural Protection Zone' in the interest of ecology, sport and tourism. Surely the promise of unspoilt natural beauty would be more appealing to visitors.

We will not allow the establishment to destroy in days the coastal sea bed that was formed by lava over thousands of years ago, home to a rich variety of marine life.

Those of us who defend surfing and the waves, not only are preserving a sport but we are protecting a natural geological heritage that is of interest to scientists, sportsmen and tourists. We would like to be able to count on your support or to have you participate in this project so we invite you to collaborate in whatever means possible. You can contact us by phone or by visiting Aloha Surf Shops in Tenerife.

Antonio Miguel García/A.D.E.S.

Addresses:

The Marine Conservation Society,
9 Gloucester Rd, Ross on Wye,
Herefordshire, HR9 5B4
Tel: 0898 66 017

The Clean Water Initiative,
186 Kensington Park Road, London W11 1EF
Tel: 071 792 3134

Surfers Against Sewage
The Old Counthouse Warehouse
Wheal Kitty, St Agnes, Cornwall, TR5 0RE
Tel: 0892 553001

Surfrider Foundation Europe
Villa Sion, 79, rue d'Espagne
62400 Biarritz, France
Tel: 59 235499

A.D.E.S.
c/ Imeldo Seris, 17
38003 Sta Cruz de Tenerife, Canary Islands, Spain
Tel: 922 242206

useful information:

184

advertisers' index

wave sport magazines

SURF

BRITAIN
Ground Swell
British Surfing Association,
Champions Yard, Penzance,
Cornwall TR18 2SS
Tel: 0736 60250
Publisher: Chris Power
Editor: Colin Wilson
Format: Tabloid
Cost: Free

Surfs Up
2 Frognall Cottages ,
Wickhambreaux , Canterbury, Kent
CT3 1SB
Tel: 0227 721706
Editor: Paul Knowles
Format: A5 mono
Cost: £1.00

Tube News
Wessex Surf Club, c/o 19 Stalham
Road, Branksome, Poole, Dorset
Tel: 0202 748052
Editor: Roger Castle
Format: A5 mono
Cost: £0.75

Wavelength Magazine
Unity Hall, Clevedon Road,
Newquay, Cornwall TR7 2BU
Tel: 0637 87629
Editor: John Conway
Format: A4 colour
Cost: £2.50

FRANCE
Surf Session
44 rue Luis Mariano, 64200
Biarritz
Tel: 59 41 21 40
Editor: Gibus de Soultrait
Format: A4 colour
Cost: FF30

Surf Time!
BP 60 - 40150 Hossegor
Tel: 58 43 94 08
Editor: Antoine Desquenne
Format: Tabloid
Cost: Free

SPAIN
Tres 60
c/ Iparraguirre, 59-2º

48980 Santurtzi, Vizcaya
Tel: 94 461 4474
Editor: Jakue Andikoetxea
Photos: Javier Amezaga
Admin: Borja Peñeñori
Staff: Paloma Vega, Marina Vega
Format: A4 colour
Cost: 600 ptas

Surfer Rule
Surfer Rule S.L., c/ San Pedro, 7
bajo, 20300 Irún, Guipúzcoa
Tel: 943 631 327
Editor: Jon Beunza
Director: Marisa Beunza
Photos: Fernando Muñoz
Format: A4 80 pages
Cost: 575 ptas

PORTUGAL
Revista Surf Portugal
Rua Nova da Trinidade, nº1/3º
esq., 1200 Lisbon
Tel: 1 346 7962
Editor: João Valente (editorial and
photographic)
Director: Henrique Balsemão
Art Director: Fernando 'Zozi'
Mendes
Advertising: Rony Carrari
Format: A4 colour
Cost: 350$00

Surf Magazine
Oceanus LDA, Apartado 23 (Sto
Antonio), 2780 Oeiras
Tel: 1 456 6072/
456 6097
Editor: Graça Afonso
Format: A4 colour
Cost: 380$00

AUSTRALIA
Surfing Life
PO Box 823, Burleigh Heads,
Queensland 4220
Tel: 02 761 388/
979 5807
Editor: Peter Morrison
Photos: Tim Baker
Format: A4 colour
Cost: AUD$4.50

Surfing World
PO Box 128, Mona Vale, NSW
Tel: 02 997 2657

Editor: Bruce Channon
Format: A4 colour
Cost: AUD$4.50

Tracks Surfing Magazine
PO Box 746,Darlinghurst, NSW,
Australia 2010
Tel: 02 331 5006
Editor: Gary Dunne
Assistant editor: Neil Ridgway
Format: Tabloid B & W
Cost: $2.95 per issue
Subscription price: AUD$ 65.00
overseas surface mail, AUD$
145.00 airmail

Waves
PO Box 746, Darlinghurst, NSW,
Australia 2010
Tel: 02 331 5006
Editor: Andrew Kidman
Format: Glossy colour
Cost: $3.95 per isssue
Subscription price: AUD$ 61.00
overseas surface mail, AUD$
102.00 airmail

AMERICA
Surfer
PO Box 1028, Dana Point, CA
92629
Tel: 714 496 592
Editor: Steve Hawk
Format: A4 colour
Cost: US$3.95

Surfing
950 Calle Amanecer, Suite C, PO
Box 3010, San Clemente, CA
92672
Tel: 714 492 7873
Editor: Nick Carroll
Format: A4 colour
Cost: US$3.50

BRAZIL
Fluir
Editora Azul S.A., Rua Pequetita,
145 7º andar, conj 71, Via
Olimpia, São Paulo
Tel: 011 212 523
Editor: Reinaldo Andraus,
Frederico d'Orey
Format: A4 colour
Cost: NCZ$12.00

SOUTH AFRICA
Zig Zag
Zig Zag Promotions, PO Box 11,
Westville 3630
Tel: 031 866707
Editor: Craig Sims
Format: A4 colour
Cost: R5.50

WINDSURFING MAGAZINES

BRITAIN
Boards
196 Eastern Esplanade, Southend
on Sea, Essex SS1 3AB
Tel: 0702 582245
Editor: Jeremy Evans
Format: A4 colour
Cost: £1.95

On Board Windsurfing Magazine
Andrew House, 2a Granville Road,
Sidcup, Kent DA14 4BN
Tel: 081 302 6150
Editor: Mark Griffiths
Format: A4 colour
Cost: £1.35

Windsurf Magazine
The Coach House, Medcroft Road,
Tackley, Oxon OX5 3AH
Tel: 0869 83677
Editor: Mark Kasprowicz
Format: A4 colour
Cost: £1.95

FRANCE
Planchemag
Editions de l'Aquarium SARL, 107,
rue du Point du Jour, 92100
Boulogne-Billancourt
Tel: 49 10 30 70
Editor: Benoît Tréguilly
Format: A4 colour
Cost: FF28

Wind Magazine
8-10 rue Pierre Brossolette,
92300 Levallois-Perret
Tel: 40 87 41 69/
87 42 77
Editor: Philippe Simon
Format: A4 colour
Cost: FF32

SPAIN
Surf a Vela
Sirpus, S.A., San Gervasio de
Cassolas, 79, 08022 Barcelona
Tel: 93 211 1146
Director: Panxo Pi-Suñer Cañellas
Editor: Pablo Zendrera Zariquiey
Format: A4 colour
Cost: 450 ptas

BODYBOARD MAGAZINES

BRITAIN
Three Sixty
Orca Communications, 60 Pentine
Avenue, Newquay , Cornwall TR7
1PE
Tel: 0637 872 654
Editor: Mike Searle
Format: Tabloid
Cost: £1.50

SPAIN
Tres 60 Body
Tres 60 Coop Ltda., c/
Iparraguirre, 59-2º, 48980
Santurtzi, Vizcaya
Tel: 94 461 4474
Editor: Jakue Andikoetxea
Photos: Javler Amezaga
Format: A4 colour
Cost: 425 ptas

PORTUGAL
Body Board Portugal
Rua Nova da Trinidade, nº1/3º
esq.,
1200 Lisbon
Tel: 1 346 7962/346 7820/347
8144
Editor: Miguel Simães, António
Fonseca
Format: A4 colour
Cost: 380$00

OTHER MAGAZINES

BRITAIN
Snowboard Magazine UK
Air Publications, Unit 1a Franchise
Street, Kidderminster,
Worchestershire DY11 6RE
Tel: 0562 827744
Editor: Mark Sturgeon and Eddie

(Shred Ready) Spearing
Format: A4 colour
Cost: £2.20

FRANCE
Vertical
Boite Postal 177, 6, rue du
Lieutenant Chanaron, 38008
Grenoble Cedex
Tel: 76 87 37 58
Editor: Jean Michel Asselin
Format: A4 colour
Cost: FF40

SPAIN
Todo Sport
Consejo de Ciento, 346 principal,
08009 Barcelona
Tel: 93 487 4188
Editor: Daniel Ortiz
Format: A4 colour
Cost: 400 ptas

AUSTRALIA
**Australian Ski and Surf and Skate
Trade Directory**
PO Box 16, Bondi Road, Bondi,
NSW 2026
Tel: 03 319 2511
Editor: Merrick Davis/ Brett Allat
Format: A5
Cost: FREE of charge to every Ski,
Surf and Skate shop Australia
wide.

photographic contributors

Alex Williams
Higher Aunemouth
Banthem
Kingsbridge
S. Devon DQ7 3AD
Tel: 0548 852381 /
0548560339

Chris Power
7 Daniel Rd
Truro
Cornwall TR1 2BZ
Tel: 0872 74262

Phil Holden
Bali Hai
Thistle Boon Drive
Mumbles
Swansea SA3 4JB
Wales
Tel: 0792 367571

Simon McComb
9 Ericy Terrace
Falmouth
Cornwall
Tel: 0326 314682
Fax: 0326 211205

Peter Cade
Keveral House
Keveral Gardens
Seaton
Tor Point
Cornwall PL1 13JH
Tel:0752 779831 ext 329 (day)
Fax:0752 790691

Rick Abbott
58 South St
Braunton
North Devon EX33 2AN
Tel:0271 814716

Tim McKeena Photography
13 Rue Dabadie
33100 Bordeaux
France
Tel: 56 929707

Tim Rainger
Low Pressure
186 Kensington Park Road
London W11
Tel: 071 792 3134

Eric Chauché
Domaine de Pyrenée
Batiment Pic du Midi
Route de Cassou
64600 Anglet
France
Tel: 59 310854

João Valente
Surf Portugal
Rua Nova da Trinidade, nº1/3º
1200 Lisbon
Tel: 1 346 7962
Fax: 1 342 1809

Javier Amezaga
Tres 60
c/ Iparraguirre, 59-20
48980 Santurtzi
Vizcaya
Tel: 94 461 4474
Fax: 94 483 6763

Borja Peñeñori
Tres 60
c/ Iparraguirre, 59-2º
48980 Santurtzi
Vizcaya
Tel: 94 461 4474
Fax: 94 483 6763

Jakue Andikoetxea
Tres 60
c/ Iparraguirre, 59-2º
48980 Santurtzi
Vizcaya
Tel: 94 461 4474
Fax: 94 483 6763

acknowledgements & further reading

SCOTLAND
AA Illustrated Guide to Britain's Coast, Drive Publications
The Surf Report: Scotland, Vol 6 No 2, Surfer Publishing Group
Surfing in Caithness, Caithness District Council

IRELAND
Ireland: the Rough Guide, Seán Doran, Margaret Greenwood and Hildi Hawkins, Harrap Columbus
The Surf Report: The North Coast of Ireland, Vol 8 No 8, Surfer Publishing Group
The Surf Report: The South Coast of Ireland, Vol 8 No 7, Surfer Publishing Group

WALES
AA Illustrated Guide to Britain's Coast, Drive Publications
The Surf Report: The Gower Peninsula, Vol 9 No 2, Surfer Publishing Group
The Surf Report: SW Wales, Vol 9 No8, Surfer Publishing Group

ENGLAND
AA Illustrated Guide to Britain' s Coast, Drive Publications
The Surf Report: Cornwall, Vol 8 No 6, Surfer Publishing Group
The Surf Report: Devon County, Vol 8 No 3, Surfer Publishing Group

FRANCE
France: The Rough Guide: Kate Ballie & Tim Salmon, Harrap Columbus
Brittany & Normandy: The Rough Guide: Greg Ward, Harrap Columbus
The Surf Report: NW France, Vol 5 No 3, Surfer Publishing Group
The Surf Report: SW France, Vol 5 No 2, Surfer Publishing Group
Guide Des Spots: Côte Basque – Sud des Landes, Association Culturelle Touristique & Surf Session
Solo/Spot Globe Surfer Tome 1, Edition Glénat

SPAIN
Spain: The Rough Guide, Mark Ellingham and John Fisher, Harrap Columbus
The Surf Report: Spain, Vol 6 No 6, Surfer Publishing Group

THE CANARY ISLANDS
Canary Island Series: Tenerife, Mary and Archie Tisdall, Lascelles
Canary Island Series: Gran Canaria and the Eastern Canary Islands Mary and Archie Tisdall, Lascelles
Canary Island Series: Lanzarote and Fuerteventura, Mary and Archie Tisdall, Lascelles
The Surf Report: Lanzarote, Vol 11 No 6, Surfer Publishing Group
The Surf Report: Fuerteventura, Vol 11 No 6, Surfer Publishing Group
Olas Idoneas de Tenerife para la Practica del Surf, A.D.E.S & A.T.A.N.

PORTUGAL
Portugal: The Rough Guide: Mark Ellingham, John Fisher, Graham Kenyon and Alice Martin, Harrap Columbus
The Surf Report: Portugal, Vol 3 No 7, Surfer Publishing Group

ITALY
Sardegna Wind and Surfer Spot: Lorenzo Merlo, Victory Project

GENERAL
Let's Go: The Budget Guide to Europe, Harvard Student Agencies Inc.
The Times Atlas of the Oceans, Times Books
The Good Beach Guide, Marine Conservation Society
Plus numerous and varied wave sport publications.

index